THE CHRIST IS JESUS

Society of Biblical Literature

Academia Biblica

Steven L. McKenzie,
Hebrew Bible/Old Testament Editor

Mark Allan Powell,
New Testament Editor

Number 18

THE CHRIST IS JESUS
Metamorphosis, Possession,
and Johannine Christology

THE CHRIST IS JESUS
Metamorphosis, Possession, and Johannine Christology

Pamela E. Kinlaw

Society of Biblical Literature
Atlanta

THE CHRIST IS JESUS
Metamorphosis, Possession, and Johannine Christology

Copyright © 2005 by the Society of Biblical Literature

Library of Congress Cataloging-in-Publication Data

Kinlaw, Pamela E.
  The Christ is Jesus : metamorphosis, possession, and Johannine christology / Pamela E. Kinlaw.
     p. cm. — (Academia Biblica ; no. 18)
  Includes bibliographical references.
  ISBN 1-58983-165-9 (pbk. : alk. paper)
  1. Jesus Christ—Natures—History of doctrines—Early church, ca. 30-600.
2. Bible. N.T. John—Theology. 3. Bible. N.T. Epistles of John—Theology. I. Title. II. Series: Academia Biblica (Series) (Society of Biblical Literature) ; no. 18

BS2601.K565 2005
226.5'06--dc22

                                                    2005002216

Printed in the United States of America
on acid-free paper

CONTENTS

ACKNOWLEDGEMENTS

This dissertation was made possible by the patient support of a multitude. At the University of North Carolina, John Van Seters and Bart Ehrman taught me to think historically about both Testaments, while from David Halperin I learned about Judaism, teaching, and integrity. At Baylor University, dissertations in the Department of Religion are achievable only with the good humor and professionalism of Clova Gibson. Naymond Keathley defines generosity of spirit, and Mikeal Parsons constantly goes the extra mile to provide opportunities for graduate students to become teacher-scholars. Bob Patterson receives the reward for the utmost patience while teaching me to think theologically. William H. Bellinger's ability to encourage all students to think deeply about the literature of the Old Testament, and to have great fun doing it, is unsurpassed. Sharyn Dowd and John Nordling generously assisted in making this dissertation into a final product, while Ralph Wood continues to teach me the meaning of true friendship.

The prayers of my faith community of Sacred Heart Catholic Church in Abilene, Texas, especially those of the Legion of Mary, were desperately needed and, it would appear, effective! This project, of course, would have been impossible without the long-suffering endurance and liberal assistance of my husband, Charles Jeffery Kinlaw.

St. Francis of Assisi once told his companions, "Brothers, it is no good going anywhere to preach unless our walking *is* our preaching." I have been blessed to have a mentor who is not only a gifted scholar and teacher, but whose walking has been his preaching for as long as I have known him. My greatest thanks go to Charles H. Talbert, who believed I could get this far, and committed the time and the energy to prove it.

Chapter 1
Historical and Methodological Studies

When a god comes onto the stage of human history and moves among human beings, how is that entry into human history conceptualized? In this dissertation, I propose to examine the Christology of the Fourth Gospel and the Johannine Epistles in its ancient Mediterranean context. The relationship between the divine and human in Christ is a key issue of the Gospel, and it is also the main source of contention between the authors and their opponents in the Epistles. Despite the many efforts to explicate the Christology of these writings, little consideration has been given to how the audience's knowledge of models concerning the union of divine beings with humans would affect its understanding that Christology. A methodology that illuminates the cultural expectations that the original audience brings to the text will help to elucidate the Christology as well.

Previous Research on the Christology of the Fourth Gospel

Christology in the Johannine literature,[1] especially in the Fourth Gospel, has not suffered from lack of attention. Paul Anderson helpfully divides the academic study of Johannine Christology into five broaddivisions, with no less than thirteen sub-categories.[2] For the specific interests of this dissertation, two of these sub-categories are particularly important: (1) the History of Religions approach, and (2)

---

[1] For the purposes of this dissertation, the designations "Johannine literature" and "Johannine writings" will not include Revelation.

[2] Paul Anderson, *The Christology of the Fourth Gospel: Its Unity and Disunity in the Light of John 6* (Tübingen: Mohr, 1996; repr.,Valley Forge, Pa.: Trinity Press, 1996), 17-32. Anderson's five divisions are: (1) comprehensive overviews; (2) text-centered approaches; (3) theological-christological approaches; (4) literary-christological approaches, and (5) historical-christological approaches.

2   T<small>HE</small> C<small>HRIST IS</small> J<small>ESUS</small>

those approaches that concentrate on Jesus' humanity/divinity.[3] A third category, the history of Johannine Christianity approach, should be considered with regard to some possible implications of this dissertation.

History of Religions Approach to Johannine Christology

Though the approach of the *Religionsgeschichte Schule* to Johannine Christology is usually associated with Rudolf Bultmann, he was in fact only the most talented biblical exegete and theologian of that school. Of the Göttingen scholars who are credited with the founding of that approach in the 1880s, it was Wilhelm Bousset who was to have the most profound influence on the study of Johannine Christology until Bultmann. Bousset's magisterial *Kyrios Christos* (1913) finds the mystical vision of the Fourth Gospel rooted in Greek soil, a mysticism reflected otherwise most clearly in the *Corpus Hermeticum*.[4] In the his 1964 introduction to the fifth edition, Bultmann is able to point out six enduring areas of significance for the study of the New Testament, all of which are directly applicable to the Christology of John, that the History of Religions school in general and Bousset in particular brought to the fore.[5]

Bultmann portrayed John's Christology as based upon a "redeemer-revealer" pattern drawn from an early oriental gnostic redeemer myth, which, Bultmann insisted, was widespread in the environment of the Fourth Gospel, as evidenced by traditions found in later Manichean and especially Mandean written sources.[6] Parallels between the seventh century Mandean texts and the thought of second century gnostics suggested for Bultmann the likelihood that the gnostic sects existed earlier than the Gospel, and he suggested that they could possibly be identified with the followers of John the Baptist.[7] Though the evangelist "de-mythologized" the myth to emphasize the fact of Jesus having been sent as the revealer and the existential decision facing each person "in his bare, undifferentiated

---

[3] Although the divisions are employed for their convenience, the overlap between them will become immediately apparent.

[4] Wilhelm Bousset, *Kyrios Christos:A History of the Belief in Christ from the Beginnings of Christianity to Irenaeus* (trans. J. E. Steely; Nashville: Abingdon, 1970, 1913), esp. 235.

[5] Bousset, *Kyrios*, 7-9.

[6] See esp. "Die Bedeutung der neuerscholossenen mandäischen und manichäischen Quellen für das Verständnis des Johannesevangeliums," *ZNW* 24 (1925): 100-46; *The Gospel of John: A Commentary* (trans. G. Beasley-Murray; Oxford: Blackwell, 1971; 1952, 1955); *Theology of the New Testament*, Vol. 2 (London: SCM, 1955), and "Die religionsgeschichtliche Hintergrund des Prologs zum Johannes-Evangelium, repr., *Exegetica: Aufsätze zur Erforschung des Neuen Testaments* (Tübingen: Mohr, 1967), 1-35. Bultmann was preceded in the use of Mandean sources esp. by Walter Bauer, *Das Johannesevangelium Erklärt* (Tübingen: Mohr, 1933). 3, 179-80.

[7] Bultmann, "Bedeutung," 97-100.

situation of being human,"[8] the gnostic background was still crucial in understanding the dualism which the evangelist transformed and in discerning the diachronic strata of the Gospel.[9]

The depiction of a gnostic background for the Gospel has been thoroughly dismantled. Though criticism commenced almost immediately,[10] the most effective critiques began with C. H. Dodd, who emphasizes the utility of Hermetic literature and Philo over Mandean sources.[11] George MacRae, for example, highlights numerous parallels between Jewish and gnostic wisdom schemas, suggesting that the Jewish sources most likely served as the source both for the Fourth Gospel and the gnostic concepts.[12] The final nail in the coffin was hammered in by Charles H. Talbert, who demonstrated the preponderance of descending-ascending redeemer figures in the Mediterranean environment without recourse to late gnostic evidence.[13]

The History of Religions approach brought to the fore another cultural model applied to Jesus, the θεῖος ἀνήρ concept. Its major influence in the study of the Fourth Gospel has been in that of the so-called "signs-source"

---

[8]Bultmann, *Theology*, 2.62.

[9]Bultmann was not the first to suggest a gnostic background especially for the prologue of the Fourth Gospel. For example, John Ashton notes that J. D. Michaelis (1788) suggested that the term *logos* was drawn from gnosticism, and Adolf Hilgenfeld (*Das Evangelium und die Briefe Johannes nach ihre Lehrbegriff dargestellt* [Halle, 1849]) considered John a gnostic writing. Consideration of the parallels with Mandean texts was advocated by Johannes Kreyenbühl and Walter Bauer's second edition of his commentary on John. John Ashton, *Understanding the Fourth Gospel* (London: Clarendon, 1991), 20-21, 26-27.

[10]See, for example, C. E. Percy, *Untersuchungen über den Ursprung der johanneischen Theologie zugleich ein Beitrag zur Frage nach der Entstehung des Gnostizismus* (Lund: Gleerup, 1939), esp. 1-20; Rudolf Schnackenburg, "Logos-Hymnus und johanneischer Prolog," *BZ* 1 (1957): 69-109.

[11]C. H. Dodd, *The Interpretation of the Fourth Gospel* (Cambridge: Cambridge University Press, 1953), esp. 10-73; 97-98; 133.

[12]George MacRae, "The Jewish Background of the Gnostic Sophia Myth," *NovT* 12 (1970): 86-101.

[13]Charles H. Talbert, "The Myth of a Descending-Ascending Redeemer in Mediterranean Antiquity," *NTS* 22 (1976): 418-39; repr. in Talbert, *Reading John: A Literary and Theological Commentary on the Fourth Gospel and the Johannine Epistles* (New York: Crossroad, 1992), 265-84. Citations will refer to the reprint. For other criticisms of the influence of gnostic patterns on John, see C. Colpe, *Die religionsgeschichtliche Schule: Darstellung und Kritik ihres Bildes vom gnostischen Erlöser-mythus* (FRLANT 60; Göttingen: Vandenhoeck & Ruprecht, 1961); E. M. Yamauchi, *Pre-Christian Gnosticism* (Grand Rapids: Eerdmans, 1973) and "Jewish Gnosticism? The Prologue of John, Mandean Parallels and the Trimorphic Protenoia," *Festschrift for Giles Quispel* (Leiden: Brill, 1981), 467-97; Pheme Perkins, "Gnostic Christologies and the New Testament," *CBQ* 43 (1981): 590-606, and S. Pétrement, *Le Dieu séparé: les origines du gnosticisme* (Paris: Cerf, 1984). For a recent comprehensive criticism of Bultmann's approach to and conclusions about the Fourth Gospel, see Jörg Frey, *Die Johanneische Eschatologie* (2 vols.; Tübingen: Mohr Siebeck, 1997), 1.119-50.

of the Fourth Gospel, usually portrayed as a more primitive source/
stratum of the Gospel.[14] Critiques of the θεῖος ἀνήρ concept have come
particularly from George MacRae,[15] Carl R. Holladay[16] and Otto Betz,[17]
though the last two commentators do not concentrate specifically on the
Fourth Gospel. MacRae suggests that the taking over of a signs source
with a θεῖος ἀνήρ Christology to explain the tension in John between the
extravagant miracles and their de-emphasizing by the Gospel writer is too
simple; the Fourth Evangelist, rather, applies various cultural categories
"to assert both the universality and the transcendence of the divine Son
Jesus."[18] Neither Holladay nor Betz find sufficient evidence for a unified
θεῖος ἀνήρ concept in the Hellenistic Judaism that supposedly provided the
source for John's use of it, and Betz makes it a point to deny the evidence
for this concept in John (as well as that of a signs-source at all).[19]

The discovery of the Qumran literature contributed to a shift to a
Jewish Palestinian background for the reaction to History of Religions:
Jewish precedents.[20] Dodd's emphasis on the use of Philo for the origins
of the Logos concept, for example, is a stream that has continued in
Johannine studies.[21] As NT scholars have very gradually come to accept
the impossibility of dividing Judaism in the Hellenistic era into two

---

[14]See, for example, H. D. Betz, "Jesus as Divine Man," *Jesus and the Historian* (ed. F. D. Trotter; Philadelphia: Fortress, 1968), 114-33. While the signs-source hypothesis has lost ground in Johannine studies, esp. following the work of G. van Belle (*The Signs Source in the Fourth Gospel: Historical Survey and Critical Evaluation of the Semeia Hypothesis* [BETL 116; Leuven: Peters, 1994]), there are some recent proponents of its existence and importance in understanding the Gospel; see esp. J. Rinke (*Kerygma und Autopsie: Der christologische Disput als Spiegel johanneischer Gemeindegeschichte* (HBS 12; Freiberg: Herder, 1997), and H. Riedel, *Zeichen und Herrlichkeit: Die christologische Relevanz der Semeiaquelle in den Kanawundern Joh 2, 1-11 und Joh 4, 46-54* (RST 51; Main: Peter Lang, 1977).

[15]George MacRae, "The Fourth Gospel and *Religionsgeschichte*," *CBQ* 32 (1970): 12-24.

[16]Carl R. Holladay, *Theios Aner in Hellenistic Judaism: A Critique of the Use of this Category in New Testament Christology* (SBLDS 40; Missoula: Scholars Press, 1977). Holladay (15-22) includes a discussion of the hypothesis, its relation to the History of Religions school, and critics of it.

[17]Otto Betz, "The Concept of the So-Called 'Divine Man' in Mark's Christology," *Studies in New Testament and Early Christian Literature. Essays Honoring Allen P. Wikgren* (ed. D. E. Aune; Leiden: Brill, 1972), 220-40.

[18]MacRae, "Fourth Gospel," 24. MacRae admits, however, his own bias toward the influence of the wisdom tradition on the Fourth Gospel (22).

[19]Betz, "Concept," 240.

[20]Consideration of Jewish sources had, of course, been carried out before this point. See, for example, Adolf Schlatter, *Die Sprache und Heimat des vierten Evangelisten* (1902); Hugo Odeberg, *The Fourth Gospel Interpreted in its Relation to Contemporaneous Religious Currents in Palestine and the Hellenistic-Oriental World* (1929), and E. C. Hoskyns, *The Fourth Gospel* (ed. F. N. Davey; London: Faber & Faber, 1947, 1940).

[21]Dodd, *Interpretation*, 54-73, 276-77. Cf. A. W. Argyle, "Philo and the Fourth Gospel," *ExpTim* 63 (1952), 385-86.

broad branches entitled "Palestinian" and "Hellenistic," a broader base of Jewish "parallels" has gradually come to the fore.[22] Another result of this shift is that the Gospel has been treated with the same study of Christology-by-titles that has been carried out in the New Testament as a whole.[23] As Culpepper points out, however, the examination of titles often treats each title as a "static entity that can be extracted from its narrative contexts and understood in detached isolation."[24] Considerable progress has been made, however, in the influence of Jewish concepts on John's Christology, such as both wisdom and Moses typologies,[25] the importance of the sending/emissary concept[26] and the prophet/king typologies.[27] No

[22]Early on, R. McL. Wilson ("Philo and the Fourth Gospel," *ExpTim* 65 [1954]: 47-49) suggested that the roots of the Logos concept in Philo and the Fourth Gospel lie in similar backgrounds to both, and, therefore, it is not necessary to postulate dependence of the Gospel on Philo.

[23]See Oscar Cullman, *The Christology of the New Testament* (trans. S. C. Guthrie & C. A. M. Hall; Philadelphia: Westminster, 1963); H. E. Tödt, *The Son of Man in the Synoptic Tradition* (trans. D. M. Barton; Philadelphia: Westminster, 1965); Ferdinand Hahn, *The Titles of Jesus in Christology: Their History in Early Christianity* (trans. H. Knight & George Ogg; London: Lutterworth, 1969); R. H. Fuller, *The Foundations of New Testament Christology* (New York: Scribner, 1965).

[24]Alan Culpepper, "The Christology of the Johannine Writings," *Who Do You Say That I Am: Essays on Christology* (ed. M. A. Powell & D. R. Bauer; Louisville: Westminster John Knox, 1999), 85.

[25]For recent examples, see Walter Grundmann, *Der Zeuge der Wahrheit: Grundzüge der Christologie des Johannesevangeliums* (ed. W. Wiefel; Berlin: Evangelisch Verlagsanstalt, 1985); Martin Scott, *Sophia and the Johannine Jesus* (JSNTSS 71; Sheffield: Sheffield Academic Press, 1992); Sharon H. Ringe, *Wisdom's Friends: Community and Christology in the Fourth Gospel* (Louisville, Ky.: Westminster/John Knox, 1999); Michael E. Willett, *Wisdom Christology in the Fourth Gospel* (San Francisco: Mellen, 1992); Elizabeth Schlüssler Fiorenza, *Jesus: Miriam's Child, Sophia's Prophet: Critical Issues in Feminist Christology* (New York: Continuum, 1994), and Ben Witherington, *John's Wisdom: A Commentary on the Fourth Gospel* (Louisville, Ky.: Westminster John Knox, 1995). On Moses typology, see, for example, Wayne A. Meeks, *The Prophet King: Moses Traditions and the Johannine Christology* (Leiden: Brill, 1967); M.-E. Boismard, *Moïse ou Jésus: Essai de christologie johannique* (BETL 84; Leuven: Leuven University Press/Peeters, 1988), and Stanley D. Harstine, *The Functions of Moses as a Character in the Fourth Gospel and the Responses of Three Ancient Mediterranean Audiences* (Ph.D. diss., Baylor University, 1999).

[26]See, for example, J. P. Miranda, *Der Vater, der mich gesandt hat* (Frankfurt: Lang Bern, 1972); Ernst Haenchen, "'Der Vater, der mich gesandt hat,'" *Gott und Mensch* (Tübingen: Mohr, 1965) 68-77; Josef Kuhl, *Die Sendung Jesu und der Kirche nach dem Johannes-Evangelium* (St. Augustin: Steyler, 1967; J.-A. Bühner, *Der Gesandte und sein Weg im vierten Evangelium: Die kultur- und religionsgeschichtliche Grundlagen der johanneischen Sendungschristologie sowie ihre traditionsgeschichtliche Entwicklung* (Tübingen: Mohr, 1977), and Peder Borgen, "God's Agent in the Fourth Gospel," *The Interpretation of John* (ed. John Ashton; London: SPCK, 1986), 67-78.

[27]See, for example, Marinus de Jonge, "Jesus as Prophet and King in the Fourth Gospel," *Jesus: Stranger from Heaven and Son of God. Jesus Christ and the Christians in Johannine Perspective* (Missoula: Scholars Press, 1977), 49-76, and Joachim Kügler, *Der Andere König: Religionsgeschichtliche Perspektiven auf die Christologie des Johannesevangeliums* (SBS 178; Stuttgart: Katholisches Bibelwerk, 1999).

commentators would argue at this point for an exclusively non-Jewish background to the Gospel.

Jesus' Humanity/Divinity Approach

"The Word became flesh" (John 1:14a) suggests for Bultmann that the emphasis was on the humanity of Jesus as needed to be Revealer to humanity.[28] Ernst Käsemann's counter that author of the Fourth Gospel was guilty of a "naïve docetism"[29] ensured that for much of the last century, opinions of Johannine Christology would alternate between these two poles. While Käsemann builds on, and gives credit to, predecessors in this argument such as F. C. Baur, Wilhelm Wrede, G. P. Wetter and Emanuel Hirsch, he chooses to focus on John 17 as the center of that which was unique to the thought of the Fourth Gospel. Käsemann reads the Gospel as so completely focussed on the glorified Christ that what passes for history in the Gospel is actually only human *reaction* to Christ; moreover, the incarnation is the encounter of earthly and heavenly, not a "complete, total entry into the earth, into human existence."[30]

Some recent works continue to emphasize the divinity of Jesus in the Fourth Gospel. For example, Boy Hinrichs sees the key to the human and divine in Jesus in the "I am" sayings, which emphasize the divinity of Jesus and offer the believer the chance to participate in eternal life through participation in this divine being through belief.[31] "I am" sayings that do not fit into this schema (those of John 10 and 15, for example) are judged to be redactional additions.[32] Jerome Neyrey suggests that John's high Christology is summarized in John 6:63: "The flesh profits nothing."[33] The "facts" of the latest stratum of the Gospel, that Jesus has and can dispense eternal life, that he both judges and raises the dead, depicts a Jesus equal to God who belongs in heaven with the Father, while the older strata of the Gospel retained the view of Jesus as sent, certainly, but as only a human being.[34] The high Christology points to a social context of a community radically dissociated from its parent community,

---

[28]Bultmann, *Theology*, 2.40-41.

[29]Ernst Käsemann, "The Structure and Purpose of the Prologue to John's Gospel," in *New Testament Questions of Today* (London: SCM, 1969), 138-167 and *The Testament of Jesus* (London: SCM, 1968).

[30]Käsemann, *Testament*, 65.

[31]Boy Hinrichs, *"Ich bin": Die Konsistenz des Johannes-Evangeliums in der Konzentration auf das Wort Jesu* (SBS 133; Stuttgart: Katholisches Bibelwerk, 1988).

[32]Hinrichs, *"Ich bin,"* 18-22, 66-82.

[33]Jerome H. Neyrey, *An Ideology of Revolt: John's Christology in Social Science Perspective* (Philadelphia: Fortress, 1988), 154-56. Cf. Neyrey, "'My Lord and My God.' The Divinity of Jesus in John's Gospel," *SBLSP* 25 (1986): 152-71.

[34]Neyrey, *Ideology*, 9-36.

a community with a focus on the heavenly which puts a heavy emphasis on the Spirit.[35]

What Käsemann particularly highlights is a problem that has dogged the study of John's Christology for decades, one which C. K. Barrett most helpfully described, the tension between the preexistent Logos and the humanity of Jesus which threatens throughout the Gospel to undermine it.[36] Barrett offers the suggestion that the author is not only naively docetic, but that he is even more naively antidocetic.[37] Other scholars, however, have seen the Fourth Gospel as portraying a more accomplished balance between the two. At about the same time, for example, F.-M. Braun[38] and Andre Feuillet[39] achieved eloquent readings of the Fourth Gospel that preserved a fully balanced human/divine person in Jesus Christ; unfortunately, their works concentrated on the theological aspects within the Gospel without reference to the historical context.

Several authors have recently argued that the Fourth Gospel never loses sight of the full humanity of Jesus. John F. O'Grady, for example, suggests that Jesus' human need for friendship and affection, the titles Logos, Son, Christ/ Messiah and the use of the "I am" sayings all can be read as keeping the importance of human life in view.[40] Udo Schnelle considers the Gospel of John a reaction to a docetism which emphasizes the mere appearance of the divine being on earth.[41] The conflict is an inner-church one rather than one with the synagogue; the synagogue conflict, Schnelle argues, is only a memory.[42] We will have cause to consider Schnelle's work later in the dissertation.

The full humanity of Jesus has been addressed also by the diverse approaches of Herbert Kohler and M. M. Thompson. In a theological exegesis, Kohler concentrates particularly on the continuity of identity between the Jesus who died on the cross and who was resurrected.[43]

---

[35]Neyrey, *Ideology*, 173-206.

[36]C. K. Barrett, "Christocentric or Theocentric? Observations on the Theological Method of the Fourth Gospel," *Essays on John* (London: SPCK and Philadelphia: Westminster, 1982), 11-12.

[37]Barrett, "History," *Essays on John*, 129-30; cf. Loader, *Christology*, 185.

[38]F.-M. Braun, *Jean le Théologian. Sa Théologie. Le Mystère de Jésus-Christ* (Paris: Gabalda, 1966).

[39]Andre Feuillet, *Le Mystère de l'amour divin dans la théologie johannique* (Paris: Gabalda, 1972).

[40]John F. O'Grady, "The Human Jesus in the Fourth Gospel," *BTB* 14 (1984): 63-66.

[41]Udo Schnelle, *Antidocetic Christology in the Gospel of John: An Investigation of the Place of the Fourth Gospel in the Johannine School* (trans. Linda M. Maloney; Minneapolis: Fortress, 1992).

[42]Schnelle, *Antidocetic*, 37-48.

[43]Herbert Kohler, *Kreuz und Menschwerdung im Johannesevangelium: Ein exegetisch-hermeneutischer Versuch zur johannesichen Kreuzestheologie* (ATANT 72; Zürich: Theologischer Verlag Zürich, 1987).

Thompson also emphasizes the humanity of Jesus in the Fourth Gospel with distinct theological interests, but through a different lens. She insists that par Käsemann in particular placed the study of Johannine Christology on a trajectory that ignores the fact that the Gospel does not seek to prove the humanity of Jesus because it *presumes* that humanity.[44] Thompson criticizes Käsemann for his focus on John 17, through which he may overlook aspects of the Johannine Jesus that would also be "at home" in the synoptic portrayals, including his parents, brothers, weariness at the well, friends, emotion at the plight of Lazarus, and his death.[45] She analyzes four themes in John with this suggestion in view: (1) Jesus' earthly origins; (2) the incarnation; (3) the signs, and (4) his death, and finds that in none of these is an interpretation necessitated "which impugns the true humanity of Jesus."[46] Thompson interprets the intention of the Gospel as struggling to establish that Jesus is the Son of God as well as being human.[47]

History of the Johannine Community Approach

Bultmann's lack of attention to the historical situation of the Johannine community is typically seen as the most severe omission of his work on the Gospel.[48] Käsemann addressed the situation only slightly more, finding the origins of the Fourth Gospel in the situation of Christian "enthusiasm."[49] In the meantime, however, some commentators were suggesting a Jewish context for the Gospel. W. C. van Unnik, for example, pointed out the essential Jewishness of the titles "Son of God" and Messiah" pointed to a mission to the synagogue, over against the History of Religions school, who decided upon the complete hostility of the Gospel toward Judaism.[50] J. A. T. Robinson came to a similar conclusion primarily by focusing on the predominance of the title "Son" over "Logos" in the body of the Gospel as well as the remarkable lack of reference to the Gentiles.[51]

For the past twenty-five years Johannine research in the United States has been dominated by the now familiar hypothesis concerning

---

[44]Marianne Meye Thompson, *The Humanity of Jesus in the Fourth Gospel* (Philadelphia: Fortress, 1988), 6-11.

[45]Thompson, *Humanity*, 3-4.

[46]Thompson, *Humanity*, 117.

[47]Thompson, *Humanity*, 13-116.

[48]Schnelle's summary criticism is typical: "[The evangelist's] goal is not a faith removed from history but an understanding of the various factual, spatial, and temporal levels of the Christ event." Udo Schnelle, "Recent Views of John's Gospel," *Word and World* 21 (2001): 359.

[49]Käsemann, *Testament*, 20-22. Ashton (*Understanding*, 92) perceptively points out that this position is "a partial return to the views of Bousset."

[50]W. C. van Unnik, "The Purpose of St. John's Gospel," *SE* 1 (1959): 382-411.

[51]J. A. T. Robinson, "Destination and Purpose of St. John's Gospel," *New Testament Issues* (ed. R. Batey; New York: Harper & Row, 1970), 191-209.

the community put forward by J. Louis Martyn and developed fully by Raymond Brown. These works attempt to trace a history of the development of christological understanding in the community in conflict with Judaism in the community's specific historical situation. Martyn links the predicted ejection from the synagogue passages in the Gospel with the insertion into the Eighteen Benedictions condemning *minim* and uses that connection as a clue to the situation of the community, specifically, that the Gospel is telling the story of the community in conflict with the synagogue.[52] Three stages, Martyn suggests, may be discerned: (1) the Early (Tranquil) Period, when the community consisted of Christian Jews, from before the Jewish War until some time in the 80s; (2) the Middle (Turbulent) Period, during the late 80s, when the synagogue instituted the *birkat ha-minim* and executed some of the community's evangelists, and (3) the Late Period, not dated by Martyn, when the Johannine community solidified its own identity and its relationship to the synagogue, the Christian Jews still in the synagogue, and other Jewish-Christian groups with whom it had hopes of unification.

Raymond Brown postulates four stages in the development of the Johannine community, stretching from before the written Gospel to the time of 3 John; he traces, moreover, the beliefs of several groups and conflicts with six groups of opponents reflected in the final Gospel product.[53] He concurs with Martyn that the Gospel can be read as an autobiography of the Johannine community and that the most formative situation for the community is the conflict with the synagogue. The traditions of the Gospel, he suggests, were interpreted in two broad directions, one that led onto the path that became the orthodoxy of the ecumenical councils, the other that led to the full-blown gnosticism of the second century, and representative positions of these two directions are exemplified by the author and opponents in the Epistles. The Johannine writings are best read, then, in their traditional order, which reflects the changes and conflicts in the community.[54]

The Brown-Martyn view of the Johannine community has recently, however, been challenged. Georg Strecker[55] and Charles H. Talbert,[56] for example, have offered alternative readings of the relationship between the Gospel and the Epistles. These readings not only challenge the assumption

[52]J. L. Martyn, *History and Theology in the Fourth Gospel* (2nd ed.; Nashville: Abingdon, 1979, 1968).

[53]Raymond E. Brown, *The Community of the Beloved Disciple* (New York: Paulist, 1979).

[54]As we will see in Chapter Four, Brown modifies his position somewhat by the time of his commentary on the Epistles.

[55]George Strecker, *The Johannine Letters: A Commentary on 1, 2, and 3 John* (ed. Harold Attridge; trans. Linda Maloney; Minneapolis: Fortress, 1996).

[56]Charles H. Talbert, *Reading John: A Literary and Theological Commentary on the Fourth Gospel and the Johannine Epistles* (New York: Crossroad, 1992).

of the chronological order in which Gospel and Epistles were written, but they also steer us away from the obsession with the conflict between the Johannine community and the synagogue and toward the christological understanding of the authors of the literature and their opponents as described especially in the Epistles. We will consider these and other challenges in some detail in Chapter Four.

I propose that a comparative History of Religions approach that takes into account the patterns of the ancient Mediterranean environment, as opposed to only Jewish precedents, will best serve to discern the foundations of the Johannine depiction of Christology and eventually to reconceptualize the development of the community. It was not the comparative approach of the History of Religions school that was in error but rather the lack of a controlling methodology. This lack, however, can now be remedied by taking into account recent progress in literary theory, especially in the area of a work of literature's reception by its audience.

METHODOLOGICAL CONCERNS: THE AUTHORIAL AUDIENCE

One of the primary difficulties of the History of Religions approach was the tendency to move from influence of background to influence of source; that is, from a writer using what "came naturally" as a product of the culture to a writer directly and intentionally utilizing a written and/or oral sources. The discomfort (to put it mildly) with the work of the History of Religions school approach was the tendency, seen especially in Bousset's work, to see the shared culture used by the evangelist as a pagan source of inspiration.[57] As Richard Seaford notes when considering the question of direct textual influence,

> It seems to me impossible that the detailed structural similarity that I have described can be wholly explained by such influence. What we have is rather a pattern of action whose powerful effect on the imagination was persistent enough to make itself felt in these two texts separated by five centuries. I suggest that the power and persistence of the pattern may derive, at least in part, from its relation with the powerful and persistent ritual of mystic initiation.[58]

The concern is a crucial one in John, and it has recently intersected with the interest in the Gospel as a coherent work of literature in its own right. Since the important study of Alan Culpepper,[59] the appreciation of John as

---

[57] Bousset, *Kyrios*, 158-60.

[58] Richard Seaford, "Thunder, Lightening and Earthquake in the *Bacchae* and the *Acts of the Apostles*," *What is a God*, 142 (article 139-51).

[59] Alan Culpepper, *Anatomy of the Fourth Gospel: A Study in Literary Design* (Philadelphia: Fortress, 1983).

a sophisticated literary text and a shift of attention from authorial intent to the reception of the text by the audience has increased.[60]

I will examine comparative literature from both the Jewish and the Greco-Roman cultural environments to reconstruct the expectations of the authorial audience using primarily the understandings of audience theory proposed by Hans Robert Jauss and Peter J. Rabinowitz. In his attempt to describe the dialectical process of the formation of literary canons, Jauss asserts that both the historicity of literature and its communicative nature "presupposes a dialogical and at once processlike relationship between work, audience, and new work that can be conceived in the relations between message and receiver as well as between question and answer, problem and solution."[61] It is possible to objectify the audience's "horizon of expectations," since we can discern the disposition an author expects from the audience through three factors: (1) the norms and poetics of the genre; (2) the relationships to known works of the literary-historical environment, and (3) the opposition between the poetic and the practical function of language.[62] The second factor will serve particularly well both in discerning models familiar to the audience in the literature of the time and, therefore, in perceiving the christological questions and answers the Johannine literature expresses.

Rabinowitz proposes a useful description of authorial audience.[63] He coined the term "authorial audience" for the readers who are *presupposed* by the text, that is, they are "*contextualized* implied readers" whom the author hoped would read the text, readers who can only be determined by examining the interrelation between the text and the context in which the text was produced. An author always makes assumptions about his or her readers' beliefs, knowledge, and familiarity with certain conventions. Social, historical and cultural assumptions are familiar to the audience, constituting their *assumed competency*, and, therefore, may not be elaborated in the text, making reconstruction a necessary element for understanding the perspective of the authorial audience. The modern interpreter attempts to engage the text with this audience by recognizing the need to make explicit as much of this assumed competency as possible, then asking how that affects the understanding of the text.

---

[60]For a recent review of the trend, see Schnelle, "Recent Views," 352-59.

[61]Hans Robert Jauss, *Toward an Aesthetic of Reception* (trans. Timothy Bahti; Minneapolis: University of Minnesota Press, 1982), 19.

[62]Jauss, *Aesthetic*, 24.

[63]Peter J. Rabinowitz, "Whirl Without End: Audience-Oriented Criticism," in *Contemporary Literary Theory* (ed. G. D. Atkins and L. Morrow; Amherst, Mass.; University of Massachusetts, 1989), 85; "Truth in Fiction: A Reexamination of Audiences," in *Critical Inquiry* 4 (1977), 126.

This assumed competency will be reconstructed by the use of comparative material from Mediterranean antiquity, both Jewish and pagan. The method will be to survey the behavior patterns of human/ divine interaction, noting the vocabulary used to describe these systems of behavior. From this, I will create a semantic field related to the behavior and thematic field and examine the Johannine literature in this light. This procedure will provide a framework to understand the expectations of the audience and, hence, to grasp how the description of the divine and human in Christ would have been heard and by which ancient pattern the audience would have understood it.

THE APPROACH OF THIS STUDY

The goal of this dissertation is to place the Christology of the Fourth Gospel, particularly its understanding of the incarnation, in an ancient Mediterranean context.[64] I will first survey Mediterranean sources to explore the question of how divine beings manifest themselves in the human realm; in this way, the patterns an ancient auditor might expect to encounter will become clear. While other Hellenistic themes have been investigated as forerunners to the New Testament concept of incarnation, such as descent from a god and "divine men,"[65] these themes can be subsumed under two general patterns: (1) metamorphosis, which involves a change in form, and (2) possession, which involves a change in substance.

Chapter Two will cover the metamorphosis models in the ancient Mediterranean world, a pattern in which a god will change his/her appearance into that of a human in order to interact with humans. This pattern generally entails a change in form and, therefore, in appearance, not a change in substance. The semantic field varies, but none of the terms connotes a change in essence—there is a continuity of mind and, therefore, of identity. In the metamorphosis phenomenon, two tendencies present themselves. The most common is a tendency to emphasize the actual physical form, but sometimes, the emphasis is upon the fact of the presentation, not as something material, but only as the appearance of it.

---

[64]While *concepts* from the ancient Mediterranean culture have been studied in the Fourth Gospel, the only *pattern* that has been thoroughly discussed is the descent-ascent pattern. In post-Bultmann scholarship, see, for example, Wayne Meeks, "The Man from Heaven in Johannine Sectarianism," *The Interpretation of John* (Issues in Religion and Theology 9; ed. J. Ashton; London: SPCK and Philadelphia: Fortress, 1986), 141-73; De Jonge, *Jesus: Stranger from Heaven and Son of God*; Talbert, "The Myth of a Descending-Ascending Redeemer in Mediterranean Antiquity;" Godfrey C. Nicholson, *Death as Departure: The Johannine Descent-Ascent Schema* (SBLDS 63; Chico: Scholars Press, 1983), and James F. McGrath, "Going Up and Coming Down in Johannine Legitimation," *Neot* 31 (1997): 107-18.

[65]For a concise review, see J. D. G. Dunn, "Incarnation," *ABD* 3.397-404.

In both tendencies, the a polymorphic capacity is present, usually for a god and occasionally for a divinized human.

In Jewish literature, the dominant representatives of God on earth, the angels, are described in the literature in ways that will assist us in building thematic and semantic metamorphosis fields to compare with the pagan literature. In the Jewish literature as well, typical vocabulary emphasizes the change of outward appearance rather than a change of inward essence. Again, sometimes the visible form is emphasized, but, perhaps more often than in Greco-Roman authors, the presentation as mere appearance is stressed. For Jewish authors, however, polymorphism is generally limited to demonic beings.

Chapter Three discusses the possession models. I will give evidence in this chapter that the phenomenon of possession is a many-sided one that is not well described by rigid categories. The model is better expressed by three continua, involving: (1) the expression of ecstatic behavior; (2) the displacement of the rational mind, and (3) the duration of the possession. As we will see, the characteristics of a possessive event have tendencies along these continua; for example, displacement of the rational mind has a strong, but not necessary, tendency to be accompanied by frenzied behavior.

The fourth chapter will concentrate on the Johannine Epistles, focusing particularly on 1 John and the christological controversy between the author and his opponents. In an examination of the Epistles, I will suggest that the audience would recognize that both the authors and opponents use a possession pattern to explain the association between the Christ and Jesus. While the opponents build upon a model of a temporary possession, however, the epistolary authors reveal an adaptation of the possession pattern that makes the primary issue one of permanence, and this focus on permanence serves to express the complete union of the human and divine. A key to appreciating the issue of permanence is the prolific use of the term μένω in the Johannine corpus, a term that suggests permanence, sometimes spatially, and always existentially. The author of 1 John stresses the permanence of the possession because it is the only means by which the believer can attain any permanent spiritual status; moreover, denying the permanence can only lead to impermanence (schism) in the community.

In Chapter Five, I will bring the conclusion of the previous three chapters together in an examination of the Christology of the Fourth Gospel. If the Gospel of John is closely related to 1 John and composed at approximately the same time, as I will suggest, and my analysis of the Epistles about the christological issue faced is correct, then in the Fourth Gospel we should see an emphasis on the tendency of possession that emphasizes permanence as well. This emphasis, moreover, we would expect to be shaped to counteract the temporary possession model; that is, the emphasis will fall on the permanence of the union between the human and divine, with no tendencies toward ecstatic behavior and none toward displacement of the human mind. One would also expect there to be a consequence of this investment in permanence that extends past an abstract theological point.

I will attempt to demonstrate that we see exactly that in the Gospel of John. While the identities of the divine being (Logos) and the human being (Jesus) are set out in the prologue, the role of the baptism has generally been under appreciated both as the event that describes *how* the divine being became flesh and also as a control through which the remainder of the Gospel would have been heard. It is not only the prologue, I suggest, that controls the audience's understanding of the Gospel but also the baptismal account. The permanence of this possessive union between the divine Christ and the human Jesus is developed and emphasized throughout the Gospel, and it is particularly explored both existentially and spatially through the use of the term μένω. The Gospel of John, in short, builds upon a pattern of permanent possession but extends both the pattern and its implications farther than does other literature. The result of this investment in the permanent unity of the divine and human is no less than the means of salvation offered to humankind through mutual indwelling, an indwelling enabled by the continuing identity of this being which is emphasized throughout its salvific death and the resurrection. Impermanence in the community, like the schism we saw in the Epistles, is decried in the narrative as a christological offense.

In his analysis of the works of Braun and Feuillet concerning the relationship between the human and divine in the Johannine Christ, Robert Kysar indicts them, along with those commentators who propose an "envoy" Christology, of finally being unable "to present a model for comprehending the way the two are related in the fourth gospel."[66] This dissertation proposes to defend such a model, one that is not only drawn from the cultural environment but also that invites the audience of the Fourth Gospel to stretch its expectations beyond what it brings to the hearing of the Gospel. The only thing they have to gain, according to the Fourth Evangelist, is eternal life.

---

[66]Robert Kysar, *The Fourth Evangelist and His Gospel: An Examination of Contemporary Scholarship* (Minneapolis: Augsburg, 1975).

CHAPTER 2
THE ANCIENT MEDITERRANEAN CONTEXT: METAMORPHOSIS

How does a divine being appear on earth to interact with humans? In this chapter, I will investigate the thematic and semantic domains of phenomena in which the external appearance of a heavenly being is emphasized, both in Greco-Roman and Jewish literature. While heavenly beings were described at times as simply appearing on earth, more often they transformed themselves into another appearance, an appearance in which either the form itself, or its substance or lack thereof, may be emphasized.

Especially in the ancient Greco-Roman literature, the manifestations of gods on earth looms as a major motif, and the diversity with which it has been described in the literature leads one scholar to call it a "kaleidoscopic reality."[1] A heavenly being may emerge before humans with no alteration in its appearance described; I will refer to this type of appearance as *direct epiphany*. This appearance is possible especially in Greco-Roman literature because the gods are pictured as like humans on "an exaggerated scale."[2] The mode of direct epiphany ranges from the dramatic, accompanied by spectacular natural phenomena, to one with an almost everyday quality.

---

[1] H. S. Versnel, "What Did Ancient Man See When He Saw a God? Some Reflections on Greco-Roman Epiphany," *Effigies Dei* (ed. D. v. d. Plas; Leiden: Brill), 43. See also B. C. Dietrich, "Divine Epiphanies in Homer," *Numen* 30 (1983): 68-69, who says concerning Homer that "the circumstances of the epiphany not only vary greatly, but they tend to be confused, contradictory even at times, and quite frequently impossible to visualize."

[2] They are stronger, more beautiful, taller, radiate like light, and so on, yet their appearance can be ascertained by such measurements as the size of a footprint. Bernard Dietrich, "From Knossos to Homer," in *What is a God: Studies in the Nature of Greek Divinity* (ed. Alan B. Lloyd; London: Duckworth, 1997), 4 and "Divine Epiphanies," 68-69; H. S. Versnel, "What," 42-43. Versnel (44) also points out that in this type of epiphany, although there is sometimes room for argument, "we may assume that generally the gods and heroes were considered to have appeared in what people believed to be their normal shapes."

Often, epiphany occurs at a time of crisis and can entail danger for the addressee. Surveying this phenomenon will help to highlight the thematic and semantic differences between it and metamorphosis.[3]

More important for our christological interests is the second phenomenon, in which heavenly beings interact with humans after altering their appearance; I will refer to this type of appearance as *metamorphosis*. Though this term is sometimes limited to the transformation of humans, while any type of appearance of a god is categorized as "epiphany," I prefer to use "metamorphosis" for both in order to highlight an important common element between the metamorphoses of humans and of gods: the metamorphosis pattern typically entails a change in form and, therefore, in appearance, not a change in substance. While the vocabulary varies, none of the terms connotes a change in essence—there is a continuity of mind and of identity. The major difference is that the change for a human is usually permanent, while that of a god is temporary. In the metamorphosis phenomenon, two tendencies present themselves. The most common is a tendency to emphasize the actual physical form, but sometimes, the emphasis is upon the fact of the presentation, not as something material, but only as the appearance of it. In both tendencies, the capacity is present, generally for a god and occasionally for a divinized human, to assume various forms (polymorphism).

In Jewish literature, the picture is comparable. The dominant representatives of God on earth in that tradition, the angels, are described in the literature in ways that will assist us in building thematic and semantic fields to compare with the pagan literature. We will also gain some assistance in building these fields when the Jewish authors discuss pagan beliefs. In the Jewish literature as well, the typical vocabulary emphasizes the outward change of the appearance, rather than a change of inward essence, and it has tendencies sometimes to emphasize the visible form, but, perhaps more often than in Greco-Roman authors, to stress the fact of the presentation as a mere appearance. For Jewish authors, polymorphism is generally limited to demonic beings.

GRECO-ROMAN LITERATURE: DIRECT EPIPHANY

Typical of the epiphanies described as simply an immediate appearance are those that occur in the heat of a hero's battle at the time of crisis. The semantic field commonly includes vocabulary of descending, standing near the person addressed and speaking, and ascending. Athena, for example, came gliding down (*delapsa*) through the high air to Cadmus

---

[3]For a summary of the debate as to exactly which types of phenomena should be included under epiphany, see Versnel, "What," 42-43. I have chosen to limit what I term "direct epiphany" to the personal, visual appearance of the god.

(Ovid, *Metam.* 3.101-02), and, in another work, came near Heracles to aid him in his battle with Cycnus (ἀγχίμολον δέ σφ᾽ ἦλθε, Hesiod, *The Shield of Heracles*, 325-26).[4] Apollo "stood close by and spoke to Telphusa" (αἶψα δ᾽ ἵκανε στῆ, Hom. *Hymn to Pythian Apollo*, 378).[5] Again, Athena descended quickly from Olympos and arrived beside the Achaians' ships (βῆ δὲ κατ᾽ Οὐλύμποιο καρήνων ἀΐξασα, Homer, *Il.* 2.167). She found Odysseus, stood beside him and spoke to him (ἀγχοῦ δ᾽ ἱσταμένη προσέφη γλαυκῶπις Ἀθήνη, Homer, *Il.* 2.172). At one point in the battles, Zeus sends the goddess Strife, who stands (στῆ) in the middle of a ship to stir up both sides (Homer, *Il.* 11.2-14; cf. 11.199-210).

At times the epiphany is limited to the person addressed. Venus revealed herself to no one except Hippomenes (Ovid, *Metam.* 10.650), while Apollo came to battle at Troy "wrapped in a cloud" and revealed his identity only to Paris (Ovid, *Metam.* 12.598-601). Apollo stood beside Hektor and talked to him (ἀγχοῦ δ᾽ ἱστάμενος προσέφη); Hektor immediately recognized the god, and Apollo promised to stand beside him and defend him (Homer, *Il.* 15.236-38).[6] The gods are not always so recognizable to the heroes, however. When Diomedes prayed to Athena, she stood close beside him (ἀγχοῦ δ᾽ ἱσταμένη) and told him that she had "taken the mist from his eyes" so that he "may recognize the god and the mortal" and thus be prevented from doing battle with immortals straight on (Homer, *Il.* 5.121-32; cf. *Od.* 16.161).

The literature also describes epiphany in more dramatic terms. Again, times of crisis provide the most typical occasions for epiphany in the literature, and the occurrences are far more varied than the stereotypical appearance of a god as a literary device to initiate a drama or as a *deus ex machina* resolution.[7] Sometimes, the heightened drama is depicted through the physical description of the divine being and the reaction of the person addressed. Athena, sent by Hera to Achilles to prevent him from acting rashly in anger, "came from the sky" (ἦλθε δ᾽ Ἀθήνη οὐρανόθεν). She stood (στῆ) behind Achilles and caught him by his hair, appearing (φαιομένη) to him only. Achilles "in amazement turned around, and immediately he knew Pallas Athena and the terrible eyes shining" (Homer, *Il.* 1.193-200). Athena then returned (βεβήκει) to Olympus" (Homer, *Il.*1.221-22).

---

[4]Quotations of Greek and Latin texts are from the *Loeb Classical Library*; full citations of the volumes used may be found in the *Bibliography*. The translations are mine, unless otherwise noted.

[5]See also Hom. *Hymn to Pythian Apollo*, 246: στῆς δὲ μάλ᾽ ἄγχ᾽ αὐτῆς.

[6]For the problem of deciding whether examples such as this one display an actual manifestation of a god or a literary technique for portraying inner motivation, see Dietrich, "Divine Epiphanies," 59 and n. 46.

[7]As, for example, the appearance Athena at the beginning of *Ajax* or of Herakles at end of *Philoctetes*.

Spectacular natural phenomena can occur with epiphanies as well. Dietrich notes that light and fire were important signals of divine birth in Greek myth, citing the birth of Zeus "signalled annually by a flash of fire" and the use of flames to mark the birth of a child by Potnia in the Eleusinian mysteries.[8] In the *Odyssey*, Zeus sent a thunderbolt to accompany an epiphany of Athena at a climatic point (Homer, *Od.* 24.520-48). Ovid is one of the writers who records a mythological tragedy with perhaps the most famous of lighteningbolts. At Juno's bidding, Semele asks Jove to reveal himself to her as he is. Distressed, Jove drew on the mists and mingled clouds, lightening, blasts of wind and thunder. Though he tried to decrease his power by taking a "lighter bolt," Semele was nonetheless destroyed by it (Ovid, *Metam.* 3.255-315). The danger to the human is obvious, and the theme of crisis remains dominant.[9]

An ancient Mediterranean audience, then, could expect literature to describe direct epiphanies, generally in situations of crisis. While the accompaniment of spectacular natural phenomena, such as lightening, would not surprise, such a depiction would not necessarily be expected. A direct epiphany, moreover, can cause danger for the human, hence the appeal of another mode of appearance.

GRECO-ROMAN LITERATURE: METAMORPHOSIS

If we define metamorphosis broadly, as I have suggested, the types of transformation familiar to an audience from Greco-Roman literature were legion. Humans may be transformed into inanimate objects or animals, and gods can change their appearance not only to that of a human, but also to that of other gods or animals. The transformation of humans, as previously mentioned, is most often a permanent change that can actually clarify the character of the former human,[10] while that of gods is temporary, for the purpose of aid or deception.[11] While our main consideration is the temporary transformation of gods to humans, it will be helpful to consider

---

[8]Dietrich, "Divine Epiphanies," 68.

[9]Frederick Brenk, "Greek Epiphanies and Paul on the Road to Damascus," in *Relighting the Souls: Studies in Plutarch, in Greek Literature, Religion and Philosophy, and in the New Testament Background* (Stuttgart: Franz Steiner Verlag, 1998), 354-63. Even in the case of Semele, Brenk suggests (357) that the intent may have been her divination, citing Philostratos' understanding of Euripides' account of Semele in *Bacchae* 1-12. In addition, Brenk points out that lightening epiphanies often serve not only divine vengeance, but also the protection of a nascent cult that is being threatened.

[10]For this issue in Ovid, see Joseph B. Solodow, *The World of Ovid's Metamorphoses* (Chapel Hill & London: University of North Carolina Press, 1988), 174-88.

[11]Dietrich ("Divine Epiphanies," 62) points out that in the Homeric epics, "a god who assumed the exact likeness of a particular hero wished to mislead more often than to communicate with mortals and inspire them."

other types of metamorphosis briefly as we search for how the process is described in the literature, developing the thematic and semantic fields.

The family of verbs most often used to describe the process of human beings changed into an animal or an inanimate object are, not surprisingly, those expressing "turning" or "changing," such as the Latin *muto*, *transformo* and *verso*, and the Greek μετεβάλλω and μορφόω. To save Adonis from being killed by a wild boar, Venus will change (*mutabitur*) his blood into an anemone by sprinkling it with nectar (Ovid, *Metam*.10.728, cf. 14.91-100). Perimele's transformation into an island by Neptune is described by Ovid as a solid island growing from her "transformed members" (*mutatis membris*, Ovid, *Metam*. 8.609-10). Venus changes (*transformat*) two humans into bulls and changes (*versae*) others who denied her divinity into stones (Ovid, *Metam*. 10.234; 242). Neptune grieves for the son "whose body (*corpus*) he had changed (*versum*) into the bird of Phaëthon" (Ovid, *Metam*. 12.581; cf. 6.672). Hermes changed (μετέβαλλεν) Battrus into a rock (Hesiod, *The Great Eoiae*, 16), and in Euripides' *The Bacchae*, Dionysius tells Cadmus that the man will be changed (μεταβαλών) into a serpent (*l.* 1330). Zeus touched Io and changed (μετεμόρφωσε) her into a white cow (Hesiod, *The Aeginius* 3). Very rarely, a simple transitive verb is employed. Sailors are changed into dolphins by Dionysus (δελφῖνες δ᾿ ἐγένοντο, Hom. *Hymn to Dionysus* 53). For frightening and mocking nymphs, a shepherd is turned into a tree (*arbor enim est*, Ovid, *Metam*.14.524; cf. 1.237). Apollo pitied Daedalion and "made him into a bird" (*fecit avem*, Ovid, *Metam*. 11.349).

The verbal transformation, however, tells us little about substance. Was the essence changed, or merely the appearance? To answer that question, we must highlight the nouns used to describe exactly *what* was changed, and the typical nouns employed are *corpus, facies, figura, forma, imago* and *specie*, all of which customarily describe the external form rather than the essence of a being. *Corpus*, for example, generally means "form" in the sense of the substantial bodies of people or animals.[12] Neptune, for example, gives the daughter of Erysichthon power to change her form (*transformia corpora*) to avoid being enslaved (Ovid, *Metam*. 8.871). Though the river-god Acheloüs claims often to have changed form (*nempe novandi est corporis*), he admits that his power to change is limited in its range (Ovid, *Metam*. 8.879-80).

Both *facies* and *figura* also express the outer form that is altered during metamorphosis. Venus changed Acmon to a bird in anger, and the others who stood around marveling at this transformation were changed into the same form (*eandem accipiunt faciem*, Ovid, *Metam*. 14.505-06). Scoffing at the gods, Pirithoüs states that it is conceding too much power to the gods to believe that "they give and take the forms of things" (*si dant*

---

[12] Glare, P. G. W. ed., *Oxford Latin Dictionary* (Oxford: Clarendon, 1982), 448.

adimuntque figuras, Ovid, *Metam.* 8.614-15). Venus' change of two people into bulls is described as the "penalty of the changed form" (*versae poena figurae*, Ovid, *Metam.*10.234). Bacchus caused the daughters of Anius to lose their human form (*figuram perdiderint*) and be changed to doves (Ovid, *Metam.*13.670-74).

Other terms to express that which is changed in metamorphosis are *forma* and *imago*. *Forma* clearly emphasizes the exterior shape of a thing.[13] *Imago* tends in that direction as well, though it is a bit more complex: it can mean either a visible form or a mental picture.[14] Hyacinthus' transformation to a lily is expressed as *formamque capit, quam lilia* (Ovid, *Metam.* 10.212). Neptune changed the form (*formamque novat*) of a woman to a fisherman (Ovid, *Metam.* 8.853), then returned her to her original form (*redita forma est*, Ovid, *Metam.* 8.870).[15] The marble statue of Picus is described in this way: "The hero's form was as you see it; although you should look at his own beauty, you would approve the true in comparison with the feigned image" (*forma viro, quam cernis, erat: licet ipse decorem adspicias fictaque probes ab imagine verum*, Ovid, *Metam.*14.322-23). In an example of a temporary metamorphosis of a human, Tiresias changed from a man to woman (*deque viro factus femina*) for seven years, then his former state returned and his innate image came back (*forma prior rediit, genetivaque venit imago*, Ovid, *Metam.* 3.326-331). Circe transformed Herakles' companions, described as various beast-like forms coming (*veniunt*) upon them, and "none kept his own image" (*nulli sua mansit imago*, Ovid, *Metam.* 14.414-15).

One interesting type of exception in the process of metamorphosis proves the point, adding to our semantic field in the meantime. When humans who had a divine parent are taken into the realm of the gods, the process reveals that the metamorphosis does not bestow divinity; rather, the human which is within must be purged from the divine.[16] A river-god washed the mortal part from the half-divine Aeneas at the command of Venus, so that "the best was restored to him" (Ovid, *Metam.* 14.600-08). Herakles changed to a god, "and no shape of Herakles that could be recognized remained" because only the aspects from his divine father remained, and none from his human mother (Ovid, *Metam.* 9.256-72). When Romulus and his wife were transformed to gods, Romulus' alteration was described as his mortal part dissolving into thin air while a beautiful form comes over him (*corpus mortale per auras dilapsum tenues pulchra subit facies*,

---

[13]Glare, *OLD*, 722.

[14]Glare, *OLD*, 831.

[15]Ovid in particular delights in describing the process of transformation gradually, artistically, and in those longer descriptions sometimes does not have the need to use the key vocabularly. Examples of this type of description may be found, for example, in *Metam.* 9.118-22; 10.699-707; 11.67; 12.201-07; 12.524-31.

[16]Solodow, *World*, 191-92.

Ovid, *Metam.* 14.823-28; cf. 9.262-70). For his wife, however, who was not half-divine, the familiar verb *muto* is used to describe the change of her mortal body and her name (14.850-51).

The descriptions are similar when gods metamorphose into something other than human; again, the vocabulary reveals that the transformation does not involve anything of essence. A verb that makes a rare appearance in this context is *induo*. Ovid describes Jove putting on the features and dress of Diana (*protinus induitur faciem cultumque Dianae*, Ovid, *Metam.* 2.425), and later as taking the form of a bull (*induitur faciem tauri*, Ovid, *Metam.* 2.850-51). Later, Jove put off that disguise and acknowledged what he was (*posita fallacis imagina tauri se confessus erat*, 3.1-2). *Verso* and *muto* suffice well for this type of metamorphosis as well. The sun god assumes the form of a nymph's mother, Eurynome, then resumes his own form and splendor (*versus in Eurynomes faciem genetricis... nec longius ille moratus in veram rediit speciem solitumque nitorem* (Ovid, *Metam.* 4.219; 230-31; cf. 10.157-58).

In Greek, two verbs most often express the process of metamorphosis. The first is ἔοικα, a perfect tense form with a present tense meaning "to be like" or "to seem," along with its participle form ἐοικώς, meaning "seeming like" or "like."[17] The second is *ειδω, which in the middle means "to appear," "to be like or to make oneself like."[18] The *Homeric Hymn to Pythian Apollo* gives examples of each in identical contexts, showing the lack of distinction between the two. At one point Apollo takes the form of a dolphin (δελφῖνι ἐοικώς, 400), and later recalls the incident at the founding of the cult: "since at the first on the hazy sea I leapt upon the swift ship in the form of a dolphin (εἰδόμενος δελφῖνι), pray to me as Apollo Delphinius" (*Hom. Hymn to Pythian Apollo*, 494). In the *Iliad*, Athena and Apollo assumed the forms of birds (ὄρισιν ἐοικότες, 7.58-60), and Apollo at one point descended to Hector in the likeness of a hawk (ἰρήκι ἐοικώς), though he appeared to Hector as a god (15.236-38).[19] Ἀλλάσσω can serve on the Greek side, as when Zeus descended and changed himself into a bull (καταλθὼν ἤλλαξεν ἑαυτὸν εἰς ταῦρον, Hesiod, *Eoiae*, 19). An intransitive

---

[17]H. G. Liddell and R. S. Scott, *A Greek-English Lexicon* (rev. ed.; Oxford: Clarendon, 1968), 601.

[18]Liddell-Scott, *Lexicon*, 483. While the line between the denotations of this term, whether "assumed the appearance" or "his own appearance was like" can admittedly be fluid (see Versnel, "What," 45 and Dietrich, "Divine Epiphanies," 56), I have chosen examples in which it seems to me the chance of understanding of the phrase as merely poetic is minimal. An example of what seems to be more (bad) simile than transformation, see *Il.* 13.754-55, where Polydamas goes forth into the battle like (ἐοικώς) a snowy mountain.

[19]Dietrich ("Divine Epiphanies," 56-58) points out that in the Homeric epics the line between true identification and mere comparison with the term ἐοικώς can be difficult, especially in cases of bird comparisons, which could often highlight the manner and speed of ascent and descent rather than an actual metamorphosis.

is found again in the *Homeric Hymn to Dionysius* 44, as when Dionysus'
metamorphosis into a lion is described (λέων γένετ'). The shape is changed
rather than the essence.

The noun family employed is also comparable, with the semantic field
signaling a change only in form. Not surprisingly, for Ovid *imago* can serve
both for metamorphosis and for artistic works such as statues and painting:
all are conceived as representations of form (*Metam.* 1.239; 5.199; 7.128-9).[20]
After travelling on a ship to Rome in the form of a serpent (*in serpente deus
praenuntia sibila misit*), Asclepius resumed his "heavenly form" (*et finem
specie caelestem resumpta*, Ovid, *Metam.* 15.670; 743). Plautus employs *imago*
in the same manner in *Amphitryon*. Mercury steps on stage and declares
that Jupiter is inside, having turned himself into the very image (*vertit sese
imaginem*) of Amphitryon. He continues, "As for me, I have assumed the
form (*sumpsi...imaginem*) of Amphyitryon's slave Sosia" (*ll.* 120-24).

When gods or other heavenly beings change their shape to interact
with humans, similar semantic and thematic patterns emerge to those we
have seen. I will survey typical examples of those patterns, highlighting
aspects that particularly distinguish the heavenly beings from the mortals.
The Latin verbal patterns are familiar from earlier sections, with the
reappearance of *verso* and *muto*, as well as the compatible terms *simulo* and
sumptio. When Arethusa changed into a stream of water (*in latices mutor*),
her pursuer, the river-god Alphaeus, laid aside the human form which he
had assumed and changed back into his own shape (*positoque viri, quod
sumpserat, ore vertitur in proprias...undas*, Ovid, *Metam.*5.637-38). Mercury
descends, changing his form, assuming on earth the figure of man (*sive
mutata iuvenum figure*, Horace, *Odes* 1.2.41-44). In pursuit of Chione,
Phoebus assumes an old woman's form (*Phoebus anum simulat praereptaque
gaudia sumit*, Ovid, *Metam.*11.310).

Familiar nouns reappear, commonly in tandem with expected verbs.
Specie serves the descriptive purpose at one point when Jupiter come in
the disguise of a human (*Iuppiter huc specie mortali*, Ovid, *Metam.* 8.626).
Mercury, having pretended to leave a scene, soon returns with changed
voice and form (*mox redit et versa pariter cum voce figura*, Ovid, *Metam.*
2.697-98); later, however, Mercury does not seek to disguise himself (*nec se
dissimulat*, Ovid, *Metam.*2.731). Pallas assumes the form of an old woman
(*Pallas anum simulat*) and is not recognized, then removes the human
form and reveals herself (*formamque removit anilem Palladaque exhibuit*,
Ovid, *Metam.* 6.26; 43-44). At times, however, the gods are at least partly
recognizable. In the story of Lycaon, king of Arcadia, Jove descends and
wanders about disguised as a man (*quam cupiens falsam summo delabor
Olympo et deus humana lustro sub imagine terras*, Ovid, *Metam.* 212-13).

---

[20]Solodow, *World*, 205-06.

Although Jove gives a sign that a god has come, Lycaon does not believe it and sets out to find the truth, with tragic results (Ovid, *Metam.* 1.198-239). Ovid's telling of the story of Bacchus and the sailors is interesting on this point. One of the sailors and the narrator of the tale relates how he gazed on the dress, face and gait (*cultum faciemque gradumque*) of a young man, the metamorphosed Bacchus, and "all seemed more than mortal" (*nil ibi, quod credi posset mortale, videbam,* Ovid, *Metam.* 3.609-10). He assures his companions that there is a divinity within the human body (*quod numen in isto corpore sit, dubito; sed corpore numen in isto est!* Ovid, *Metam.* 3.611-12).

In Greek, verbal forms from the root *εἰδω are again typical, as is ἔοικα. A typical expression in this pattern is found in the *Iliad*, as when Ares entered (μετελθών) the Trojan ranks in the likeness (εἰδόμενος) of Adamas to encourage them (Homer, *Il.* 5.461-62). Also in the *Iliad*, Apollo assumes the form (δέμας) of Periphas, and in his likeness (ἐεισάμενος), speaks (17.323-26). In a Homeric hymn, Apollo takes the form of a man (ἀνέρι εἰδόμενος, *Hom. Hymn to Pythian Apollo*, 449).[21] In the *Homeric Hymn to Dionysius*, the god appears (ἐφάνη) on the shore, seeming like a young man (ὡς νεηνίη ἀνδρὶ ἐοικώς, *ll.* 2-3; cf. Homer, *Il.* 13.352-57; 24.345-48). In the *Iliad*, Aphrodite appears to Helen, likening herself to an old woman (γρηΐ δὲ μιν ἐϊκυῖα παλαιγενέϊ, Homer, *Il.* 3.386), and Apollo likens himself in every way (πάντα ἐοικὼς) to Agenor (21.600).[22]

The nominal form εἶδος is typical of the process as well, as is the noun δέμας. Εἶδος typically means "that which is seen, a "form," "shape" or "figure," and δέμας is used to express a "bodily frame."[23] In the *Homeric Hymn to Demeter*, the goddess is described as "disfiguring her form for a while" (εἶδος ἀμαλδύνουσα πολὺν χρόνον) when she disguised herself as an old woman (*l.* 94); the change of appearance back to that of a goddess is described similarly (εἶδος ἄμειψε γῆρας ἀπωσαμένη, *ll.* 275-76). The characteristic verbs often appear in conjunction with the noun δέμας. Poseidon likens himself both in form and voice to Kalchas" to encourage the Argives (εἰσάμενος Κάλχαντι δέμας καὶ ἀτειρέα φωνήν), then leaves in the form of a hawk (Homer, *Il.* 13.43-45). Athena several times "likens herself in voice and appearance to Mentor" (Μέντορι εἰδομένη ἠμὲν δέμας ἠδὲ καὶ αὐδήν, Homer, *Il.* 22.205-206; 24.502-503; 24.548). Again in the *Iliad*, Athena descends from heaven (οὐρανόθεν καταβᾶσα) and comes to Odysseus in the likeness of a woman (δέμας δ᾽ ἤϊκτο γυναικι, 20.30-31; cf. 16.157; 21.284-86). In a Homeric hymn, Apollo takes the shape of a young man (ἀνέρι εἰδόμενος)

---

[21] It should also be noted that a god can make his or her voice only like that of a hero; for example, to deliver a message from Zeus to the Trojans, Iris likens her voice to that of Polites' (εἴσατο δὲ φθογγὴν; ἐεισαμένη; Homer, *Il.* 2.795; 807).

[22] A similar term that serves is in *Il.* 4.86, where Athena merges among the Trojans in the likeness of a man (ἀνδρὶ ἰκέλη).

[23] Liddell-Scott, *Lexicon*, 482; 378.

yet is addressed as being more like the immortals in shape and form (ἐπεὶ οὐ μὲν γάρ τι καταθνητοῖσι ἔοικας οὐ δέμας οὐδὲ φυήν ἀλλ' ἀθανάτοισι θεοῖσιν, *Hom. Hymn to Pythian Apollo*, 448-65).

Μορφή is a typical noun for external appearance, generally meaning "form" or "shape."[24] For example, in Sophocles' *Oedipus the King* (*ll.* 740-44) Jocasta tells Oedipus that Laius was a tall man, with nearly white hair, "and in his form (μορφῆς) not unlike you" (cf. *ll.* 699-700). In Euripides' *The Bacchae*, Dionysius describes his appearance as a "shape changed from god to mortal" (μορφὴν δ' ἀμείψας ἐκ θεοῦ βροτησίαν, *l.* 4). Later, the god describes the transformation using several of our distinctive nouns and verbs: "For this reason I have changed to mortal form (εἶδος θνητὸν ἀλλάξας) and transformed my shape into human (μορφήν τ' ἐμὴν μετέβαλον εἰς ἀνδρὸς φύσιν, *ll.* 53-54). At the beginning of *The Women of Trachis*, Deianeira describes how the river-god Achelous came to woo her "in three shapes" (ἐν τρισὶν μορφαῖσιν), sometimes manifest (ἐναργής) as a bull, other times as a serpent, and again as part man and part bull (*ll.* 9-14).

Metamorphosis: Polymorphism

It is apparent in the previous examples that the gods have the power to take different forms at different times; an epithet of Dionysius, in fact, is one "of many shapes" (πολυμόρφος, *Orphic Hymns* 29.8).[25] Those associated with the sea in particular have this ability. The sea god Proteus, for example, could rapidly assume shapes in quick succession, capable of "every type of transfiguration" (μεταβολὰς παντοίας, Homer, *Od.* 4.454-56). In the *Iliad*, Poseidon appears to Ajax as Calchas (13.45), to King Idomeneus as Thoas (13.216-18) and to Agamemnon as an old man (14.136). When the gods are not recognizable, it is not only because humans have a "mist" over their eyes (Homer, *Il.* 5.121-132) and the gods are so quick (Homer, *Od.* 10.573), but also because the gods can take any shape (παντὶ ἔϊσκεις, Homer, *Od.* 13.313).[26]

---

[24]Liddell-Scott (*Lexicon*, 1147) lists the Latin *forma* as possibly a cognate.

[25]Anne-France Morand, "Orphic Gods and Other Gods," in *What is a God? Studies in the Nature of Greek Divinity* (ed. Alan B. Lloyd; London: Duckworth, 1997), 172; 178 n. 6. A fragment attributed to Sophocles preserved in Clement of Alexandria, *Stromata* 5.14.111,4-6 (H. Attridge, *Fragments of Pseudo-Greek Poets* in *The Old Testament Pseudepigrapha* [2 vols.; ed. James H. Charlesworth; Garden City, N. J.: Doubleday, 1985], 2.826-27 describes Zeus' ability to take different forms to copulate with humans: "For Zeus wed the mother of this man, not in golden form, nor clothed with feathers of a swan, as he made pregnant the maid of Pleuron, but completely as a man." The episode is probably the conception of Herakles.

[26]Cf. *Hom. Hymn to Demeter* 111. The transformation, however, is not always completely successful; sometimes, there seems to be something about the nature of the deity that is yet apparent to some mortals. See Homer, *Il.* 2.56-59; 2.790-791; 3.385-399; 15.236-238; 17.323-326; Ovid, *Metam.* 3.574-698; 22.210; Virgil, *Aen.* 1.315-328.

Our standard Latin vocabulary reappears when Ovid describes gods, heroes and nymphs as shape-shifters. Neptune gave Periclymenus the "power to assume any form he pleased and to put it off again at will" (*cui posse figuras sumere, quas vellet, rursusque reponere sumptas Neptunus dederat*, Ovid, *Metam*.12.556-58). The god Vertumnas, to woo the wood-nymph Pomona, can change to many forms (*per multas figuras*, Ovid, *Metam.* 14.652), having the ability to assume whatever form he wishes (*formasque apte fingetur in omnes*, Ovid, *Metam.* 14.685; cf. 766-67). As the river-god Acheloüs tells Theseus, some of the greatest heroes have had their form changed once and it remained in its new state (*forma semel mota est et in hoc renovamine mansit*, Ovid, *Metam.* 8.728ff.), while others have been given the power to assume many forms (*in plures ius est transire figuras*, Ovid, *Metam.* 8.727-30). Acheloüs describes a change to the form (*formatus*) of a snake, then to a bull (*tauri forma; tauro mutatus*, Ovid, *Metam.* 9.62-63; 80-81). Thetis changed to many forms to avoid sex with Peleus (*quod nisi venisses veriatis saepe figuris ad solitas artes; illa novat formas*, Ovid, *Metam.* 11.241, 260), then admitted failure and revealed her true form (*exhibita estque Thetis*, Ovid, *Metam.*11.264).

Metamorphosis: Nonmaterial Emphasis

In some examples of the metamorphosed appearance of the gods, the stress is on the *mere* appearance rather than physical form, in the sense of a vision or phantom. The line between the two emphases can be fluid, but the vocabulary sometimes helps to distinguish between them. *Specie*, for example, can be used of reported portents of phantom ships (*navium speciem*) in the sky (Livy 21.62.4; cf. 42.2.4), of a nocturnal vision (*nocturnae spicea*, Tacitus, *Hist.* 11.4) and of the phantom appearance and ghost (*species et umbrae*) of an innocent murder victim, though one real enough to drive the guilty haunted man to his death (Livy 40.56.9). Ovid describes the healing god Asclepius during the sleep of an ill person: "Then did the health-giving god in your dreams seem to stand (*consistere visus*) before your couch...in the same way as he is accustomed to do in a temple" (Ovid, *Metam.* 15.653-65).

In the *Metamorphoses*, Ovid records the story of Iris asking Sleep to "fashion a shape that will seem real form" (*quae veras aequant imitamine formas*) and have it go "in semblance" (*sub imagine*) of the king to Alcyone (11.626). Sleep then rouses Morpheus, so-named because he is the most accomplished "imitator of the human form" (*artificem simulatoremque figurae*, 11.634). Morpheus arrives at his destination and takes the shape of Ceyx, pale like the dead (*in faciem Ceycis abit sumptaque figura luridus*, 11.652-654). When he tells the wife of the king that he is the shade of her husband, she reaches out to grab him, but holds only air (11.655-75). She was suddenly awakened by her own crying out and "by the image (*specie*) of her husband" (11.677). Morpheus, then, can transform himself into a human form, and he can make that form like a "shade" (*umbra*) without solid physical presence.

In Greek, the terms εἰκών, ὄψις and especially εἴδωλον, φάντασμα and φαντασία generally represent this emphasis. Both εἰκών and ὄψις can indicate either a form, an appearance of a person or thing, or a nonmaterial presence.[27] Athena is once described merely as a "shape" that came (ἦλθεν εἰκών) to stop the homicidal spree of the maddened Herakles (Euripides, *The Madness of Herakles ll.* 1002-06). Ariston made violent love to Perictone, but failed to win her; when he ceased his violence, he saw a vision (ὄψιν) of Apollo, and he left her unmolested until her child was born (Diogenes Laertius, *Plato* 3.2). King Croesus saw a vision in a dream (ὄψις ὀνείρου) which came to him during the night and told him that his son would die young and by an iron weapon (Herodotus, *Hist.* 1.38.1).

Εἴδωλον, φάντασμα and φαντασία more consistently emphasize a nonsubstantial appearance.[28] In *Ajax* (*ll.* 125-26), Achilles laments, "I see that all of us who live are nothing but ghosts, or a fleeting shadow" (ὁρῶ γὰρ ἡμᾶς οὐδὲν ὄντας ἄλλο πλὴν εἴδωλ᾽ ὅσοιπερ ζῶμεν ἢ κούφην σκιάν). The distinction between this emphasis and that on physical form can be seen in Oedipus' prayer to the Eumenides: "Take pity on this wretched ghost of the man Oedipus, for indeed this is not his former form" (οἰκτίρατ᾽ ἀνδρὸ ς Οἰδίπου τόδ᾽ ἄθλιον εἴδωλον οὐ γὰρ δὴ τό γ᾽ ἀρχαῖον δέμας, Sophocles, *Oed. col.* 109-110). Apollo made a spectre (εἴδωλον) in the likeness of Aeneas and in armor like his (Homer, *Il.* 5.449), and the εἴδωλον of Herakles recognized Odysseus in the netherworld (Homer, *Od.* 11.615).

Metamorphosis: Continuity of Mind and Identity

A theme of metamorphosis is that of *continuity*: characteristics of the being's essence continue in its altered form. Again, the crucial aspect to grasp about metamorphosis as it will concern Christology is that the change is not one of essence. To this end, examples that show the same mind throughout, no matter what type of metamorphosis, are instructive. In the human metamorphosis realm, we have examples of humans retaining physical features, emotions, mind, and/or bodily

---

[27]Liddell-Scott, *Lexicon*, 485 and 1282, respectively.

[28]Liddell-Scott, *Lexicon*, 483 and 1916, respectively. Versnel ("What," 47-48) describes εἴδωλον and φάντασμα thus: "Now, *eidolon* is any unsubstantiated form, a phantom, and also an image in the mind, fancy. *Phasma* comes very close to this: in the mysteries *phasmata* of the gods are shown in order to impress the awe-struck audience who think they are real gods. During the battle of Marathon according to one report it was not Theseus himself but the *phasma* of Theseus that was observed (Plut. *Thes.* 35,7). No wonder these terms function especially in the atmosphere of death and the uncanny."

functions.[29] While there are important exceptions, the transformation of form is generally a permanent one.

Ovid in particular has a profound interest in this continuity and so is especially explicit.[30] Even with physical human characteristics, some continuity can remain. Though changed into a tree, Dryope is described as "hidden" in the tree trunk, and we are told that the branches of the tree long kept the warmth of her "transformed body" (*corpore mutato*, Ovid, *Metam.* 9.392-93; cf. 9.319-24). The category of nymphs is an interesting one. One Homeric hymn tells us that they "rank neither with mortals nor with immortals," since they interact primarily with the gods and eat divine foods, but nonetheless die as do mortals, though after a longer lifespan (*Hom. Hymn to Aphrodite*, 259-75). The nymph Lotis continues to bleed even after she takes refuge in the shape of a flower, "changed as to features but yet keeping her name" (*contulerat versos, servato nomine, vultus*, Ovid, *Metam.* 9.344-48).

More importantly, the mind, feelings, attachments and memory can remain after the transformation. When Juno, for example, turned a nymph into a bear, Ovid points out that "still her human mind remained" (*mens antiqua manet, Metam.* 2.485). Acteon, having been changed into a stag by Diana, groans and cries when he sees his features, and "only his former mind remains" (*mens tantum pristina mansit*, Ovid, *Metam.* 3.193-203). Callisto, having been changed into a bear by Artemis, "thought fit to go into the forbidden precinct of Zeus, being ignorant of the law" (δόξαι εἰσελθεῖν ἀγνοήσασαν τὸν νόμον, Hesiod, *Astron.* 3). Though Cadmus and his wife are turned to serpents, they neither fear nor wound humans, "remembering what they once were, mild creatures" (*quidque prius fuerint, pacidi meminere dracones*); moreover, in their altered form (*versae formae*) they continue to find comfort in their grandson (Ovid, *Metam.* 4.602-5; cf. 11.741-48; 14.549-66). Glaucus was once mortal, but when changed to river-god, he still recalls his past life despite the fact that Ovid says his mind was not the same (*Metam.* 13.906-968; cf. 14.275-305). Cephalus recalls how Aurora helped him by temporarily changing his form, a change he could feel occuring (*inmutatque meam [videor sensisse] figuram*) so that he could enter unrecognized into Athens (Ovid, *Metam.* 7.721-724).

Physical and emotional continuity sometimes comes in tandem. "When Myrrha is turned into a tree after her crime of incest, she loses her former feelings with her body but continues to weep, and her tears trickle from the

---

[29]Occasionally, Ovid gives evidence that the change is substantial; for example, Picus is changed to bird and "nothing of his former self remained to Picus except his name" (*nec quicquam antiquum Pico nisi nomina restat*, Ovid, *Metam.*14.389-96)

[30]The psychological dimensions of this continuity, the "edge of cruelty in the comedy of transformation," is explored interestingly by Harold Skulsky in *Metamorphosis: The Mind in Exile* (Cambridge, Mass. and London: Harvard University Press, 1981); quotation is from p. 30.

tree" (*quae quamquam amisit veteres cum corpore sensus, flet tamen, et tepidae manant ex arbore guttae*, Ovid, *Metam.* 10.499-500). Since she is pregnant, the tree swells in the midst of the trunk, and she gives birth in that form (Ovid, *Metam.* 10.503-518). The Heliades drip blood from where their mother grabs at them during their transformation and tears off branches; one of them says that the "body you are mutilating in this tree is mine" (Ovid, *Metam.* 2.359-363). When the hero Acis changed into a river-god, blood first flows from his previous wounds, then water flows from them as he begins to change. Suddenly his appearance is as a youth standing in the water with newly-sprung horns wreathed in rushes. "The youth, except that he was larger and his face was dark blue like water, was still Acis, changed to a river-god, and his waters kept their former name" (*Acis erat, sed sic quoque erat tamen Acis, in amnem versus*, Ovid, *Metam.* 13.896-7).

In the *Metamorphosis* of Apuleius, the protagonist Lucian is changed into an ass and yet can recall and narrate his entire experience. He shows human characteristics, moreover, while he is in the form of an ass (e.g. 3.26; 4.2; 4.6; 7.16). Lucian insists that even though he is now an ass, he "still retained a human sense and understanding" (*iumentum sensum tamen retinebam humanum*, 3.26) and his mind "was not through and through bestial" (4.2). He challenges the reader on this very point: "I will test my wit (*ingenium*) and give you the chance to consider if I was an ass in mind (*mente*) and in purpose" (*sensu*, 4.6).

We have already seen many examples of the continuity of essence when gods make the temporary change to a human form. I would like to highlight one more extraordinary example, the story of Demeter as told in the *Homeric Hymn to Demeter*. In this well-known tale, the goddess in her grief over her daughter traveled around towns and fields "disfiguring her form for a time" (εἶδος ἀμαλδύνουσα πολὺν χρόνον, l. 94). She was unrecognized, since "gods are not easily discerned by mortals" (χαλεποὶ δὲ θεοὶ θνητοῖσιν ὁρᾶσθαι, l. 111). During the entire episode, the goddess is described as only herself, feeling the same emotions of grief over her daughter (*ll.* 181-83), her head reaching the roof as she entered the home (*ll.* 188-89), drinking only meal and water with mint (*ll.* 208-09), and, instead of breast-feeding the child in her care, anointing him with ambrosia, breathing on him and keeping him in a fire at night, as if he were the child of a god (*ll.* 236-38). Interestingly, however, Demeter fits in among humans amazingly well; as Helene Foley points out, she "even laughs at human jokes and develops a fondness for the mortal maid Iambe, who is able to share them with her. A goddess, she ironically receives (although she does not accept) from mortals advice on how to endure the lot given by the gods."[31] In this hymn, the fact that metamorphosis is merely an

---

[31] Helene Foley, *The Homeric Hymn to Demeter: Translation, Commentary, and Interpretive Essays* (ed. H. P. Foley; Princeton: Princeton University Press, 1994), 88.

outward change does not prevent meaningful interaction between the god and human.[32] Eventually, she returns to her natural form (θεὰ μέγεθος καὶ εἶδος ἄμειψε γῆρας απωσαμένη, *ll.* 275-76).

To summarize, in the Greco-Roman material, the metamorphosis pattern almost always entails a change in form and, therefore, in appearance, not a change in substance; accordingly, while the vocabulary varies, none of the terms connotes a change in essence, and none necessitates a permanent alteration. We can discern distinctions, however, between a transformation that results in a physical presence and one that results in a phantom presence, and we can see in both the ability that some have to take a multitude of forms.

JEWISH LITERATURE: INTRODUCTION

In the Jewish literature, we see the similar thematic and semantic patterns to those in the Greco-Roman literature. As in the Greco-Roman section, I will here treat direct epiphany first, then metamorphosis, highlighting the tendencies in metamorphosis not only of the change of external form, but also of polymorphism and nonmaterialism. The differences between the Greco-Roman and Jewish literature are primarily two: (1) here metamorphosis is described more often of angels than of God, and (2) polymorphism is customarily limited to demonic beings. Continuity of identity remains throughout the process.

JEWISH LITERATURE: DIRECT EPIPHANY

Descriptions of epiphanies of Yahweh in the Old Testament range from mundane to dramatic. On the one side are expressions such as we find in Ps 17:15, "As for me, I shall behold your face in righteousness; when I awake I shall be satisfied, beholding your likeness," or in Exod 6:3, "I appeared to Abraham, Isaac and Jacob." More dramatic is the desciption in Numbers:

> Then the Lord came down in a pillar of cloud, and stood at the entrance of the tent, and called Aaron and Miriam; and they both came forward. And he said, "Hear my words: When there are prophets among you, I the Lord make myself known to them in visions; I speak to them in dreams. Not so with my servant Moses; he is entrusted with all my house. With him I speak face to face – clearly, not in riddles; and he beholds the form of the Lord." (12:5-8)

---

[32]Foley notes that "the *Hymn* is unique in archaic Greek poetry for the degree of humanization its gods experience, and precisely this humanization results in the establishment of the Mysteries at the end of the poem" (88) and that "the Mysteries are a produce of divine suffering and of the convergence of divine and human experience" (102).

An epiphany can occur with many witnesses as well, as at the mountain when Moses, Aaron, Nadab, Abihu and 70 elders "saw the God of Israel. Under his feet there was something like a pavement of sapphire stone, like the very heaven for clearness" (Exod 24.10-11). Those who recounted the story of Genesis at Qumran obviously felt no compunction toward such epiphanies, quoting Abraham, "And God appeared to me in a vision at night and said to me…" (1Qap Gen 21).[33] *Jubilees* looks forward to a future time when God "will descend and dwell with them [Israel] in all the ages of eternity" (1:26).[34]

The comfort level with such direct epiphany varies, however; for example, the description in Exodus 33:18ff. is restrained, with Moses only allowed to see God's glory by the back as God passes by. After Ezekiel's dramatic initiatory vision, he metaphorically steps back to describe it as merely "the appearance of the likeness of the glory of the Lord" (1:28). The restraint continues in the LXX, which, for example, softens Exodus 24:10-11: "and they saw the place where the God of Israel stood."[35] The discomfort appears as well in the many examples of what at first appears to be an angel later described as God himself; for example, the "angel of God" appeared to Hagar, who responded, "have I really seen God and remained alive after I saw him?" (Gen 16:7-14), and in Judges, the "angel of the Lord" asserts that he had told the Israelites, "I will never break my covenant with you" (2:1).

On the whole in Jewish literature, however, the angelic epiphany is the most typical. One need not cite the many examples of angelic direct epiphanies in the OT. In later Judaism, angelic epiphanies continue to be described.[36] *Second Baruch* 6:4-9 describes angels appearing and removing ritual implements from the Temple before the Babylonians destroy it.[37] In the *Ladder of Jacob* 3:3-4, Jacob says that Sariel the archangel came to him and "his appearance was very beautiful and awesome," but the patriarch claims that his previous vision at the ladder was so terrifying to him that he is not at all afraid of the angel

---

[33]Quotations from the Qumran manuscripts are taken from Geza Vermes, *The Dead Sea Scrolls in English* (3rd ed.; N.Y.: Penguin, 1987).

[34]Quotations from *Jubilees* are taken from *Jubilees*, trans. R. H. Charles, revised by C. Rabin in *The Apocryphal Old Testament* (ed. H. F. D. Sparks; Oxford: Oxford University Press, 1989), 1-140.

[35]Translations from the LXX are based on the text of Alfred Rahlfs, *Septuaginta* (Stuttgart: Württembergische Bibleanstalt, 1935, 1979) and are mine unless otherwise noted.

[36]For more information on the appearance of angels as serving mediating functions, see Loren T. Stuckenbruck, *Angel Veneration and Christology: A Study in Early Judaism and in the Christology of the Apocalypse of John* (WUNT 2.20; Tübingen: Mohr [Siebeck], 1995), 45-204.

[37]All quotations from 2 Baruch are taken from *2 (Syriac Apocalypse of) Baruch*, trans. A. F. J. Klijn in Charlesworth, *Pseueipigrapha*, 1.615-52.

(cf. *T. Iss.* 2:1).[38] Likewise, in *4 Baruch* Jeremiah pleads with destroying angels whom he and Baruch have watched descend from heaven with torches and stand on the walls of Jerusalem (3:1-4).[39] Later, Abimelech is led by an angel who came and took hold of his hand (6:1). In *3 Maccabees* 6:18, two angels descended (κατέβησαν) "clothed in glory and of awe-inspiring appearance, visible (φανεροί) to all except the Jews" to save the Jews from the trampling elephants. In *2 Enoch*, Gabriel flies down at night to address Nir, then taking the child Melkisedek on his wings and placing him in the paradise of Edem (Recension A 72:1-9).[40]

As in the Greco-Roman literature, light and fire accompany epiphany in Jewish literature, whether the epiphany is of God or angels. In perhaps the most famous OT theophany, that of the burning bush, the angel of the Lord appeared to Moses in fire that came out of the bush; God then calls to Moses and says, "'I am the God of your father, the God of Abraham, the God of Isaac, and the God of Jacob.' And Moses hid his face, for he was afraid to look at God" (Exod 3:2-6; cf. Exod 19:16; Ps 96 [97].4). In the *Apocalypse of Abraham*, the voice of God comes down from the heavens to Abraham in a stream of fire, and Abraham sees God in heaven as a fire with a voice like the sea in its midst (8:1; 17:1).[41] The *Sybilline Oracles* describe "swords of fire upon the earth" preceding the appearance of God "magnificently standing by" (*Sib. Or.* 3.673, 705).[42] God appears in the Greek *Life of Adam and Eve* in a chariot of light, and even the sun and moon cannot shine before the "light of all" (*L.A.E.* 35-36).[43] In the *Testament of Job* 3.1, an angel calls to Job as a great voice in a great light (καὶ ἐν τῇ νυκτὶ Κοιμωμένου μου ἦλθέν μοι μεγάλη φωνὴ ἐν μείζονι φωτὶ, cf. *Jos. Asen.* 14:3-4).[44]

JEWISH LITERATURE: METAMORPHOSIS

In the Jewish literature, we see familiar terms used for external appearance in general. In the *Testament of Benjamin* 10:1, Benjamin states, "when Joseph was in Egypt I earnestly desired to see his appearance and the form of his face" (τῷ εἴδει, καὶ καλὸς τῇ ὄψει). Μορφή denotes "countenance" in Daniel; for example, when Baltasar became well, his

---

[38]*Ladder of Jacob*, trans. H. G. Hunt in Charlesworth, *Pseudepigrapha*, 2.401-12.

[39]*4 Baruch*, trans. S. E. Robinson in Charlesworth, *Pseudepigrapha*, 2.413-26.

[40]*2 Enoch*, trans. F. I. Andersen in Charlesworth, *Pseudepigrapha*, 1.91-222.

[41]*Apocalypse of Abraham*, trans. R. Rubinkiewicz in Charlesworth, *Pseudepigrapha*, 1.681-706.

[42]*Sybilline Oracles*, trans. J. J. Collins in Charlesworth, *Pseudepigrapha*, 1.317-472.

[43]*A Synopsis of the Book of Adam and Eve* (ed. G. A. Anderson and M. E. Stone; 2nd rev. ed.; Atlanta: Scholars Press, 1999).

[44]*Testamentum Iobi; Apocalypsis Baruchi Graece* (eds. S. P. Brock & J.-C. Picard; Leiden: Brill, 1967).

reason returned and his "form (μορφή) returned" (Dan 4:33). In fear at the handwriting on the wall, his form/countenance (μορφή) changed (Dan 5:6, 9, 10; cf. 7:28).

Our familiar vocabulary for external appearance is abundant in the writings of Philo, though the situation can sometimes become a bit cloudy due to the philosopher's adaptation of the Platonic concept of forms. Philo uses μορφή for external rather than internal realities; for example, he professes that the inward meaning of a story appeals to the few people who study soul characteristics rather than "bodily forms" (σωμάτων μορφάς, *Abraham* 147.3-4), an unjust man is described as no man at all, but rather "a beast in human form" (ἀνθρωπομόρφου θηρίου, *Abraham* 33.3-4; cf. *Moses* 1.43.4; 2.165.5; *Spec. Laws* 3.99.11-14), and he comments that the creation story distinguishes the species created "male and female," even though their individual members had not yet "taken shape" (τῶν μορφὴν λαβόντων, *Creation* 76.2; cf. 135.4; *Migration* 3.4). The verbal form is often used for the fashioning of idols,[45] though Philo can use it for a more substantial change, as in the case of a virtue like piety when something is added or subtracted to it and thereby transforms its shape (μεταμορφώσει τὸ εἶδος, with εἶδος here having more the denotation of "nature," *Spec. Laws* 4.147.4); also, the soul has multiple forms (πολυμόρφῳ, *Unchangeable* 2.1-2) and the term is used for God's giving form to creation.[46] It is difficult to discern a major difference between this term and εἶδος for Philo, since Adam saw Eve as having both an εἶδος and a μορφήν like his own (*Creation* 151.7) and little distinction between μορφήν and ἰδέας (*Spec. Laws* 1.47.48; 1.90.4). He often speaks of the fact that God has neither human passions nor human form (ἀνθρωπόμορφον).[47]

Another intriguing set of examples from Philo concern the attempts of Gaius to "liken himself" (ἐξομοιοῦν, *Embassy* 78.1) first to demi-gods, such as Dionysius, Heracles and the Dioscuri, then to full-blown deities like Apollo, Hermes and Ares (*Embassy* 74-113). While trying to convince others that he was on the order of a demi-god, Gaius is described by Philo as recasting his one body "into manifold forms" (εἰς πολυτρόπους μορφάς) by using different costumes at different occasions, as if in the theater. Philo argues, however, that the interior vice of Gaius meant that he could never truly partake of immortality; even if it appeared that Gaius were a god (ἔδοξας γεγενῆθαι θεός), his evil practices would have caused him to change (μεταβαλεῖν) into mortal existence (*Embassy* 91.5-8). Worse yet, Gaius decided to impersonate gods who are "divine on both sides," dressing first

---

[45] *Decalogue* 7.3; 66.6; 72.6; *Spec. Laws* 1.21.5; 2.256.1; *Embassy* 290.3; 346.5.

[46] *Dreams* 1.210.3; 2.45.3-7; *Flight* 12.3; *Confusion* 63.4-5; *Eternity* 41.9.

[47] *Sacrifices* 95.8-10; *Posterity* 4.2; *Unchangeable* 56.1; 59.4; *Planting* 35.5; *Confusion* 135.2; *Prelim. Studies* 115.4-5; *Names* 55.1.

like Hermes, then removing that dress to "change his figure and dress into Apollo's" (εἰς δὲ Ἀπόλλωνα μετεμορφοῦτο καὶ μετεσκευάζετο, *Embassy* 93.5-95.3). Yet Gaius, like an actor, deceived the spectators with the "deceptive appearances" (φαντασίαις ψευδέσιν) he assumed (*Embassy* 111.5-112.1).

Josephus also uses our familiar terminology for outward appearance. He describes Moses, for example, as being a child of such beauty that he has "divine form" (μορφῇ θεῖον, *Ant.* 2.232.5). Josephus' uses of these terms in the context of idolatry are noteworthy. Egyptian gods transformed into the forms of animals (μεταβαλόντας εἰς μορφὰς θηρίων, *Ag. Ap.* 2.128.3). God's "form and magnitude" (μορφὴν δὲ καὶ μέγεθος) surpasses description so that no image of him (εἰκόνα) is allowed (*Ag. Ap.* 2.190.5). He criticizes the Greeks for turning passions into both the nature and forms of gods (φύσιν καὶ μορφὴν ἀνέπλασαν, *Ag. Ap.* 2.248.3). Again in the overlap between art and idolatry, Greek artists mold figures of their own imaginations (μορφήν ἐπινοῶν), whether they use clay or paint (*Ag. Ap.* 2.252.3). A similar problem existed in the palace of Herod with forbidden representations (μορφάς) of animals (*Life* 65.5).

One of the challenging areas in the Jewish realm of metamorphosis are the simplest descriptions of angels that look like humans. The *Testament of Levi* describes "seven men in white clothing" (καὶ εἶδον ἑπτὰ ἄνδρας ἐν ἐσθῆ τι λευκῇ, 8.2), presumably angelic beings, who appear in a dream. In *Joseph and Aseneth*, heaven was torn, a great light appeared, and "a man came to her from heaven and stood at her head and called to her" (ἄνθρωπος ἐκ τοῦ οὐρανοῦ. Καὶ ἔστη ὑπὲρ κεφαλῆς αὐτῆς καὶ ἐκάλεσεν αὐτήν, 14:3-4).[48] The discomfort with that description is apparent in that the "man" is called in various texts and versions "one similar to a man," "a man of light," "the man of God," "an angel," "the angel of the Lord," "a bright angel," and a "voice."[49] Almost immediately another being appears to Aseneth as "a man resembling Joseph in every way" (ἀνὴρ ὅμοιος κατὰ πάντα τῷ Ἰωσήφ) but dressed as a king, with a face like lightening, eyes like the sun, and other dramatic physical characteristics that give him away as an angel, as does his encouragement to her to "be not afraid" (14.8-11). In *2 Enoch* the protagonist relates that as he is dreaming and weeping, "two huge men appeared to me, the like of which I had never seen on earth." He describes their appearance in detail:

Their faces were like the shining sun;
their eyes were like burning lamps;
from their mouths fire was coming forth;

---

[48]*Joseph et Aséneth* (ed. and trans. Marc Philonenko; Leiden: Brill, 1968).

[49]After listing these variants, C. Burchard suggests that the "man" was promoted to an "angel," since 19:5, 9 attests "man" in "virtually all witnesses" (*Joseph and Aseneth*, trans. C. Burchard in Charlesworth, *Pseudepigrapha*, 224, note h).

their clothings was various singing;
their wings were more glistering than gold;
their hands were whiter than snow.

Then he awoke and realized that they were actually standing before him
(1:4-6, J recension).[50]

We can determine that these "men" are metamorphosed angels
based on more extended descriptions of the pattern. In the *Apocalypse
of Abraham*, Abraham describes how "the angel he [God] sent to me in
the likeness of a man came, and he took me by my right hand and stood
me on my feet" (10:4).[51] In an example from Jewish literature, an angel is
sent to give assistance to Tobit and his family; when his son Tobias went
out searching for a traveling companion, he "found the angel Raphael
standing in front of him, but he did not perceive that he was an angel of
God. Tobias said to him, "Where do you come from, young man?" (Tob
5:4-5). Clearly, Raphael appeared in human form, but his essence remained
spiritual, since he admits later that he "really did not eat or drink anything
– but what you saw was a vision" (ὁράσιν; 12:19); that is, it was merely an
external appearance of eating and drinking.

A clear and extended example of the phenomenon is presented by
Recension A of the *Testament of Abraham*. Commanded by God to tell
Abraham of his approaching death, Michael comes to Abraham "in the
manner of a handsome soldier" (δίκην σρατιώτου εὐπρεπεστάτου, 2:2).[52]
Abraham immediately admits that the man's appearance is extraordinarily
attractive (2:4; 4:3), but he does not recognize him as an angel. Though the
archangel is consistently refered to in the text as "the incorporeal one"
(ἀσωμάτος, 3:6; 9:2; 11:9; 15:4, 6; 16:2), his metamorphosed presence is quite
physical: Abraham washes his feet, for example, and Michael weeps with
the humans, though *his* tears, upon falling into a basin, become precious
stones (3:9-11; 5:11; 6:7). The title of "incorporeal one," therefore, refers to
the archangel's essence, rather than to his metamorphosed form. Michael
ascends quickly to heaven, complaining to God that he does not wish
to announce the death to such a fine man; God, however, orders him
to return and do what Abraham says and eat what Abraham eats (4:7).
Michael reminds God that because angels are incorporeal, they neither
eat nor drink, so God promises to send an "all-devouring spirit" that will
eat from Michael's hands and through his mouth (4:10). Upon his return,
Sarah recognizes the archangel as one of those three "heavenly men" who

---

[50]Translation by F. I. Andersen in Charlesworth, *Pseudepigrapha*, 1.106 .

[51]Translation by R. Rubinkiewicz in Charlesworth, *Pseudepigrapha*, 695.

[52]*The Testament of Abraham: The Greek Recensions* (Texts and Translations 2; Pseudepigrapha
Series 2; trans. M. E. Stone; New York: SBL, 1972).

visited them previously (Gen 18:1-8), at which time Abraham suggests that he had indeed thought those were the feet of one of those angels (6:1-6).

On a fanciful note, Philo imagines a personification of the virtue "nobility" that would "take a human shape" (εἰς ἀνθρωπόμορφον ἰδέαν) and address rebellious ones (*Virtues* 195.1-3). Μορφήν appears in Philo's recount of the burning bush, in the midst of which was a μορφήν of great beauty, which, Philo says, might be thought to be an image (εἰκόνα) of God, though he prefers to call it an angel (*Moses* 1.66.1-6). The idea of the image of God reappears in *On the Creation*, where Philo suggests that the whole creation is a copy of the divine image (μίμημα θείας εἰκόνος; 25.7-8). Several of our typical vocabularly terms come together in the context of metamorphosis as Philo recounts the story of the angelic visit to Abraham and Sarah, when the angels, though incorporeal, "changed to human shape" (εἰς ἰδέαν ἀνθρώπων μεμορφῶσθαι, *Abraham* 118.4-5).

Philo can employ φαντασία for a vision, a dream or an external presentation. In the tale of Joseph, the king's vision during the night is called a φαντασία at one point and an ὄψις soon after, and, immediately, a φαντασία again (*Joseph* 102-103). Life itself, in fact, has sensation, impulse and φαντασία, with φαντασία here meaning "appearance" or "presentation" (*Unchangeable* 41-44). Moses at the burning bush says, "I bow before your admonitions, that I could never have received your vision manifested (τὸ τῆς σῆς φαντασίας ἐναργὲς εἶδος), but I beg that I may at least see the glory that surrounds you" (*Spec. Laws* 45.3-4); we see as in Josephus, there is a tendency in Philo to retreat from direct epiphanies of God. In *On Dreams*, Philo points out that to those still in the body, God must appear in the likeness of angels but without altering his own nature (ἀγγέλοις εἰκαζόμενον οὐ μεταβάλλοντα τὴν ἑαυτοῦ φύσιν), "but communicating to those who receive the impression of his presence a semblance in a different form, so that they take the image not to be a copy, but the original form itself" (ἀλλὰ δόξαν ἐντιθέντα ταῖς φαντασιουμέναις ἑτερόμορφον ὡς τὴν εἰκόνα οὐ μίμημα, ἀλλ' αὐτὸ τὸ ἀρχέτυπον ἐκεῖνο εἶδος ὑπολαμβάνειν εἶναι, 1.232.4-10 [Thackeray, LCL]). Philo offers the traditional "external" uses of this vocabulary, but he offers also the use of it to express more abstract ideas of form and shape.

One extended description that employs several of our key terms is Philo's description of the heavenly visitors to Abraham and Sarah. According to Philo, after Sarah's episode of laughter with the strangers, she saw in them a "different and grander aspect, that of prophets or angels, changed (μεταβαλόντων) from their spiritual and soul-like nature (οὐσία) into a semblance of human form" (εἰς ἀνθρωπόμορφον ἰδέαν, *Abraham* 113). He also uses φαντασία for an unreal appearance, as when the angel visiting Abraham and Sarah gave only the appearance (φαντασίαν) of eating and drinking (*Abraham* 118.2). Their angelic οὐσία remains, though the appearance is human.

Josephus uses μορφή in his retelling of the story of Saul and the witch of Endor, as the witch says that she saw someone "arise in a form like God" ([ἀνελθόντα] τῷ θεῷ [τινα] τὴν μορφὴν ὅμοιον, *Ant.* 6.333.3-4); the shape describes only an outer appearance, for the true identity of this "form" is the spirit of Samuel (τῆς Σαμουήλου ψυχῆς, *Ant.* 6.334.3-4). He employs μορφή for the phantasm (angel of the Lord) that appeared to Gideon "in the shape of a young man" (φαντάσματος...παραστάντος νεανίσκου μορφῇ, *Ant.* 5.213.5-6); note in Josephus the reluctance for angels to have material form.[53] This passage introduces another noun favored by Josephus in this situation: φάντασμα. He uses the term again, for the angel appears in the likeness of a young man (φάντασμα ἐπιφαίεται...νεανίᾳ καλῷ παραπλήσιον) to announce the birth of a son to the wife of Manoch (*Ant.* 5.277.3-4). Due to Manoch's disbelief, a second appearance of the angel is required, and the angel does not eat the bread and meat Manoch offers as hospitality, but instead uses a rod to consume it with fire then ascends to heaven on the smoke (ἀνιὼν εἰς οὐρανὸν, *Ant.* 5.284.3-4).

Less attractive heavenly beings, as well, disguise themselves as men and have a physical presence. In the *Testament of Reuben*, the Watchers are described as transforming themselves into a man (μετεσχηματίζοντο γὰρ εἰς ἄνδρα) and appearing to women while they were cohabiting with their husbands (5:6; cf. 4QAgesCreat; 1Qap Gen; *1 En.* 6-8). In the *Life of Adam and Eve*, that greatest of fallen angels metamorphoses into an angel and weeps to deceive Eve a second time (*transfiguravit se in claritatem angelorum*, *Vita* 9:1; λαβὼν σχῆμα ἀγγέλου, *Apoc* 29:15; cf. *Apoc* 17:1). The use of the term σχῆμα is an interesting one. Not used for metamorphosis in the Greco-Roman literature, it was, however, used for one's bearing or appearance, and for an appearance as opposed to a reality.[54] In Euripides' play, Ion tells queen Creusa that there is nobility in her "form" (μορφῇ) and her appearance (σχῆμ') shows she is well-born (*Ion*, *ll.* 236-40). Plato uses the term in the example of "a front and a show" (πρόθυρα μὲν καὶ σχῆμα, *Rep.* 365C), and in the case of advising not to "contrive pretence" but to honor virtue (σχήμασι, *Epi.* 989C).

An angelic being is often described as ascending when the purpose has been accomplished. The ascent is typical whether the appearance was one of direct epiphany or of metamorphosis. Sometimes the ascent occurs visibly, as we have seen (Jos. *Ant.* 5.284.3-4), but sometimes not; Michael,

---

[53]Wilhelm Michaelis (*Theological Dictionary of the New Testament* [ed. Gerhard Friedrich; trans. & ed. Geoffrey Bromiley; Grand Rapids: Eerdmans, 1967], 5.338) notes that Josephus' apparent belief that God is invisible leads him to "qualify" OT theophanies, e.g. in *Ant* 5 he omits the ὤφθη passages Gen 12:7; 17:11; 26:2, 24; 35:9, etc.

[54]Liddell-Scott, 1745.

for example, is once described as "becoming invisible" (ἀφανὴς ἐγένετο) as part of his ascent (T. Ab. 8:1).[55]

Metamorphosis: Polymorphism

In the Jewish literature, the polymorphic ability is emphasized as a talent of evil beings. In the *Testament of Job*, Satan first metamorphoses (μετασχηματίσθεις) his form into that of a beggar (6:4), then into king of the Persians (17:2), then became like (ὁμοιώθη) a great whirlwind (20:5) and, finally, metamorphosed (μετασχηματίσθη) into a peddler of bread (23:1). Comparably, in the *Testament of Abraham*, Death is dramatically described as a shape-shifter. In order to take the soul of the righteous Abraham who is understandably resisting death, God commands Death to "conceal your fierceness, cover your decay, and cast off your bitterness from yourself, and put on your youthful beauty and glory" so as not to terrify him (16:4-5). Death immediately goes to Abraham in "great glory and youthful beauty," preceded by a sweet aroma and a radiant light that give him an "appearance of sunlike form" (ὄψιν ἡλιόμορφον,16:8, 10; cf. 16:12; 17:7).[56] Abraham asks to see his real form, and Death "put off all the bloom of youth and beauty and glory and the appearance of sunlike form that he had worn, and he put on a robe of tyranny and made his appearance gloomy and more fierce than any type of wild beast and more unclean than any uncleanness. And he showed Abraham seven fiery heads of dragons and fourteen ferocious faces," revealing each one individually (17:12-14). After Death metamorphoses back to the pleasant appearance, Abraham demands, "teach me all your metamorphoses" (μεταμορφώσιες); that is, what each one means (19:5).[57]

In the *Testament of Solomon*,[58] the demon Ornias can "transform into three forms" (εἰς τρεῖς μορφάς μεταβαλλόμενος): "sometimes I am a man who desires the bodies of effeminate boys, and when I touch them, they suffer immense pain. Sometimes I become a creature with wings up to the

---

[55]See, for example, Tob 12:19-20a; Jud 13:20; *Jos. Asen.* 17; *T. Job* 4.2.

[56]The description of transformation here reveals again the diversity of vocabulary that can serve, though, also again, we see that the terms refer to the external rather than to the essence: "conceal (κρύψον) your fierceness, cover (σκέπασον) your decay, and cast off (ἀποβαλοῦ) your bitterness from yourself, and put on (περιβαλοῦ) your youthful beauty and glory."

[57]Recension B has a more limited story of the metamorphoses of Death, only changing from youthful beauty, with which Michael adorns him, to his original form of decay, with two heads (13-14).

[58]C. C. McCown, *The Testament of Solomon* (Leipzig: Hinrichs, 1922). While most scholars now consider this testament the work of a Greek-speaking Christian in Egypt, rather than a Jewish work with a Christian editing, there is enough doubt concerning authorship, and the topic of this passage so apt to our current discussion of polymorphism, that I have elected to include it at this point. For a summary of the authorship debate, see Charlesworth, *Pseudepigrapha*, 1.943.

heavenly regions. Finally, I assume the appearance (ὄψιν) of a lion" (2:3-4). In that same work there appears "a spirit who had the shape of a woman (ἦλθε πνεῦμα ὡς γύνη μέν τὸ εἶδος ἔχον)," Enersigos, "called by countless names" (15:1-2). She continues,

> I can change my appearance, first being taken for a goddess, and then becoming one who has some other shape" (ἐγὼ μὲν μεταβάλλομαι ὡς θεὰ λεγομένη, καὶ μεταβάλλομαι πάλιν καὶ γίνομαι ἔτερον εἶδος ἔχομαι,15:3). I hover near the moon and because of this I assume three forms (μορφάς). Sometimes, I am conjured up as Kronos by the wise men. At other times, I descend around those who bring me down and appear in another form. The capacity of the heavenly body is invincible, incalculable, and impossible to thwart. At times, changing into three forms (εἰς τὰς τρεῖς μορφὰς μεταβαλλομένη), I descend and become like that which you now see. (15:4-5)

In Jewish circles, therefore, it appears that polymorphism was a talent viewed as having only a deceitful purpose.

Metamorphosis: Nonmaterial Emphasis

We see similar thematic and semantic patterns to the Greco-Roman literature when the Jewish texts emphasize the nonmaterial quality of the appearance. Pseudo-Philo employs a term familiar to us in this context, *species*, when he narrates the encounter between Saul and the witch of Endor: "And Saul said to her, 'What is his appearance (*species*)?' She said, 'You are asking me about divine beings. For behold his appearance is not the appearance of a man (*Ecce enim species eius non est hominis*). For he is clothed in a white robe with a mantle placed over it, and two angels are leading him" (*L.A.B.* 64:6).

In Job 4:12-21, Eliphaz was in deep sleep when "a spirit (רוח) glided by my face; the hair of my flesh bristled. It stood still, but I could not see its appearance (מראהו). A form (תמונה) was in front of my eyes. There was silence, then I heard a voice: 'Can mortals be righteous before God...?'" (Job 4:15-17). As Marvin Pope points out, "the word רוח is never used of an apparition in the OT, but here the spirit is given a semblance of form."[59] This episode has been called a theophany particularly on the basis of comparisons with Abraham's deep sleep (Gen 15:12) and Elijah's "sound of sheer silence" (1 Kgs 19:12).[60] Note again some discomfort with an appearance of God's external form when the LXX translates, "And a spirit (πνεῦμα) came before my face, and my hair and flesh quivered. I arose and

---

[59]Marvin Pope, *Job* (AB 15; Garden City, N. J.: Doubleday, 1965), 37.

[60]For a more detailed argument supporting this passage as a theophany, see David J. A. Clines, *Job* (Word 17; Dallas: Word, 1989), 131.

did not perceive it. I looked, and there, was no form (οὐκ ἦν μορφή) before my eyes, but I heard only a breath and a voice, saying, 'What, shall a mortal be pure before the Lord?'" (Job 4:15-17). When the book of Wisdom describes the effects of the plague of darkness in Egypt, it says that "sad phantoms (φάσματα) with gloomy faces appeared," as did "monstrous apparitions (φαντασμάτων) during sleep" (17:4, 15). For the children of Israel, however, there was "a great light, whose voice they heard, but did not see the form (μορφήν, 18:1)." Φάσμα is used for a dream in Job 20:8 and for a prophetic vision in Isaiah 28:7.

Jewish Literature: Continuity of Mind and Identity

We have seen no evidence for any essential change of identity when these beings metamorphose. On the contrary, several texts seem to go out of their way to show particularly that the angelic essence remains. Recall that Michael's tears become precious stones (*T. Ab.* 3:9-11). This effort is especially clear in the repeated affirmation that metamorphosed angels, like the Greco-Roman gods, do not eat perishable human foods. Raphael, we remember, produced only a "vision" of eating and drinking (Tob 12:19; cf. Philo, *Abraham* 118.2), and Michael has to remind God that angels cannot eat or drink so that God can make other provisions (*T. Ab.* 4:10; cf. Jos. *Ant.* 5.284.3-4). Since evil beings metamorphose for the purpose of deceit, their character or identity certainly has not been transformed by the metamorphosis.

In summary, the Jewish literature describes the external transformation of heavenly beings into human shape employing similar thematic and semantic patterns as Greco-Roman literature uses to describe the metamorphoses of its gods. At times, again like the Greco-Roman literature, the emphasis is on the non-material nature of the appearance. Polymorphism, however, is emphasized in the case of evil beings, or at least those with evil intent. Continuity of mind and identity from one state to another remains central to the metamorphic process.

CONCLUSION

The metamorphosis pattern generally entails a change in form rather than one of essence. At times, the pattern shows a tendency to emphasize a nonmaterial aspect to the metamorphosed being. At other times, a polymorphic capability is stressed. The semantic fields both in Latin and in Greek include words that emphasize the outer transformation, such as *verso, transformo, specie, figura,* *εἰδω, εἶδος and δέμας. The typical Greek field for a nonsubstantial appearance include εἴδωλον, φάντασμα and φαντασία, while the Latin generally adds terms to the characteristic field to reveal the lack of material substance.

Not everyone in the ancient Mediterranean world, however, expected the gods to present themselves "in person" on earth in a metamorphosed form. To describe the interaction between divine and human, another model was available, one that encompassed even more diversity than does the metamorphosis model. In this second model, the power of the gods was imparted directly to human beings through the mechanism of possession.

CHAPTER 3
THE ANCIENT MEDITERRANEAN CONTEXT: POSSESSION

> Then what do we expect? Do we wait for the immortal gods to converse
> with us in the forum, on the street, and in our homes? While they do not,
> of course, present themselves in person, they do diffuse their power far
> and wide—sometimes enclosing it in caverns of the earth and sometimes
> imparting it to human beings (Cicero, *De Div.* 1.79 [Falconer, LCL]).

The phenomenon of possession is another way that a god can make
his/her presence known and effective on earth, this time, as Cicero
points out, literally through human beings. The phenomenon has
typically been studied under the context of prophecy,[1] and, despite the
undeniable helpfulness of this work, the phenomenon has thereby been
categorized a little narrowly from the beginning of the query. The word
"possession" is in academic and common parlance often limited to the
complete overtaking of the mind and body of a human by a god or spirit,
visibly identifiable by wild, frenzied physical behavior and lack of control
of one's mental faculties. I will give evidence in this chapter, however,
that the phenomenon of possession is a multi-faceted one that is not well
described by rigid categories.

The possession phenomenon is better expressed by three continua.
One should visualize three horizontal lines for the continua. The first line
is the continuum between extremely frenzied behavior on the end to the

---

[1]Some of the best and most recent examples are: David E. Aune, *Prophecy in Early
Christianity and the Ancient Mediterranean World* (Grand Rapids: Eerdmans, 1983); Allen R.
Hunt, *The Inspired Body: Paul, the Corinthians, and Divine Inspiration* (Macon, Ga.: Mercer
University Press, 1996); Jannes Reiling, *Hermas and Christian Prophecy: A Study of the 11th
Mandate* (NovTSup 37; Leiden: Brill, 1973); Christopher Forbes, *Prophecy and Inspired Speech
in Early Christianity and its Hellenistic Environment* (Peabody, Mass.: Hendrickson, 1997).

viewer's left, to no frenzied behavior at all on the right. The second line
depicts the continuum between complete displacement of the rational mind
on the left, to a complete retention of rational faculties, including complete
recall of the event, on the right. The final line expresses the continuum
between a very occasional possession on the left, to permanent possession
on the right. As we will see, the characteristics of a possessive event have
tendencies along these continua; for example, in the Greco-Roman world,
displacement of the rational mind has a strong tendency to be accompanied
by frenzied behavior and also tends to be an occasional phenomenon.

In this chapter, I will attempt to characterize the primary tendencies
under three major categories while noting the exceptions that make
the possession phenomenon even richer and more fluid than has been
previously expressed. The tendency of an occasional possession that
involves displacement of the human mind and is usually recognizable by
frenzied behavior and lack of recall is the type of possession I will call
"ecstasy."[2] Second, the tendency of an occasional possession that does not
involve displacement of the human mind and is less often accompanied
by frenzied behavior I will call "inspiration." Third, the tendency of a
permanent possession that does not involve displacement of the human
mind and is generally not accompanied by frenzied behavior I will call
"indwelling."[3] Under each topic, I will describe the phenomenon, then
address the questions, "possession *of* whom?" and "possession *by* what or
whom?" while highlighting distinctive vocabulary.

GRECO-ROMAN LITERATURE: ECSTASY

Ecstasy was often immediately recognizable by the extremely odd
or "frenzied" behavior of the person possessed, described by Latin
vocabulary such as *furor* and by Greek vocabulary such as μανία and
words related to ἔνθεος. Perhaps the most famous examples arise from
the mystery rites of Cybele and Dionysus. Diodorus of Sicily describes
the Corybantes as possessed (ἐνθουσιάσαντας) when celebrating the rites of
Cybele (5.49.3). Livy describes men in the Bacchanalian rite as prophesying
while fanatically tossing their bodies, as if insane (*viros, velut mente capta,
cum iactatione fanatica corporis vaticinari*; 39.13.12). The rites in general were

---

[2]I intend no disparagement by the use of this term; for the problem of "esctasy" seen as
"an infelicitous form of prophetic inspiration" by biblical scholars, see Aune, *Prophecy*, 20-21.

[3]Hunt (*The Inspired Body*, 21-22) delineates the phenomena helpfully, but differently
than I, into three types, in which: (1) the will and consciousness is eliminated; (2) the will is
eliminated, and the consciousness is passive so that there is recall of the event afterwards,
and (3) the will and consciousness remain intact so that the recipient speaks the content of
what is revealed as a divine message. I have not adopted his categories, though mine clearly
overlap with his, because I am not convinced of the importance of the distinction between
his types two and three.

apparently characterized by frenzied dancing, shouting and, at times, cymbals and drums (cf. Livy 39.10.7; 39.15.9-10; Catullus 63.1-2, 18).[4]

Frenzy characterizes behavior at the oracular shrines as well. Diodorus of Sicily describes the importance of frenzied behavior in the founding of the Delphic oracular shrine, when first goats, then people, who approached the chasm would become possessed (ἐνθουσιάζουσι, ἐνθουσιάζειν). The goats leapt about and made odd noises, and some people threw themselves into the chasm and disappeared as a result of the possession (διὰ τὸν ἐνθουσιασμόν). Because of the tragic results of this behavior, it was decided that a device would be built on which a prophetess could safely sit and prophesy to those who approached (16.26.2-5).[5]

What exactly causes the frenzy? Some disagreement surfaces by the first century concerning whether the frenzy is caused by the possession itself or whether it is part of the resistance of the human to being possessed.[6] Virgil describes the Sibyl as storming around the cavern, raving wildly as she tries to shake the god from her, though Apollo of course wins the struggle and "shakes the reins while she rages and turns the spur" within her until the frenzy (*furor*) ends (*Aen.* 6.42-53, 77-102). Lucan relates a story of a Delphic priestess who dreaded the possession and its painful madness so much that she tried once to feign the possession (5.115-40), but her posturing was obvious because there were none of the inarticulate cries to show that her mind was possessed by the frenzy (*instinctam sacro mentem testata furore*). When Lucan relates that the priestess did not shout and her hair did not bristle, it is clear that these effects of the possession are expected ones (5.141-60).

More texts attribute the frenzy to a madness, and, though the vocabulary varies, the madness is often indicated in Latin by *furor* or by expressions that indicate the retreat of the rational mind. In Ovid's *Metamorphoses*, the prophetic daughter of the centaur "began to feel the prophetic madness and was warmed by the god enclosed in her breast" (*vaticinos concepit mente furors incaluitque deo, quem clausum pectore habebat*) before prophesying (2.640-41). Though no specific description of the behavior is provided in Cicero's *De Divinatione*, divination is presented as divided into two types, one by "art," practiced by those who discern from signs through observation, reason and deduction, and the second by "nature," which occurs under the influence of a mental disturbance

[4] Forbes, *Prophecy*, 134-35. The sceptical Livy explains away the ecstatic phenomena on the basis of the wine consumed and the chemicals used in the torches.

[5] Joseph Fontenrose (*The Delphic Oracle*; Berkeley: University of California Press, 1978) maintains that there is no evidence for the frenzied behavior of the Delphic priestess. Forbes, however, has demonstrated that while Fontenrose is correct for the classical period, the Hellenistic period provides a different picture (*Prophecy*, 108-09).

[6] Forbes, *Prophecy*, 137-38.

44 THE CHRIST IS JESUS

(*concitatione*) or of unrestrained and free emotion (*soluto liberoque motu*). The second occurs especially while dreaming or by a frenzy (*per furorem*), which includes oracles spoken under divine influence (*quae instinctu divine afflatuque funduntur*, 1.34; cf. 1.80).

The term μανία and, again, terms that signal the removal of the rational faculty, suffice in Greek texts. In the *Phaedrus* 244A-245A, Socrates points out that the greatest blessings come to humans "through madness, when it is given as a gift by the gods" (διὰ μανίας θείᾳ μέντοι δόσει διδομένης); he cites the examples of great benefactions from the Delphic oracle and the Sibyl, of relief from diseases caused by ancient guilt, and of poetry from the Muses. He points out that the very name of divination, μαντική, is derived from the word for frenzy / madness, μανία (*Phaed.* 244C; Latin *furor*; cf. Cicero, who prefers *divinatio*, in *Div.* 1.1). In *Agamemnon*, Clytemestra calls the priestess Cassandra mad (μαίνεται, *l.* 1064), and the chorus describes her "frenzied in soul, possessed by some god" (φρενομανής τις εἶ θεοφόρητος, *l.* 1140). Dio Chrysostom points out that if one thinks he is mad (μαίνεσθαι), for that reason one should all the more listen to him, implying an association between divine guidance and madness (*2 Tars.* 34.4). Plutarch quotes Heraclitus describing the Sibyl as speaking with "mad lips" (μαινομένῳ στόματι, *Mor.* 397A), and also quotes Euripides, that "Bacchic rout and madness contain much prophecy" (τὸ γὰρ βακχεύσιμον καὶ τὸ μανιῶδες μαντικὴν πολλὴν ἔχει, *Mor.* 432E from *Bacch.* 298).[7]

The Bacchic rites as described by Euripides, in fact, provide considerable evidence of this phenomenon. In *The Bacchae*, Dionysus drives the ritual participants out to the countryside as mad (μανίαις) with frenzied hearts (παράκοποι φρενῶν, *ll.* 32-33) and makes maddened maenads prophesy by frenzy (βακξεύσιμον; μαντικήν, *ll.* 298-301). He also inspires with madness their pursuit of Pentheus (θεοῦ πνοαῖσιν ἐμμανεῖς, *l.* 1094), while Pentheus himself is made mad by the god (ἔκστησον φρενῶν ἐνεὶς ἐλαφρὰν λύσσαν, *ll.* 850-51). Pentheus' mother is described as foaming at the mouth, with eyes rolling wildly and out of her mind, possessed of Bacchus (ἐκ βακχίου κατείχετ') as she tore at her son (*ll.* 1122-24). Later, they know nothing of what has happened, as Agave's words indicate: "I do not understand this, yet I come to my senses, changing to my former mind" (γίγνομαι δὲ πως ἔννους, μετασταθεῖσα τῶν πάρος φρενῶν, *ll.* 1269-72).

At times, a more specific description that amounts to the displacement of the rational human mind is given, shown by the subject's lack of knowledge of what was occurring during the episode and inability to remember the event once he/she had returned to normal.[8] In the *Apology*,

---

[7]Heraclitus fragment source cited in *LCL* Vol. 5, p. 273 n. b; Euripides, *Bacchae*, 298.

[8]Hunt (*Inspired Body*, 20 n. 11) uses the term "'irrational' to signify places where the human νοῦς or understanding is displaced, taken over, possessed, inactive, or thwarted."

Socrates describes the work of the poets in these terms: since they compose because they are inspired (ἐνθουσιάζοντες), like prophets and oracles, they know nothing of what they say (ἴσασιν δὲ οὐδὲν ὧν λέγουσι, 22B-C). By this means, everyone knows that these priceless words come not from a human but directly from a god (Plato, *Ion* B-E).[9] In the *Meno*, Socrates uses the same phrase of oracles, prophets and great statesmen, all of whom may be called divine, enraptured, inspired and possessed of God (θείους τε εἶναι καὶ ἐνθουσιάζειν ἐπίπνους ὄντας καὶ κατεξομένους ἐκ τοῦ θεοῦ) when they succeed in speaking great things though they know not what they are saying (99C). The *Timaeus* gives us more detailed information, stating that no one when in his/her rational mind attains possessed and true prophecy (οὐδεὶς γὰρ ἔννους ἐφάπτεται μαντικῆς ἐνθέου καὶ ἀληθοῦς); rather, one's rationality must be laid low in sleep, by disease, or by some divine possession (διὰ τινα ἐνθουσιασμόν, 71E). In this case, when one returns to the right mind, he/she can and should recollect and consider any messages or visions received, but while remaining in the frenzy (μανέντος, μένοντος), one should not attempt interpretation of the prophecy (71E-72A).

This understanding of a possession that results in displacement continues in Hellenistic times, as we see in discussions of possession at oracular shrines. Plutarch presents Plato's description in the *Phaedrus* of two types of madness (μανία), one as a result of disease, another "not uninspired nor intrinsic" (οὐκ ἀθείαστος οὐδ' οἰκογενής), which displaces the rational mind (ἔπηλυς ἐπίπνοια), is created and begun by a higher power, and is called ἐνθουσιαστικόν because it shares in a more divine power (θειοτέρας δυνάμεως, *Mor.* 758 D-E). Here, Plutarch lists several types of possession: the prophetic from Apollo, the Bacchic from Dionysus, and the rites of Cybele and Pan are similar (758 E-F).

Other descriptions follow suit. In Lucan's account of the true inspiration of a priestess, we see the familiar portrayal of the god Apollo "expelling her former mind" (*mentemque priorem expulit*) and ordering her human nature to withdraw, and her frantic throwing herself about the cave, hair bristling, groaning and shouting inarticular sounds before uttering the articulate prophecy (5.166-93). The effects of the possession, moreover, can be lasting. Plutarch insists that when the priestess is somehow disturbed, she should not go into the oracle, since even the death of the priestess can and has resulted in such circumstances (*Mor.* 427D-438B). Aristides later notes that the priestesses of the oracles at Delphi and Dodona know only what the god wants them to know, and for as long as he wishes it: they do not know anything of the communication before the god relates it, nor anything of what they themselves have said afterward (*Defence of Oratory*, 42-43).

---

[9]For more on the inspiration of poets, see Plato, *Leg.* 682A and *Crat.* 396D; Longinus, [*Subl.*] 8.1-4; 9.7-9; 13.2; 15.1-8.

To whom does possession typically occur? In *De Divinatione*, Quintus argues that the soul has an inherent power of foreknowledge given by God that, when vigorously developed is called frenzy (*furor*) and happens when the soul withdraws from the physical body and is "violently stimulated by a divine impulse" (*divino instinctu concitatur*; 1.66). Later, he emphasizes the necessity of the separation of the soul from the body, as in frenzy and dreams; whether it is dreams, subterranean vapors, or Phrygian songs that lead the soul to leave the body with its influence of the physical senses and wordly anxieties, "the frenzied mind" (*furibunda mens*) can then see the future in advance (1.113-15; cf. 129; 2.100-101). Note that here, the mind is not replaced so much as it leaves the body to see farther than it possibly could while trapped in the body. In Plutarch's *Obsolescence of Oracles*, however, the suggestion is made that the soul uses a natural ability which is generally ineffectual when commingled with the mortal, but can function fully when it leaves the body (*Mor.* 432A).[10] The soul, then, can sometimes disclose this power in dreams, when near death; that is, when the body is cleansed of impurities and achieves a relaxation of reason which encourages a change "we call inspiration" (ἐνθουσιασμόν; *Mor.* 432C).

Who or what exactly is the possessor? Normally, as we have seen, a god. The line between gods and *daimons*, however, was not generally a rigid one, and there is some evidence that either could be used for the possessing entity. In *The Bacchae*, Dionysus is called a *daimon* twelve times, and, as Versnel notes, this use in the play combines "the negative elements of contemporary fake gods, who are as a rule referred to as *daimons*, and the awe-inspiring aspects of its authentic meaning in Homer and elsewhere," as emphasizing "specific and unique action by a god with special reference to the speaker."[11]

By the first century B.C.E., the suggestion that *daimons* were actually the possessing entities claims more attention. In *Obsolescence of Oracles*, Lamprias argues that it should not be surprising to think that an oracle decreases, because the god gives nothing imperishable to humans. It is, moreover, "extremely silly and childish" to think that a god enters a human body and uses the human like a ventriloquist's dummy, "for if he becomes entangled in humans' needs, he does not spare the majesty nor guard the dignity and greatness of his excellence" (*Mor.* 414E). The possession is rather carried out by the *daimons*, beings midway between gods and people (*Mor.* 415A), the nature of whom is to interpret, to minister and to avenge

---

[10]For a description of this process, in the case of a man whose soul left the body at the oracle of Trophonius in Boeotia (the "myth of Timarchus"), see Plutarch, *Mor.* 590A-592E .

[11]H. S. Versnel, *Ter Unus. Isis, Dionysus, Hermes: Three Studies in Henotheism* (Studies in Greek and Roman Religion 6; Leiden: Brill, 1990), 158-59 n. 246. Cf. R. Schlesier, "Daimon und Daimones bei Euripides," *Saeculum* 34 (1983): 267-79.

injustice (*Mor.* 416F, 417A), though they often take on the name of a god with whom they are closely associated (*Mor.* 421E). Much of the mischief carried out for and against gods that is related in stories, the argument goes, was actually done for these *daimons* (*Mor.* 417E-F). From those beings, a few because of excellence (ἀρετήν) are purified and share completely in divine attributes, though some surrender and become clothed (ἐνδυομέναις) again with human bodies and have a life like a mist (*Mor.* 415C). The poet Hesiod is then cited in support of the controversial argument that the *daimons'* long lives may eventually come to an end, and the idea is presented as well that they are susceptible to human emotions and necessary changes, but have godlike power (*Mor.* 415C, 416C-D, 418E).[12]

On a complementary note, Cicero also cites evidence of the negative way such possession and behavior was sometimes seen by this time. In the dialogue *On Divination*, set between Cicero and his brother Quintus, Cicero begins his challenge of Quintus' support of divination by possession by asking, with distinct sarcasm, what weight should be given to a frenzy (*furor*) "which you call divine" (*quem "divinum" vocatis*) that enables "the crazy man to see what the wise does not, and invests the man who has lost the human mind with that of the gods?" (*quae sapiens non videat, ea videat insanus, et is qui humanos sensus amiserit divinos adsecutus sit*; 2.110). He maintains that a certain pronouncement by the Sibyl, supposedly made while frenzied, was so vague that it could apply to many times and places, and that the pronouncement, since it was made in the form of an acrostic poem, was clearly the product of diligent work rather than of frenzy or insanity (*non furentis, adhibentis diligentiam, non insani*, 2.112). His sarcasm continues as he points out that sometimes the oracles are so esoteric that the interpreters need interpreters, that no one believes one particular oracle because everyone knows that Apollo never spoke Latin, and that the Delphic oracle is now regarded with only contempt and is ceasing to function because people are far less credulous now (2.115-7). Dream divination, as well, is not to be believed, since non-existent things are seen by men who are drunk, crazy, or asleep and optical allusions are seen even by those awake and in their right mind; generally, such belief should be considered superstitious and the product of a weak mind (2.120-25).

In the Greco-Roman evidence of ecstasy, then, we see that generally "mad" behavior by the possessed, whether general prophets to oracular

---

[12]The topic of *daimons* is not only a complicated one in the classical and Hellenistic worlds generally but also in Plutarch's writings specifically. I am not here arguing that the above is necessarily Plutarch's opinion, only that the dialogue presents this view as one current in the culture. For more on *daimons* in Plutarch, see Frederick E. Brenk, *In Mist Apparelled: Religious Themes in Plutarch's Moralia and Lives* (Leiden: Brill, 1977), esp. 49-66; 85-183. A good and concise summary of the dialogue may be found in Kathleen O'Brien Wicker, "De Defectu Oraculorum (Moralia 409E-438E)," *Plutarch's Theological Writings and Early Christian Literature* (ed. H. D. Betz; Leiden: Brill, 1975), 131-34.

priestesses, was explained by the displacement of the human mind by the divine or by the struggle to prevent that displacement. This displacement is a necessary part of the schema because human and divine minds could not coexist in a person at the same time because of the perishable and changeable nature of the mortal, a problem that contributed to the replacement of gods in possession with demigods. We also see some negative attitude toward the entire business.

JEWISH LITERATURE: ECSTASY

In the Old Testament there are some examples that are comparable to the odd behavior described in the Greco-Roman milieu, though the descriptions are "muted" compared to the Greco-Roman material we have encountered.[13] In fact, while several prophets describe some symptoms of ecstasy, the displacement of their minds is not clearly indicated.[14] Isaiah speaks of severe pain and a reeling mind (Isa 21:3-4), and Elijah runs in front of Ahab's chariot (1 Kgs 18:46). Ezekiel is lifted up by the spirit in the "heat" of his spirit (Ezek 3:14),[15] and Daniel falls into a trance (Dan 8:18) and feels great pain, shakes and cannot breathe (Dan 10:16-17). Zechariah is awakened "as one is awakened from sleep" by an angel (Zech 4:1).

---

[13]Cf. Jer 4:19; 15:18; 20:9-10; Hab 3:16; Dan 7:15; 8:17-18; 8:27; 10:8-9, 15-17. The description as "muted" comes from John R. Levison, *Of Two Minds: Ecstasy and Inspired Interpretation in the New Testament World* (Dead Sea Scrolls & Christian Origins Library 1; N. Richland Hills, Tex.: BIBAL, 1999), 11-12. A substantial literature has developed using anthropological knowledge of possession and trance states in various cultures to the phenomenon in the Old Testament; for a good discussion, see Peter Michaelsen, "Ecstasy and Possession in Ancient Israel: A Review of Some Recent Contributions," *SJOT* 2 (1989): 28-54. I have bypassed direct discussion of the phenomenon in this manner because for christological purposes I am interested more in how the phenomenon is portrayed in the literature than I am in the social or psychological analyses of the prophets or their role in their own historical context.

[14]J. Lindblom in *Prophecy in Ancient Israel* (Philadelphia: Fortress, 1963), 33, distinguishes between two types of OT prophecy: (1) "possession," in which "the deity itself, or the divine substance, takes its abode within man, penetrates him, acts and speaks in him, so that the divine *ego* dominates and more or less pushes out the human *ego*," and (2) "personal inspiration," in which the divinity does not enter the human *ego* but stands outside and "comes to him, appears to him, speaks to him, affects him with its powers, seizes him, or that he has fellowship with the divinity, has intercourse with it, and is influenced by it," which includes the phenomenon of "ecstasy." While the similarities between my schema and Lindblom's are readily apparent, my schema differs in that I would recognize these as different types of the same phenomenon of possession. I also agree with Lindblom that the possession phenomenon (my terminology) is more of a continuum than one with rigid dividing lines (*Prophecy*, 35), though I try to draw the lines distinctly for the sake of a working schema.

[15]John R. Levison, *The Spirit in First Century Judaism* (Leiden: Brill, 1997), 35, ventures with Lindblom (*Prophecy*, 134-35, 174-75) that "heat of my spirit" may suggest loss of mental control. Levison has published several extremely helpful articles on the topic, which are listed in my bibliography, but I will cite primarily this recent monograph that gathers much of that research in one place.

Jeremiah is like a drunkard (Jer 23:9), and when he tries not to prophesy destruction, he feels like there is a fire in his bones, and he cannot refrain (Jer 20:9). Hosea is simply described as mad (LXX μανία, Hos 9:7).

More dramatically, the "hand" of the Lord occasionally "falls" upon a prophet with described results similar to ecstasy. This hand of the Lord falling upon the prophet is a signature of Ezekiel, but also occurs two times in Kings and once in Isaiah.[16] The most dramatic and, perhaps, ecstatic examples from these are Ezekiel's resulting dumbness rather than immediate prophesying (Ezek 33:22), Elijah's resulting romp in front of Ahab's chariot (1 Kgs 18:46), and the music that set the stage for Elisha's prophesying (2 Kgs 3:15). While all of these experiences have some general similarities to descriptions of ecstatic behavior provided by Plato, Cicero and Plutarch, none indicate a lack of understanding of what was said to or by him, nor a lack of recall of the event; moreover, these examples, with the exception of Hosea described with μανία, do not use the vocabulary that we saw in the Greco-Roman examples.

A notable exception to this ecstatic quietism in the OT is the experience of Saul with the roving band of prophets. In 1 Sam 10:5-13, after Samuel anoints Saul, he tells Saul that at Gibeath-elohim he will meet a band of prophets playing musical instruments, and they will be prophesying. Then "the spirit of the Lord will spring upon you, and you will prophesy along with them and be turned into another man" (ἐφαλεῖται ἐπὶ σὲ πνεῦμα Κυρίου, καὶ προφητεύσεις μετ' αὐτῶν, καὶ στραφήσῃ εἰς ἄνδρα ἄλλον, 10:6), clearly a change of substance. After Saul's disobedience at Gilgal, however, "the spirit of the Lord departed from Saul, and an evil spirit from the Lord tormented him" (1 Sam 16:14). Saul himself recognizes the change in the situation, as we see in 18:12: "For Saul was afraid of David because the Lord was with him but had departed from Saul." This possession was occasional as well, because "whenever the evil spirit from God came upon Saul, David took the lyre and played it with his hand, and Saul would be relieved and feel better, and the evil spirit would depart from him" (1 Sam 16:23). Again, we see the intimations of ecstasy, this time in an undeniably negative manner, when "an evil spirit from God rushed upon Saul, and he raved within his house" and tried to kill David (MT 1 Sam 18:10; cf. LXX 19:9-10, "an evil spirit from God was upon Saul," ἐγένετο πνεῦμα θεοῦ πονηρὸν πρὸς Σαούλ).

Though not expressed the same way as in the Greco-Roman descriptions, these examples indicate the displacement of his rational mind, an intimation of which continues when Saul met the band of prophets, and "the spirit of God came upon him (καὶ ἐγενήθη καὶ ἐπ' αὐτῷ πνεῦμα θεοῦ). As

---

[16]Cf. Ezek 1:3; 3:14, 22; 8:1; 33:22; 37:1; 40:1; 1 Kgs 18:46; 2 Kgs 3:15; Isa 8:11 (though the Isa passage differs in the LXX).

he was going, he began prophesying, until he came to Naioth in Ramah. He too stripped off his clothes, and he too began prophesying before Samuel. He lay naked all that day and all that night" (1 Sam 19:23-24). Again, this behavior indicates ecstatic possession. We also see, however, movement in one of our expected continua, because the spirit that originally came upon Saul was possibly expected to be a permanent one, a situation that was changed because of Saul's disobedience.

Certain streams of later Judaism are less reticent to describe ecstasy. The Jewish Sibyl, for example, apparently underwent ecstatic possession, variously described in the text. The most elaborate description comes at the beginning of Book 2:

> When indeed God stopped my most perfectly wise song
> as I prayed many things, he also again placed in my breast
> a delightful utterance of wondrous words.
> I will speak the following with my whole person in ecstasy
> For I do not know what I say, but God bids me utter each thing.
> (*Sib. Or.* 2.1-5)

Book 3 opens with the Sibyl asking for relief from God, to no avail: "But why does my heart shake again? And why is my spirit lashed by a whip, compelled from within to proclaim an oracle to all?" (3:1-6; cf. 3.162-163, 295-98, 489-91).

With Philo we take another step forward in discerning the elements of ecstatic possession in Hellenistic Judaism. In the case of Samuel's mother Hannah, Philo takes the opportunity presented by her name, which means "grace," to explain an element of ecstasy. When grace fills the soul, he explains, the soul rejoices, smiles, and dances "because it is possessed" (βεβάκχευται, *Drunkenness* 146). To those looking on who are unenlightened, however, it may seem drunk, disturbed or disordered (μεθύειν καὶ παρακινεῖ ν καὶ ἐξεστάναι, 146). It is not only the soul of the possessed that is stirred but also the body, which becomes flushed by the overwhelming joy of the experience (147).

According to Philo, Abraham's understanding departed when he was possessed, since "when the mind is divinely possessed and becomes filled with God, it is no longer within itself, for it received the divine spirit to dwell within it," because "ecstasy, as its very name clearly shows, is nothing else than the departing and going out of the understanding" (*QG* 3.9).[17] In the context of discerning between mere diviners and true prophets, Philo

---

[17] On the basis of the Armenian and its general consistency with the Greek from which we have quotations, Ralph Marcus (*LCL* p. 191 n. l, m) suggests the original terms as follows: λογισμοῦ or διανοίας for the understanding that departs, ἐνθουσιάζει for "divinely possessed" and θεοφόρητος γίνεται for "filled with God."

asserts that the prophet's pronouncements are never his own, because "he is an interpreter prompted by another in everything he prophesies, when not knowing (ἀγνοίᾳ) he is filled with inspiration (ἐνθουσιᾷ), as the reason withdraws and surrenders (μετανισταμένου μὲν τοῦ λογισμοῦ καὶ παρακεχωρηκότος) the citadel of the soul to a new visitor and tenant, the divine spirit" which plays the human voice like a musical instrument to express the message (*Spec. Laws* 4.48-49; cf. 1.65). The similarity of Philo's description to the Greco-Roman model is clear.

The example of Moses also provides Philo with an opportunity to expound upon the phenomenon of prophetic inspiration. Moses, according to Philo, engaged in three types of prophecy: (1) those oracles spoken by God with the prophet as interpreter; (2) those in which the revelation comes by means of question and answer, and (3) those proclaimed by Moses "when possessed by God and taken out of himself" (ἐπιθειάσαντος καὶ ἐξ αὐτοῦ κατασχεθέντος, *Moses* 2.188.1-4). In this third type, God has given to the prophet Moses God's own power of foreknowledge to reveal the future, and it is in this type that the speaker "appears in divine possession" (ἐνθουσιῶδες ἐμφαίνεται) and so is a prophet strictly defined (2.190.5-8; 2.191.9-11). Being "out of himself" and "appearing" as possessed indicates ecstasy even though there are no specific descriptions that would fall on the far left of our "ecstatic behavior" continuum. The possession of Moses is described by several semantic combinations: (1) he experiences a possession by God (ἐστὶν αὐτῷ τῆς θεοφορήτου κατοκωχῆς, 2.246.5); (2) he has inspiration from God (θεοφορηθεὶς ἐθέσπισε, 2.264.9; κατεχόμενος ἐθέσπισεν, 2.270.2; cf. 2.275.4) with his mind guided by the divine spirit (θεῖον ἦν πνεῦμα τὸ ποδηγετοῦν, 2.265.4), and (3) he simply is "possessed by God" (θεοφορηθείς, 2.273.8).

Philo continues to portray Moses' possessive states in dramatic manner. He describes Moses when under inspiration in the face of the "Golden Calf" incident as follows: "he no longer remained (μένων) the same man, changed both in form and in mind, and, inspired (ἐξαλλάττεται τό τε εἶδος καὶ τὴν διάνοιαν καὶ ἐπιθειάσας), he said..." (2.272.1-3). Again Moses is described as changing temporarily when he is possessed (ἐνθουσιᾷ), which "transforms (μεταβαλών) him into a prophet" (2.280.2-3). There is a change of substance, but a temporary one. Particularly interesting for our purposes and picking up important vocabulary μένω, the importance of which we become clear in the chapters specifically on the Johannine literature, is a passage in which Philo describes the divine spirit that was upon Moses (ἐπ᾽ αὐτῷ) also going upon the seventy elders (Num 11:17); the divine spirit upon humans, he explains, is temporary. Philo describes the situation with a play on the verb μένω: "Though indeed it is possible for the divine spirit to abide in a soul (μένειν...ἐν ψυχῇ), it is not possible for it to remain permanently (διαμένειν), as we have said" (*Giants* 28). Why not? Moses answers the question himself, according to Philo, when he says, "'because they are flesh (σάρκας)' it is not possible for the divine spirit to abide permanently" (καταμεῖναι, 29; cf. QG 4.29). In the descriptions of Moses, we see movement in third continuum: the spirit's possession of Moses occurs on a fairly regular basis, but the possession still is not permanent one.

In the Judaism of this period, we find evidence of an "ecstatic perspective" on possession in the reshaping of biblical stories, a perspective that John R. Levison argues is colored by the Hellenistic environment. Levison shows that the concept of inspiration in Philo, Josephus and Pseudo-Philo has been richly influenced by the Greco-Roman environment in the areas of ecstatic behavior and displacement of the human mind.[18] Levison examines particularly the retelling of biblical accounts of Saul, Kenaz, Joshua and Balaam by one or more of these Hellenistic Jewish authors to see how the retellings shift the emphases, add to, or subtract from the biblical text. While we have seen that the case of Saul comes closer to an explicit description of ecstasy than any other possessions in the Old Testament, Levison argues that the OT account has too little detailed description of the displacement of the mind, presence of an angelic spirit, or foretelling the future to provide a complete precursor for the portrayals of these Greco-Roman elements by Josephus of Saul, of Kenaz by Pseudo-Philo, and of Balaam by Philo and Josephus.[19]

For our purposes, the most important aspects of these accounts are the descriptions of the displacement of the mind in each account. In the Josephus account of Saul and the band of prophets, Josephus adds that "on account of the great spirit, he became senseless" (ὑπὸ τοῦ πολλοῦ πνεύματος ἐλαυνόμενος ἔκφρων γίνεται, Ant. 6.223). In the retelling of the Balaam tale by Josephus and Philo, both add to the text the displacement of Balaam's mind, nowhere specifically indicated in the biblical text. Josephus says that when possessed, Balaam was "no longer his own master but was conquered (νενικημένος) by the divine spirit to deliver it" (Ant. 4.118).[20] Josephus has Balaam himself explain that the spirit speaks such words through the possessed as it wishes, which the speaker does not perceive (Ant. 4.119) and since when God has entered the possessed, "nothing in us is yet our own" (οὐδεν γὰρ ἐν ἡμῖν ἔτι...ἡμέτερον, Ant. 4.121).[21] Philo describes the angel telling Balaam that he (the angel) would prompt the necessary words of the prophecy without the consent of Balaam's mind (Moses 1.274). Balaam gives his second oracle under possession

[18]Primarily in Levison, Spirit in First Century Judaism (previously cited).

[19]Levison, Spirit, 38-40.

[20]Levison, Spirit, 31.

[21]Levison, Spirit, 32.

as "comprehending nothing, as if his reason had been removed" (μηδὲν συνιεὶς ὥσπερ μετανισταμένου τοῦ λογισμοῦ, *Moses* 1.283).[22]

Pseudo-Philo contains "ecstatic" adaptations of the Joshua and Kenaz stories. His expansion of the account of Joshua's commissioning adds that Joshua was clothed with Moses' garments of wisdom, girded with his belt of knowledge, and the prediction is made that Joshua "will be changed and become another man" (*immutaberis et eris in virum alium*, L.A.B. 20.1).[23] When Joshua clothed himself thusly, "his mind was inflamed and his spirit was moved" (*incensa est mens eius et spiritus eius commotus est*, L.A.B. 20.3). The image of the mind as "inflamed" recalls descriptions of the ecstatic possessed mind by Cicero (*Div.* 1.114) and Plutarch (*Mor.* 432E-F).[24] Pseudo-Philo also offers an intriguing story of Kenaz, a final prophecy that does not occur in the biblical account: "a holy spirit leapt upon and dwelled in Kenaz (*insiluit spiritus sanctus habitans in Cenaz*) and elevated his understanding (*extulit sensum eius*), and he began to prophesy" (L.A.B. 28.6); later, "he was awakened, and his sense returned to him" (*reversus est sensus eius in eum*, L.A.B. 28.10).[25] As 1 Samuel 10:6 describes Saul as being transformed into another person, so Kenaz and Joshua are described by Pseudo-Philo as transformed into military heroes (L.A.B. 27.9-10; 20.2).

Who, in general, is the one possessed? On this topic we see a shift in emphasis between the biblical and later writers like Josephus and Philo. In the OT, a person is often chosen with relatively little prior comment on the relation between that person's character and the choice as a prophet/ leader. Josephus and Philo, on the other hand, go out of their way to emphasize the good character, the virtue, of the person possessed by God. When he relates the story of Balaam, Josephus adds certain emphases to the biblical description. For example, Balaam is described as "the best diviner of his day," and he not only invited the envoys to stay overnight to wait for his decision, but "received them with exceeding hospitality" (*Ant.* 4.104-105). Balaam explains to the envoys not only that God would not let him go, but that this was the God who had given him the ability to speak the truth and the renown from that talent, and he counsels the envoys to renounce their hatred of the Israelites (*Ant.* 4.105-107). To the biblical description of Saul as tall and handsome, Josephus adds a comment on his

---

[22] Levison, *Spirit*, 30-31.

[23] Latin text from Guido Kisch, *Pseudo-Philo's* "Liber Antiquitatum Biblicarum" (Notre Dame, Ind.: University of Notre Dame, 1949).

[24] Levison, *Spirit*, 120-21.

[25] In the relation to the "elevation" of Kenaz's mind, Levison (*Spirit*, 107) argues that rather than Kenaz being "out of his mind" in ecstatic sense, the setting of his experince among elders echoes Ezekiel's being lifted by the spirit (Ezek 8:3); Kenaz, therefore, was probably lifted to receive a vision.

virtuous character (ἀγαθὸς τὸ ἦθος, *Ant.* 6.45). To God's counsel to Samuel not to choose Saul's successor by his beauty, "for God looks on the heart" (1 Sam 16:7), Josephus adds that God seeks "virtue of soul...adorned with piety, justice, and courage and obedience, from which beauty of the soul comes" (*Ant.* 6.160).

Philo emphasizes that no worthless person can be inspired of God (ἐνθουσιᾷ) nor, therefore, can be an interpreter of God, but only a wise and just person (*Heir* 259). Any apparent ecstasy or madness that overtakes the impious will become a curse that will cause them to grope in darkness like blind men (*Heir* 250). Philo asserts that even as a child Moses applied himself with modesty and gravity to hearing and seeing whatever would benefit the soul (*Mos.* 1.20), and as an adolescent, he put great energy into restraining his passions, reducing them to obedience with heavy chastisement (*Mos.* 1.26).

Who is the possessor? In "The Angelic Spirit in Early Judaism," Levison contends that certain passages in the LXX depict the spirit of God as an angelic spirit.[26] Not surprisingly, he suggests, Philo and Josephus make at times a similar exegetical move to identify the spirit possessing Balaam with an angelic spirit.[27] In Philo's account, the angel tells Balaam that he will return and prophesy through Balaam (*Mos.* 1.274). When the actual prophesying is described, Philo writes that Balaam spoke the oracles "which another had put into his mouth" (*Mos.* 1.277), whereas in the biblical account in Num 23:5, it is God who is said to have "put a word in Balaam's mouth." Philo also uses the same verb for prophesying, θεσπίζειν, in the angel's prediction and in the account of the actual event. Josephus makes the same identification by stating that the angel of God confronted Balaam in a narrow place, but calls that angel a "divine spirit" when the ass becomes conscious of it (*Ant.* 4.108). For both, according to Levison, God as the possessor has been altered to an angelic spirit as possessor.

While the account of Saul's possession by good and evil spirits provides some ground for the Hellenistic conceptions, Levison points out that the exegetical moves are better explained by the Greco-Roman milieu in which *daimons* were at times considered the actual possessors of those under the sway of ecstasy.[28] Philo's dependence on such Platonic conceptions such as I discussed above from *Symposium* 202-203 becomes particularly obvious when he notes that Moses generally calls "angels" those beings who serve as ministers and helpers, who take care of humans,

---

[26]Jdg 13:24-25; 1 Kgs 22:19-24; Isa 63:7-14; Mic 2:7, 11; 3:8; Hag 2:5, and Jud 16:14. Levison, "The Angelic Spirit in Early Judaism," *SBL Seminar Papers, 1995* (SBLSP 34; Atlanta: Scholars Press1995), 474-80.

[27]Levison, *Spirit*, 28-30.

[28]Levison, *Spirit*, 38-53.

and "whom other philosophers call 'daimons'" (Giants 6, 12; cf. Som. 1.141; Plant. 14). The influence of these Platonic ideas continues in the time under discussion, as we have seen not only from Philo, but in the discussion on the possession of oracular priestesses by daimons as discussed in Plutarch. Philo, Josephus and Pseudo-Philo accomplish, then, attributing a predominantly Greco-Roman concept of ecstatic possession, including the displacement of a person's rational mind, to biblical characters without necessarily attributing that possession directly to God.[29]

GRECO-ROMAN LITERATURE: INSPIRATION

Think again of the three horizontal lines of the possession continua: one from extremely frenzied behavior on the left to none on the right; the second from complete displacement of the rational mind to none, and the third from a very occasional phenomenon to a permanent possession. In the tendency I call "inspiration," frenzied behavior is unlikely, and displacement of the mind apparently does not occur, since awareness and memory of the event are intact. It is still of an occasional nature.

In the Greco-Roman world, just as in the metamorphosis category I called "direct epiphany," there are examples of direct influence of gods upon humans that give little description of the actual process; the effects, however, appear to be examples of inspiration. For example, Greco-Roman texts sometimes describe a god as simply speaking in order to press a human into action. Apollo stands beside Hector and speaks to him, then "breathed (ἐμπνέσθε) huge strength into the shepherd of the people" (Homer, Il. 15.236-238, 262). At other times, exactly how the god inspires the person is not described. Athena can stand beside and encourage (παρισταμένη, ὤτρυν') Odysseus to collect bits of bread from the suitors (Homer, Od. 17.360-361). During a battle with the Trojans, Homer says that Athena "sped through the host of the Achaians urging them to go on. In each heart she kindled the strength to make war and do battle unceasingly" (Homer, Il. 2.450-452; cf. 11.5-12 and Ovid, Metam. 5.46).[30] Mars can give strength and bravery to the hearts of the Latins (Virgil, Aen. 9.717-718), and the mind of Zeus, stronger than that of humans, can "drive on (ἀνῆκεν) wrath" in the heart of Patroklos (Homer, Il. 16.688-691).[31]

---

[29]Possession for Philo, however, does not always include displacement of the mind, as we will see below.

[30]Cf. Homer, Il. 2.166-182; 5.121-132; 11.195-210; Od. 15.9.

[31]Cf. Homer, Il. 11.2-14; Od. 17.360-361; Virgil, Aen. 1.297-304, 717-719; 11.725-728; 12.554-556. In the Homeric epics, Dietrich ("Divine Epiphanies," 59) cautions that in these cases, "the gods were really an epic way of expressing the hero's own ardour, besides of course offering a convenient poetic tool to advance the plot." Versnel ("What," 49-51) suggests that the immediate presence of the gods without visual form could still be referred to as "epiphanies."

A phenomenon we can clearly delineate as inspiration appears to be less expected than ecstasy in the Greco-Roman world, but it is occasionally described. Dio Chrysostom records an example of inspiration that, conversely, also reveals the dominance of ecstasy in the Greco-Roman understanding of possession. He describes an old woman he met in a sacred grove, who prophesies in a manner different from the majority of people "said to be inspired" (τῶν λεγομένων ἐνθέων), since she did not "gasp and spin the head about and try to terrify with a look, but spoke with total self-control and mastery" (1 Regn. 56). Plato can use the ἔνθυς terminology for philosophic inspiration. In the Cratylus 396D, Cratylus suggests that Socrates is speaking as if he is inspired. Socrates concurs and describes own temporary inspiration, claiming that an inspired (ἐνθουσιῶν) fellow seeker with "daimonic wisdom" (τῆς δαιμονίας σοφίας), with whom he spent time earlier in the day, had seized his soul. Though Socrates presumably is speaking metaphorically, the passage depicts the potential expectation of a temporary possession that could be seen in someone with no apparent ecstasic behavior.

In an example of the nature of the phenomenon as a continuum, however, in Plutarch's Oracles at Delphi, Theon presents a somewhat different perspective on the mechanism of possession. He first suggests that the god incites and provides a vision to the priestess, creating a light in her soul to see the future (Mor. 397B-C). He later adds that the body and soul of the possessed is unable to keep quiet while possessed, but, is tossed about and makes itself more and more troubled (Mor. 404E). The god, however, makes his/her words known through the mortal not by completely displacing, but in combination with the aptitudes of the mind of that particular human, so that the unlettered should not be expected to speak eloquently while under possession, nor the poet in prose (Mor. 404F-405A). There is, then, some evidence of ecstatic behavior, but none of displacement.

The discussion of Socrates' daimon in Plutarch's "On the Sign of Socrates" is particularly interesting, since it also gives us insight into who was the typical person expected to experience inspiration. In this dialogue, Socrates is said to have often expressed the opinion that a person who claimed visual communications with heaven was an imposter, whereas the assertions of one claiming he heard a voice should be seriously examined (Mor. 588C). The speaker then asserts that those who heard Socrates say this then assumed that perhaps Socrates' "sign" was the hearing or innate understanding of a voice. Giving us a glimpse into the type of person expected to receive such possession, he goes on to speculate that anyone hears this voice better when the mind and passions are quieted in sleep, but Socrates is distinguished in having had a mind pure and free from passion, "commingled (καταμιγνύς) little and only of necessity with the body" so that he could hear and respond to the voice of the *daimon* immediately (*Mor.* 588D-E). This process contradicts, the speaker tells us, the popular belief that a person can only receive such communication while asleep; on the contrary, "*daimonic* men" (δαιμονίοις) whose "disposition is undisturbed and soul is calm, who indeed we call both holy and *daimonic*" (ἱερούς καὶ δαιμονίους) can indeed receive this communication when awake (*Mor.* 589B-D).

The typical expectation in the Greco-Roman world, then, appears to be a possession that tends more toward the ecstatic than the inspired, though both are described as possession by a god or *daimon*. In inspiration, when we hear of Socrates being able to hear and respond to the *daimon* immediately, that implies that the *daimon* speaks to him in an occasional manner; otherwise, I assume that since the permanence of the possession is not made explicit, the possession is still viewed as temporary.

JEWISH LITERATURE: INSPIRATION

A Jewish audience expected to be confronted with the inspiration phenomenon more than did the Greco-Roman. The vocabulary here varies widely, reflecting the colorful diversity of the phenomenon; as Lindblom notes, "the ancient narrators do not use any standardized formula for describing the divine inspiration."[32] As in the Greco-Roman material, the message is sometimes described as "coming" to a person with little specificity. "The divine word," Lindblom points out, "plays a dominating role in the description of the divine influence upon the prophets. It may be said that the divine word and the divine saying are the most characteristic terms for expressing the content of a prophetic revelation."[33] The characteristic LXX vocabulary is the simple γίνομαι. For example, the word of the Lord came to (ἐγένετο ῥῆμα κυρίου πρός) Elijah, telling him to proceed to Zarephath (1 Kgs 17:8; cf. 18:1).[34] A bit more specific is the depiction of the Lord placing his word into someone's mouth. The Lord puts a word into Balaam's mouth (Num 23:5; cf. 23:16), and he promises to do the same for the future prophet he will raise up (Deut 18:18).

Other interesting variants appear. A visual aspect is depicted in Isaiah 2:1, "The word that Isaiah son of Amoz *saw* concerning Judah and Jerusalem." More dramatically, as discussed earlier, the "hand" of the Lord occasionally "falls" upon a person to give the prophecy, but the result does not always include any behavior that can readily be recognized as ecstatic. Despite the disappointing lack of clarity in the texts that describe these processes, it is undeniable that the prophet is understood as temporarily speaking not his

---

[32]Lindblom, *Prophecy*, 54.

[33]Lindblom, *Prophecy*, 55.

[34]As is well-recognized, this formula is common in the OT; for only a few other examples, see Hos 1:1; Joel 1:1; Mic 1:1; Zeph 1:1; Zech 1:1, and Jon 1:1.

own words but those of God, so the process may be considered possession. Also, in a similar vein to Plutarch's explanation in *Mor.* 404F-405A, "the revelatory state of mind did not destroy the individuality of the prophets. A prophet's revelations reflect his own personality."[35]

More specific to our interests are the instances when it is the spirit of God that is explicitly said to affect the human. Again, the vocabulary varies widely. The spirit of the God, for example, simply "was/came upon" Balaam (καὶ ἐγένετο πνεῦμα θεοῦ ἐν αὐτῷ, Num 24:2) and Isaiah: "The spirit of the Lord God is upon me (πνεῦμα Κυρίου ἐπ' ἐμὲ), because the Lord has anointed me" (61:1-2). It "fell upon" Ezekiel (ἔπεσον επ' ἐμὲ πνεῦμα κυρίου,11:5; cf. 3:24), while Micah claims, "I am *filled* with power, with the spirit of the Lord, and with justice and might" (ἐγὼ ἐμπλήσω ἰσχὺν ἐν πνεύματι κυρίου καὶ δρίματος καὶ δυναστείας, 3:8). In a different twist, Isaiah says, "and now the Lord God has sent me and his spirit" (καὶ νῦν κύριος ἀπέσταλκέν με καὶ τὸ πνεῦμα αὐτοῦ, 48:16).

Two types of biblical examples indicate inspiration given for tasks other than prophecy. The first type is represented by only one example. Exodus 31:1-3 relates that, "the Lord spoke to Moses, 'See, I have called by name Bezalel son of Uri son of Hur, of the tribe of Judah, and I have filled him with divine spirit of wisdom, understanding and knowledge in every kind of craft" to make the tabernacle and its accoutrements. Presumably, this would not displace the mind of the artisan, nor would it be present for any longer than necessary to complete the task.

The other type occurs in the book of Judges. The judges Othniel and Gideon are described as receiving the spirit to lead Israel. With respect to Othniel, "the spirit of the Lord was upon him (καὶ ἐγένετο ἐπ' αὐτὸν πνεῦμα κυρίου), and he judged Israel; he went to war" (Jdg 3:10). Othniel dies with no mention of spirit leaving during his lifetime. With Gideon, the semantic field expands: "but the spirit of the Lord clothed (πνεῦμα θεοῦ ἐνέδυσεν) Gideon, and he sounded the trumpet, and the Abiezrites were called out behind him." These examples are difficult, since the spirit is not described as coming upon them again nor as leaving them during their lifetimes. The case of Samson, however, may be decisive. In three cases, the spirit leapt upon Samson (ἥλατο ἐπ' αὐτὸν πνεῦμα Κυρίου), each time for a particular task: to kill a lion (14:6); to kill the men of Ashkelon (14:19), and to kill the Philistines (15:14). I would conclude that while the examples of the judges were seen as temporary possession for a task, the case of Gideon and Othniel at least open the door to an idea of a permanent possession to enable leadership, a concept we will explore more fully under the topic of "indwelling."

---

[35]Lindblom, *Prophecy*, 197.

In later Judaism, Josephus at one point discusses his own inspiration, conveniently experienced as the Romans were bearing down upon him. The general-turned-historian claims that he was assisted by some divine providence (δαιμονίῳ τινὶ συνεργέᾳ χρησάμενος, B.J. 3.341) to hide and temporarily elude capture. Josephus claims that he both had prophetic dreams and was an interpreter of dreams; he was, moreover, inspired (ἔνθους γενόμενος) to read prophecy. When he put the prophecy together with his dreams, he prayed to God, "You have made choice of my spirit (τὴν ἐμὴν ψυχὴν ἐπελέξω) to announce the things that are to come." He then willingly surrendered to the Romans (B.J. 3.351-54).[36]

Philo also depicts his own writing as sometimes inspired. In *The Migration of Abraham*, the philosopher relates to the audience how at times he will pursue an idea, only to have its path closed to him, "my understanding incapable of a single idea" (*Migration* 34). At other times, however, he sits down to work with a mind that seems blank, when suddenly, ideas come under the influence of "possession as seized by Corybantic frenzy (ὡς ὑπὸ κατοχῆς ἐνθέου κορυβανιᾶν), and knowing nothing, neither place, those persons present, myself, words spoken, lines written" (*Migration* 35; cf. *Cherubim* 27).

Philo also describes the philosopher's ascent of the mind with the vocabulary of possession. David Winston suggests that Philo distinguishes between ecstatic prophecy and mystic vision, with the latter referring not to "a psychic invasion" but to a "psychic ascent." [37] Winston notes, however, that both are "nevertheless characterized by an inspired frenzy like that of Corybants and Bacchants, a going out of one's self, forgetfulness of self, sudden seizure, and bodily transformation."[38] The passage in Philo that particularly supports Winston's interpretation is from *Creation* 69-71 (on Gen 1:26), where Philo concludes that the "image and likeness of God" refers to the mind, the reigning element of the soul, so that the love and pursuit of wisdom can lead the mind to soar and even to see archetypal patterns and "be seized by a sober intoxication like those filled with Corybantic frenzy, and is inspired, possessed by a longing far other than theirs and a nobler desire" (μέθη νηφαλίῳ κατασχεθεὶς ὥσπερ οἱ κορυβαντιῶντες ἐνθουσιᾷ ἑτέρου γεμισθεὶς ἱμέρου καὶ πόθου βελτίονος). According to Winston, however, the frenzy mediates the prophecy in the ecstatic prophecy, but in

---

[36]Hunt (*Inspired*, 54) says, "Josephus may use this phrase (ἔνθους γενόμενος; B.J. 3.351-3) to defend his actions, which may have been viewed as cowardly or traitorous, by using language that would connote to his Roman audience the impression of a decision made under ecstatic possession rather than made simply as a human." Hunt suggests that all examples of possession using this particular vocabulary tends to the ecstatic.

[37]David Winston, "Two Types of Mosaic Prophecy according to Philo," *SBL Seminar Papers*, 1988 (SBLSP 27; Atlanta: Scholars Press, 1988), 454.

[38]Winston, "Two Types," 454.

the ascent it is only an accompaniment.[39] Winston argues as well that the initiative lies with God in ecstatic prophecy, while in psychic ascent "it is in the hands of man."[40]

Winston's points seem sound with the exception of the final one. John Levison has pointed out that while Philo is almost completely indebted to Plato for his doctrine of the ascent of the mind, the Jewish thinker parts company with the Greek by insisting that the mind is "rendered buoyant, not by recollection, but by the spirit."[41] He cites primarily Philo's statement in *On Planting* 24, that since winds wreak all sorts of havoc in the natural world, "it is strange if a light substance like the mind is not rendered buoyant and raised to the utmost height by the native force of the Divine spirit...Above all it is strange if this is not so with the mind of the genuine philosopher."[42] Indeed, Levison helpfully describes how closely Philo connects the divine spirit with wisdom. Philo explains God's transference of spirit to the seventy elders, "God must do this because the seventy elders 'cannot be in real truth even elders, if they have not received a portion of that spirit of perfect wisdom,'" and that spirit brings about, in Philo's words, "the perfect consummation of knowledge."[43] Levison further refines our understanding of Philo's conception of inspiration by pointing out that when the crucial element received from the inspiration is *wisdom*, the mind is not specifically described as "evicted" and that the preposition "upon" is used, but, when the *prophetic* ability is received, the mind is described as "evicted" and the preposition "in" is used (cf. *Giants* 27, "the spirit upon him [Moses] is the wise, the divine").[44]

Jewish apocalyptic literature also depicts the inspiration of the chosen few. In *1 Enoch*, the spirit is "poured over" Enoch so that he might reveal the future to his children (91:1). The seer has full recall, however, as we can see in his description of the process in 82:7: "True is the matter of the exact computation of that which has been recorded; for Uriel—whom the Lord of all the creation of the world has ordered for me (in order to explain) the host of heaven—has revealed to me and breathed over me concerning the luminaries, the months, the festivals, the years, and the days."[45]

Several times before he has visions, Ezra mentions that his spirit, heart, or soul is troubled (*4 Ezra* 3:1-3; 5:21-22; 6:36-37; 9:27-28). In *4 Ezra* 14:22, Ezra prays to receive the Spirit so that he might write the history

---

[39]Winston, "Two Types," 545-55.

[40]Winston, "Two Types," 455.

[41]Levison, *Spirit*, 157.

[42]Levison, *Spirit*, 157.

[43]Levison, *Spirit*, 141; Philo, *Giants* 24-26.

[44]Levison, *Spirit*, 146-47.

[45]*1 Enoch*, trans. E. Isaac (Charlesworth, *Pseudepigrapha*, 1.5-89).

and the laws; shortly (14:38-41), Ezra receives his inspiration by drinking a full cup of something of a color "like fire." Upon drinking it, "wisdom increased in my breast, and my spirit retained its memory; and my mouth was opened, and was no longer closed."[46] While Ezra's troubled spirit may indicate a hint of ecstastic behavior, Ezra retains his awareness during and memory of his actual inspiration. Likewise, in 2 Baruch 20:4, the Lord instructs Baruch to "remember everything which I commanded you and seal it in the interior of your mind."

Taking this long span of literature into account, who were those inspired, and by whom or what were they inspired? The inspired were seen as those chosen by God for the special mission of revealing his will to his people. For Philo, this select group includes the philosopher who desires and has the ability for communion with another realm. By whom are these chosen ones possessed? Usually it is God's spirit who inspires, but we have taken note of Hellenistic examples in which that spirit has become an angelic one, not unlike the Greco-Roman possession by *daimons* rather than by the gods themselves.

In this possession tendency I am calling "inspiration," therefore, the audience would be led to expect little ecstatic behavior, no displacement of the rational mind, and a range from very occasional to a regular pattern. The vocabulary varies, and occasionally overlaps with that of ecstasy, showing that the two (ecstasy and inspiration) are two tendencies of the same phenomenon. The next movement in our continuua, bringing us to our final tendency, will be a dramatic one in that third continuum.

GRECO-ROMAN LITERATURE: INDWELLING

In our final tendency, we see points converging on one end of each continuum. Frenzied behavior is not described, nor is any displacement of the rational mind. Nor, however, is there any indication in the text that the possessing spirit has departed. In light of the apparently permanent state, which presumably ends with the human's death, I call this third tendency "indwelling."

Exceptionally wise people were seen to have some added impetus of the divine in their soul. Seneca, for example, asks Lucilius that if he sees someone happy, unafraid and peaceful in the midst of adversity, untouched by passions (the Stoic ideal, in other words), would he not say, "a divine power has descended upon that person"? (*Eps.* 41.4). This type of soul, Seneca says, "is stirred from a force from heaven...propped up by the divine," and still in part cleaves to the regions from which it descended (*Eps.* 41.5). Even taking into account the Stoic notion of the divinity of

---

[46]Translations are from Michael Stone, *Fourth Ezra: A Commentary on the Book of Fourth Ezra* (Hermeneia ; Minneapolis: Fortress, 1990).

the soul, this description is at least analogous to one of an experience of inspiration that is more applicable to some people than to others.

A related phenomenon in Greco-Roman literature that at least resembles a permanent possession is in the ascent of the philosopher's mind. Whereas Philo retreats from permanent possession, Plato seems to describe just such a hope. In the *Phaedrus* 249C-E, Plato relates what he considers a higher form of possession than that of the Delphic oracle he previously discussed. The philosopher is described as possessed (ἐνθουσιάσμος), his mind communing with god and lifted high above human concerns. Rather than being displaced, the mind can in this type of possession dwell in the realm of the absolute through the recollection of the forms the soul once beheld. It is only just, Plato argues, that the philosopher's mind only has the wings to make this ascent, "for he is always, according to his ability, able in memory to be with that by which God is divine" (249C). This type of man is the only one who becomes perfect, but since his attention is always turned to the divine, others "consider him disturbed (παρακινῶν) and do not know that he is inspired" (ἐνθουσιάζων, 249D).

JEWISH LITERATURE: INDWELLING

I suggest that when the possessing spirit is not described as leaving, we can assume that the audience heard at least the possibility that the spirit was the permanent "possession" of that person for as long as the person required it.[47] At times, the text clearly describes this permanence. We will see as well that the permanent possession of the spirit is given for a specific task that furthers God's will for his people, though it is most often oriented toward some type of leadership necessary for the establishment of a new stage in the community's life. The semantic field tends to overlap with the rest of the possession phenomenon, with one important exception.

One of the most striking examples of the connection between the spirit and leadership is that of the seventy elders in Numbers. Recall that for Philo, this example provided an opportunity to expound on the temporary nature of the divine possession of human beings. But what is indicated in the biblical text? In Num 11:17, God informs Abraham, "I will come down and talk with you there, and I will take some of the spirit that is on you and put it on them (ἀφελῶ ἀπὸ τοῦ πνεύματος τοῦ ἐπὶ σοὶ καὶ ἐπιθήσω ἐπ' αὐτούς), and they shall bear the burden of the people along with you so that you will not bear it all by yourself." The result is narrated in 11:25-26:

---

[47] My hesitation to make this assumption with the example from the book of Judges has already been noted above.

Then the Lord came down in the cloud and spoke to him (Moses), and took some of the spirit that was on him and placed it upon (παρείλατο ἀπὸ τοῦ πνεύματος τοῦ ἐπ' αὐτῶ και ἐπέθηκεν ἐπὶ) the seventy elders; and when the spirit rested upon them (ἐπανεπαύσατο τὸ πνεῦμα ἐπ' αὐτούς), they prophesied. But they did not do so again. Two men remained in the camp, one named Eldad, and the other named Medad, and the spirit rested on them (ἐπανεπαύσατο ἐπ' αὐτους); they were among those registered, but they had not gone out to the tent, and so they prophesied in the camp.

The fact that Philo felt it necessary to insist on the temporary nature of the possession hints that an audience would have assumed this to be a permanent power of leadership that is indicated by, but stretches far beyond, prophetic ability. The leadership of this "stiff-necked" people to their promised land requires a permanent possession of the spirit, one that is never described in the text as retreating, nor as needing to come upon the elders again.

The crucial connection between the permanent possession by the spirit and leadership of the community continues in the case of Joshua, who is decribed as "filled with the spirit of wisdom (ἐνεπλήσθη πνεύματος συνέσεως) because Moses had laid his hands on him; and the Israelites obeyed him, doing as the Lord had commanded Moses" (Deut 34:9). The permanence is underlined in Joshua 1:5 when the Lord tells him that "no one shall be able to stand against you all the days of your life. As I was with Moses, so I will be with you; I will not fail you or forsake you" (cf. 1:9). I suggest that the audience would make a connection between the filling with the spirit and God's commitment to Joshua in his leadership position.

The preceding examples clearly indicate that this possession by the spirit extends beyond enabling a prophetic ability. One exception proves the rule: in the passing of prophetic power from Elijah to Elisha. The Lord instructs Elijah to "anoint Elisha son of Shaphat of Abelmeholah as prophet in your place" (1 Kgs 19:16). Elijah cast (ἐπέρριψε) his mantle over Elisha (LXX 1 Kgs 19:19). When Elijah is about to be taken up, Elisha asks Elijah, "Please let me inherit a double share of *your* spirit" (2 Kgs 2:9). After Elijah is taken up, Elisha is seen at a distance by a band of prophets at Jericho and they declare "the spirit of Elijah has rested on Elisha" (ἐπαναπεπαυται τὸ πνεῦμα Ἡλιοὺ ἐπὶ Ἐλισαιέ, 2 Kgs 2:15). Note that the same verb is used here as in the case of the seventy elders, a form of ἀναπαύω. The prophetic spirit here, though, is that of Elijah, not the one of leadership given permanently by God.

The most crucial example in this vein is that of David's anointing by Samuel. At that time, "the spirit of the Lord leapt upon David from that day forward" (ἐφήλατο πνεῦμα Κυρίου ἐπὶ Δαυὶδ ἀπὸ τῆς ἡμέρας ἐκείνης καὶ ἐπάνω, 1 Sam 16:13). While employing the same vocabulary used for inspiration in the case of Samson, the text goes out of its way to point out that for David, the situation is of a far more permanent sort. In his reshaping of this story, Josephus makes the connection between the possession by the spirit and its sign, prophesying, by adding that after Samuel anoints David and goes on his way, "the deity abandoned Saul and passed over to David, who, when the divine spirit had moved its habitation to him, began to prophesy" (πρὸς δὲ τὸν Δαυίδην μεταβαίνει τὸ θεῖον καταλιπὸν Σαοῦλον. καὶ ὁ μὲν προφητεύειν ἤρξατο τοῦ θείου πνεύματος εἰς αὐτὸν μετοικισαμένου, Ant. 6.166). Josephus also perhaps highlights the permanence of the spirit's new residence by using the word μετοικίζω, which means "to move to another habitation" or "to resettle." We are continuing to move toward the right end of our third continuum.

The ultimate leader requires the ultimate indwelling of the spirit. In the biblical writers, we begin to see the move toward the permanent possession of the spirit as a characteristic of the expected messiah. When Isaiah looks to that ideal leader, for example, he describes the indwelling: "the spirit of the Lord shall rest on him, the spirit of wisdom and understanding, the spirit of counsel and might, the spirit of knowledge and the fear of the Lord" (ἀπαύσεται ἐπ' αὐτὸν πνεῦμα τοῦ θεοῦ, πνεῦμα σοφίας καὶ συνέσεως, πνεῦμα βουλῆς δαὶ ἰσχύος, πενῦμα γνώσεως καὶ εὐσεβείας, 11:2). Note again the appearance of a word from the παύω family.

The connection between wisdom and spirit in Isaiah is crucial, since Jewish literature describes wisdom in terms similar to those used in the realm of possession. In Baruch, God gave (ἔδωκεν) Wisdom to Israel, after which she "appeared (ὤφθη) on earth and lived among humankind" (ἐν τοῖ ς ἀνθρώποις συνανεστράφη) as "the law that endures forever" (3:36-4:4). In 1 Enoch 42:1-2, Wisdom is described as going forth to dwell among humans but finding no dwelling-place, so she "returned to her place [in heaven], and took her seat among the angels."[48] In Philo, wisdom is identified with the tent of meeting in which "the wise man tabernacles and dwells" (ἐν ᾗ κατασκηνοῖ καὶ ἐνοικεῖ; Alleg. Int. III.46). In these last three examples, wisdom does not possess a human, but the language is reminiscent of possession as wisdom comes to reside, apparently permanently, in the human realm.

In Isaiah 11:2 a connection is drawn between the permanent possession of the spirit and the gift of wisdom. We saw the association of spirit and wisdom as early as Joshua. The wisdom books, not surprisingly, make the strongest links between the two. The Wisdom of Solomon (7:7) says, "therefore I prayed, and understanding was given me; I called on God, and the spirit of wisdom came to me (καὶ ἦλθέν μοι πνεῦμα σοφίας)." This spirit of wisdom "passes into holy souls (εἰς ψυχὰς ὁσίας μεταβαίνουσα) and makes them friends of God and prophets" (7:27). The possession appears

[48]Translations from The Book of Enoch, trans. R. H. Charles (Oxford: Clarendon, 1912).

to be permanent: "for God loves nothing so much as the person who lives with wisdom" (συνοικοῦντα; 7.28). The connection continues in Wisdom 9:17-18: "Who has learned your counsel, unless you have given (ἔδωκας) wisdom and sent your holy spirit from on high (ἔπεμψας τὸ ἅγιόν σου πνεῦμα ἀπὸ ὑψίστων)? And thus the paths of those on earth were set right, and people were taught what pleases you, and were saved (ἐσώθησαν) by wisdom." Wisdom entered the soul (εἰσῆλθεν εἰς ψυχήν) of Moses, for example, to lead the people from Egypt (10:16). We are now far to the right of our first two continua, far from ecstatic behavior and displacement of the rational mind.

While the Wisdom of Solomon describes wisdom's salvific activity during the exodus, Sirach uses the wisdom myth to portray the Law, but with terminology that echoes that of possession. Wisdom dwelt in heaven (ἐν ὑψηλοῖς κατεσκήνωσα), and then came (ἐξῆλθον) to earth seeking a place to dwell (24:3-7). God told her to dwell *in* Jacob (ἐν Ιακωβ κατασκήνωσον), *in* Israel, *in* the holy tent, *in* Jerusalem, *in* an honored people (24:8-12), that is, as the wisdom of the Law (24:23-34); this appears to be a permanent indwelling.

The consistent image of a specific leader imbued with the spirit and with wisdom is Joseph. In Genesis 41:38-39, Pharoah said to his servants, "Can we find anyone else like this—one in whom is the spirit of God?" So Pharaoh said to Joseph, "Since God has shown you all this, there is no one so discerning and wise as are you." Later, the *Testament of Simeon* maintains that "Joseph was a good man, one who had within him the spirit of God (ἔχων πνεῦμα θεοῦ ἐν αὐτῷ), and being full of compassion and mercy he did not bear ill will toward me, but loved me as well as my brothers" (4.4). In *Joseph and Aseneth*, Joseph is described as a pious man, self-controlled, a virgin, one "powerful in wisdom and experience, and the spirit of God is upon him, and the grace of the Lord is with him" (καὶ ἀνὴρ δυνατὸς ἐν σοφίᾳ πνεῦμα θεοῦ ἐστιν ἐπ' αὐτῷ καὶ χάρις κυρίου μεν' αὐτοῦ, 4.7; cf. *Jub*. 40.5).

The two streams of permanent possession, messianic and wisdom, that are joined as early as Isaiah 11:2 continue to flow together later in Judaism. The *Psalms of Solomon* 17:37 describe the messiah thus: "He will not weaken in his days upon his God, for God made him powerful in the holy spirit (ἐν πνεύματι ἁγίῳ) and wise (σοφόν) in the counsel of understanding, with power and righteousness. And the blessing of the Lord will be with him in strength and he will not weaken" (cf. 18:7-9). Note the promise of permanence following immediately on the heels of the possession of the holy spirit that results in wisdom. In *1 Enoch*, the messiah is described using wisdom and indwelling terminology:

> So wisdom flows like water and glory is measureless before him forever and ever. For his might is in all the mysteries of righteousness, and oppression will vanish like a shadow having no foundation. The Elect

One stands before the Lord of the Spirits; his glory is forever and ever and his power is unto all generations. In him dwells the spirit of wisdom, the spirit which gives thoughtfulness, the spirit of knowledge and strength, and the spirit of those who have fallen asleep in righteousness (49:1-4).

The *Testament of Levi* says that God "will raise up a new priest to whom all the words of the Lord will be revealed" (18:2) "and the knowledge of the Lord will be poured out on the earth like the water of the seas" (ἐκχυθήσεται, 18:5). The description continues, "the glory of the Most High shall burst forth upon him (ἐπ᾽ αὐτὸν ῥηθήσεται). And the spirit of understanding and sanctification shall rest upon him" (πνεῦμα συνέσεως καὶ ἁγιασμοῦ καταπαύσει ἐπ᾽ αὐτόν, 18:7). Notice that various combinations with the base παύω, all with the idea of "resting upon," appear to be characteristic of the permanent possession of the spirit.[49]

In looking to the future, the literature also describes the hope that the entire community will experience in the indwelling of the spirit. Ezekiel's valley of the dry bones revived leads to God's promise that "I will place my spirit within you (δώσω πνεῦμά μου εἰς ὑμάς), and you will live" (37:14). Isaiah holds the promise "here is my servant, Israel, whom I uphold, my chosen, in whom my soul delights; I have put my spirit upon him (προσεδέξατο αὐτὸν ἡ ψυχή μου); he will bring forth justice to the nations" (42:1). Isaiah reaffirms the promise later, when he records, "as for me, this is my covenant with them, says the Lord: my spirit that is upon you, and my words that I have put in your mouth, shall not depart out of your mouth, or out of the mouths of your children, or out of the mouths of your children's children, says the Lord, from now on and forever" (59:21). Joel uses the possession imagery for this hope as well: "Then afterward I will pour out my spirit (ἐκχεῶ ἀπὸ τοῦ πενύματός μου) on all flesh; your sons and your daughters shall prophesy, your old men shall dream dreams, and your young men shall see visions. Even on the male and female slaves, in those days I will pour out my spirit" (2:28-29). Susannah 63 promises that "the younger ones will live reverently, and there will be in them a spirit of knowledge and understanding for all time" (πενῦμα ἐπιστήμης συνέσεως εἰς αἰῶνα αἰῶνος).[50]

In the Jewish literature, who is the one possessed, and who or what is the possessor? As in the case of inspiration, the key is the necessity of furthering God's plan for his people. At times, that calls for leadership reinforcement for Moses, then, a king. Later, a messianic expectation took over who would be the paragon of wisdom and require the indwelling of

---

[49]Levison (*Spirit*, 182) says on all these: "Although these authors subtly modify the Isaianic vision by underscoring strength (*1 En, PsSol* 17) or adding the element of sanctification (*TLevi*), they do not permit these emphases to eclipse the sapiential character of the spirit."

[50]Levison (*Spirit*, 180), says this passage "predicts a permanent supply of this spirit."

the spirit. Who or what was the possessor? The spirit that is from God is the consistent response, though often the attribute that is emphasized is that of wisdom.

CONCLUSION

Possession is a multi-faceted phenomenon. By using three continua, we can see that there are three distinct tendencies, however, in the varied experiences of possession. In the Greco-Roman world, the primary expectation was that of ecstasy. In the Jewish culture, inspiration was the most expected phenomenon, but there was a distinct hope for an ideal leader who would not only have the indwelling of the spirit for himself but also would initiate an age in which it would be for all people.

When a god appeared on earth, some people in the ancient Mediterranean world expected it to happen by metamorphosis. Sometimes, the body clearly was expected to be one of no material substance. But, like Cicero, some thought that a god at times imparted his/her power to a human. That "imparting," however, could be a temporary or a permanent one; it could cause a displacement of the human mind (or not), and ecstatic behavior (or not). Equipped with this map of metamorphosis and possession in the ancient Mediterranean world, we are ready to recognize the differences in christological schemas that led to a rivalry between the authors of the Johannine literature and their opponents. Standing amid these tensions, we are prepared to meet the Johannine Jesus.

CHAPTER 4
THE JOHANNINE EPISTLES

This fourth chapter will concentrate on the Johannine Epistles, focusing particularly on 1 John and the christological controversy between the author and his opponents. Two questions have dogged the understanding of this controversy: (1) the relation of 1 John to the Fourth Gospel, and (2) how closely the opponents can be identified with docetic thought. In this chapter I will first consider the likely order of composition of the Johannine writings, concluding that we can at least consider 1 John and the Gospel to have been written at approximately the same time as the Fourth Gospel and, therefore, that the Epistle can be utilized to understand the situation of the Gospel. Second, I will examine the phenomenon of docetism and demonstrate how the metamorphosis and possession patterns explain many of the difficulties scholars have faced in understanding docetic Christology. Finally, the christological controversy in the Epistles will be considered in depth.

After an examination of the Epistles, it will become clear that both the authors and opponents use a possession pattern to explain the association between the Christ and Jesus. While the opponents employ the model of a temporary possession, however, the authors reveal an adaptation of that pattern that makes the primary issue one of permanence, and this focus on permanence serves to express the complete union of the human and divine in Christ. A key to appreciating the issue of permanence is the prolific use of the term μένω in the Johannine corpus. The authors support their argument with a multi-faceted use of that verb, a term that suggests permanence, sometimes spatially, and always existentially. The author of 1 John stresses the permanence of the possession because only through that enduring state can the believer attain any permanent spiritual status; moreover, denying the permanence can assuredly lead to schism in the community.

ORDER OF THE WRITINGS

Since the order of the four Johannine writings, especially the relationship between 1 John and the Gospel, is an important question in attempting to understand the Christology of the author and opponents therein, we should briefly survey the major opinions. With respect to the Epistles, while major treatises such as the commentary of Raymond Brown argue for the traditional order of 1, 2, 3 John,[1] a number of works have suggested otherwise. The order 2, 3, 1 John has been supported recently by commentators such as I. Howard Marshall, Charles H. Talbert, John Christopher Thomas, George Strecker, and Udo Schnelle.[2] Talbert, for example, argues that when read in the sequence 2, 3, 1 John, the Epistles create an organized picture of a community or groups of related communities in crisis: in 2 John 10 the opposing teachers still seem to have access to the community, and 3 John 9-10 reveals a power struggle about how to treat these competing teachers in the communities; 1 John 2:19, however, makes clear that a schism has occurred.[3] A coherent picture then presents itself of one author of the Johannine community who claims some level of authority on the basis of a connection with the eyewitness tradition (1 John 1:1-5), struggling against an organized group of preachers who travel to the communities teaching christological ideas that the author believes to be erroneous. The disagreement first increases to a mutual lack of hospitality, then to a schism in which the two groups become institutionally separate.[4] Thomas, on the other hand, argues that 3 John is the earliest because there is no hint of the christological conflict, and that 2 John follows, revealing "an initial attempt to warn a particular community, at some distance from the Elder, of the impending visit of the false teachers."[5] Like Talbert, Thomas points out that 1 John 2:18-27 and 4:1-6 show that the false teachers had

---

[1]Raymond E. Brown, *The Epistles of John. The Anchor Bible*, Vol. 30 (N.Y.: Doubleday, 1982), 30-32. With respect to major commentaries, see also Rudolf Schnackenburg, *The Johannine Epistles* (trans. Reginald and Ilse Fuller; New York: Crossroad, 1992 from *Die Johannesbriefe*, 1953); Stephen S. Smalley, *1, 2, 3 John* (WBC 51; Waco: Word, 1984), xxii; John Painter, *1, 2, and 3 John* (SP 18; Collegeville, Minn.: Liturgical Press, 2002), 18-19. Painter supports the thesis that 2 John was written very shortly after 1 John and accompanied the first epistle as a "cover letter."

[2]I. Howard Marshall, *The Epistles of John* (Grand Rapids: Eerdmans, 1978), esp. 3-4; Charles H. Talbert, *Reading John*, 4; Georg Strecker, *The Johannine Letters* (Minneapolis: Fortress, 1996), xxxvii-xlii; Udo Schnelle, *Antidocetic Christology in the Gospel of John* (Minneapolis: Fortress, 1992), 46-53; John Christopher Thomas, "The Order of the Composition of the Johannine Epistles," *NovTest* 37 (1995): 68-75. An exhaustive list of the commentators who support the various reconstructions of the order of the Epistles can be found in Thomas, 68-69, nn. 2-4.

[3]Talbert, *Reading John* 9-12; cf. Marshall, *Epistles*, 74-75; 88-91; 151-52, esp. 151 n. 10.

[4]The contributions of Strecker and Schnelle to this question are discussed below.

[5]Thomas, "Order," 72-73.

already left the community; moreover, it reveals a more comprehensive and well-thought response to the developing heresy. For these reasons, it is chronologically the third of the Epistles.[6]

The other major question of order concerns how the Gospel of John relates to the Epistles. The majority opinion, especially following the now-familiar work of Raymond Brown, gives priority to the Fourth Gospel. Brown's commentary *The Epistles of John* builds on his previous works on the Gospel of John and the Johannine community.[7] In his reading of the gospel, Brown sees members of the Johannine community battling outsiders who hold a lower Christology than theirs, a situation that eventually led to their expulsion from the synagogues. These struggles are reflected in the basic form of the gospel, composed about 90 C.E. Due to the stress of the battles and the crucial importance of the proper understanding of the high Christology, the community began to quarrel within itself over its most definitive issue; 1 and 2 John reflect this inner Johannine struggle. The same author, but one different from that of the Gospel, Brown asserts, wrote the Epistles. First John was written as an exposition on the Christology of the Gospel, and this author wrote with knowledge of the tradition of the Gospel so complete that he could mimic the structure of it in the structure of his own Epistle.[8]

Brown and other scholars, however, provide one caveat in their assertion that the Gospel preceded 1 John. By the time of his commentary on the Epistles, Brown asserts that they were all written at about the same time, around 100 C.E., though the emerging church structure revealed in 3 John leads him to think that it was logically last, if not chronologically.[9] Though he then proceeds to discuss the development of the thought and situation in the letters as if it has been established that the order in which they were written is 1, 2, 3 John, Brown admits that the length at which the opponents' views are rebutted in 1 John makes it seem *logically* later than the brief allusions of 2 John. He then argues that the author of 1 John lived close to the recipients of the letter and in a community in which the strife had begun; 2 John, then, was written to a community in an outlying community at which the opponents have not yet appeared.[10] He allows, moreover, that 1 John could have been written before the last edition

---

[6]Thomas, "Order," 72-74. Thomas (74, n. 16) accepts the priority of at least "the bulk of the Fourth Gospel."

[7]Raymond E. Brown, *The Gospel According to John* (AB 29 & 29a; New York: Doubleday, 1966, 1970); *The Community of the Beloved Disciple*.

[8]Brown, *Gospel*, 73; 91; 122-129.

[9]Brown, *Gospel*, 30.

[10]Brown, *Epistles*, 31.

of the Gospel and have thus influenced that final edition.[11] The time of composition of the Gospel and Epistles in the later Brown, then, poses no problem to their sharing a common problem of Christology.

Others persuasively argue that the issue is far from concluded as well. In his 1984 commentary, Kenneth Grayston eloquently points out the towering presence of the Gospel over the First Epistle, and the resulting "intellectual and spiritual pressure to approach the Epistle after experiencing the Gospel," while "in fact the Epistle may be the most sensible approach to the top."[12] Grayston argues that in several passages, 1 John appears to contain "first attempts" at material later elaborated in the Gospel. Why, for example, if the author of 1 John had the teaching about the Paraclete in John 13-17, would he have failed to use it against his opponents?[13] Like Brown, therefore, Grayston allows for the possibility that the final form of the Gospel was influenced by the situation addressed in the Epistles.[14]

Strecker, on the other hand, asserts that there is no evidence that the authors of the Epistles were familiar with any form of the Gospel. On the basis of internal criteria such as primitive apocalyptic Christology, sender, situation, and other correspondences, he claims that 2 and 3 John are the initial documents of the community and were written by the same author (the "presbyter," who was a chiliast) around 100 C.E.; 1 John and the Gospel follow, composed by two separate authors, neither being the presbyter, during the first half of the second century C.E.[15]

Schnelle systematically challenges eight influential arguments for the priority of the Gospel and shows them to be at best inconclusive. He concludes that since in 1 John there is no quotation from the Gospel, "the often-suggested shifts in theological emphasis between the Gospel and the letter are either nonexistent or rest on a particular interpretation of the Gospel that prejudices the desired result."[16] Schnelle suggests the *acute christological dispute* of 1 John as a methodological starting point for

---

[11]Brown, *Epistles*, 32; 69. Others have also suggested that the author of 1 John may have had a hand in the final production of the Gospel. For a complete list, see James Brownson, "The Odes of Solomon and the Johannine Tradition," *JSP* (1988): 63, n. 9. Marshall (*Epistles*, 41), for example, states that the redaction issues of the Gospel seriously complicate the issue, but he asserts that "the Gospel and Epistles stand so close together in terms of theological outlook that they must have been written by authors who stood very close to each other.

[12]Kenneth Grayston, *The Johannine Epistles* (NCB; Grand Rapids: Eerdmans, 1984), 11.

[13]Grayston, *Johannine*, 13-14.

[14]Grayston, *Johannine*, 12-14. Graytston (7) suggest that 2 John is probably "secondary," but that 1 and 2 John were "more or less contemporary responses to the same disturbance. Third John 9-10 refers to 2 John (160), which places 3 John as the final production of the three."

[15]Strecker, xxxvii-xlii; cf. "Die Anfänge der johanneischen Schule," *NTS* 32 (1986): 31-47.

[16]Schnelle, *Antidocetic*, 52-63.

arguing the priority of that letter to the Gospel, and he then finds enough anti-docetic references in the Gospel to argue that the Gospel is addressing the christological dispute of 1 John.[17]

Talbert also argues that the Gospel contains themes that reflect the struggles between the author and his opponents in the Epistles. He draws attention particularly to the following themes: (1) the true humanity of God's Son from the water through the blood; (2) the subordination of the Spirit to Christology; (3) the need of Christians for post-baptismal cleansing and for Jesus' intercession; (4) the original disciples as eyewitnesses of the incarnation, especially of the "blood;" (5) the command to love one another, and (6) the result of loving one another, that they may all be one. The appearance of these themes in the Gospel suggests that the Gospel is best viewed as having been written soon after or at approximately the same time as 1 John.[18]

Another conclusion has been recently highlighted by Wendy E. Sproston North.[19] She argues that the Gospel and First Epistle clearly use some of the same material, in the same language peculiar to this literature, with different applications of that material.[20] She concludes that each author is using community tradition and interpreting it to meet current needs independently, a process that "explains the pattern of striking but intermittent contact between them."[21] This last option in particular leads us to recognize that, despite the academic orthodoxy following the early Brown, the issue is far from settled and that we need to continue testing hypotheses to explain the relationship between the Gospel and the Epistles.

This chapter will consider the Epistles in the order 2, 3, 1 John. The Gospel, the subject of the next chapter, will be considered as written in very close proximity to the Epistles and as reflecting a similar christological debate, whether 1 John and the Gospel are literarily dependent one on the other, or, are independent and dependent on a common stock of tradition

---

[17]Schnelle, *Antidocetic*, 60. We will have more opportunity to discuss Schnelle's hypotheses in the following chapter.

[18]Talbert, *Reading John*, 56-57. In discussing the common themes in the Gospel and Epistles, Talbert cites Smalley (*1, 2, 3 John*, xxx), who includes a chart of the common themes between 1 John and the Farewell Discourse of the Gospel. Smalley argues, not unlike Sproston North and Lieu (below), that the "fairly frequent points of contact" are "a natural correspondence of theological *themes*" (emphasis his).

[19]Wendy E. Sproston North, *The Lazarus Story within the Johannine Tradition* (JSNTSS 212; Sheffield: Sheffield Academic Press, 2001).

[20]North, *Lazarus*, 36.

[21]North, *Lazarus*, 37. She points out (p. 38 n. 43) that neither Strecker, Brown nor Judith Lieu (*The Theology of the Johannine Epistles*, Cambridge: Cambridge University Press, 1991) exclude this interpretation of the evidence. In my reading of Lieu (*Theology*, 101), Lieu seems to reach exactly the same conclusion as North, citing as well that the "apparently similar material is used in distinct ways."

to defend their understanding of the Christ event. In this manner, I hope that an examination of the christological issues will serve the secondary purpose of shedding some light on the order of the works. Concerning the question of authorship, this paper will assume the majority opinion that the Epistles are probably written by the same author, while the Gospel shows enough stylistic differences, despite many common themes, to consider it from a different hand of the same community.[22]

Docetism and the Epistles: State of the Question

Docetism has proven to be notoriously difficult to define. While some scholars have attempted a precise definition, others defended using docetism as an umbrella term for certain diverse schemas opposed by the church fathers. Progress on the docetism front has been hindered by the fact that one of the most important works among those who have attempted a precise definition is a Heidelberg dissertation that has remained unpublished, Peter Weigandt's "Der Doketismus im Urchristentum und in der theologischen Entwicklung des zweiten Jahrhunderts" (1961). Weigandt delineates seven types of gnostic Christology but defines as docetic only a monophysitic type in which the savior is completely divine because the divine Christ can have absolutely no contact with matter. This docetism may be found, according to Weigandt, in Ignatius' description of his opponents (*Eph.* 6.2; *Trall.* 6.2) as well as in the theology of Saturninus, Cerdo, Marcion and in the *Acts of John*.[23]

Other studies concur with Weigandt's, though they typically address the complexity of docetism differently. For example, the major *Studia Patristica* article of J. G. Davies accepts this narrow definition of docetism but tries to delineate the complexity of the phenomenon on the basis of whether the source of the ideas focus on one of four doctrines: the Godhead, a cosmology, an anthropology, or a Christology.[24] Norbert Brox recognizes that there are two different christological patterns in the docetic evidence, but argues that a pattern in which the human Jesus was inhabited temporarily by the heavenly Christ is a "separationist Christology" that should be separated from a "purely docetic Christology."[25]

---

[22]The question of authorship is not crucial to this argument; it is only important that the writings come from the same community or "school," which has been thoroughly demonstrated and on which there is broad agreement. For recent overviews of the question, see Schnelle, *Antidocetic*, 41-47 and Painter, *1, 2, and 3 John*, 44-50.

[23]Weigandt did not have the opportunity to examine the Nag Hammadi documents.

[24]J. G. Davies, "The Origins of Docetism," *Studia Patristica* 6 (1962): 13-35. The thesis of Davies' article is that "the earlier in time the docetic strand, the greater the apparent influence of Judaistic thought; conversely the later in time, the greater the influence of Graeco-Oriental speculation" (35).

[25]Norbert Brox, "'Doketismus'—eine Problemanzeige," *ZKG* 95 (1984): 301-14.

On the other end of the definition spectrum is Michael Slusser. In "Docetism: A Historical Definition,"[26] he examines not only Weigandt but also other descriptions from that of F. C. Baur to the articles of standard reference works. Baur defined the phenomenon broadly:

> Either objectivity is denied to the human in Christ, or at least the human is so separated from the divine that there is no personal unity between the two. The first is the purely docetistic view, since it holds that Christ was man only in appearance; but the second has at least this in common with genuine Docetism, that it declares the divine-human unity of the Savior to be mere appearance. For while it distinguishes between the Christ and Jesus, takes Jesus for a real human being, and lets him act in visible fashion for human salvation, it is mere illusion if one takes Jesus for the real person of the Savior, for the genuine subject of saving activity.[27]

Against several of the reference works and especially against Weigandt, Slusser argues for a broad definition. As Slusser points out, Klaus Koschorke claims to follow Weigandt's definition of docetism, yet in fact he effectively broadens the definition when he claims that "there is a single fundamental theme at work in these somewhat contrary positions: the conviction that the Savior in his own real being is entirely withdrawn from the sphere of suffering and passing-away. And precisely this marks the opposition with 'church' belief."[28]

Slusser concludes that the broad conceptions of the phenomenon provided by Baur and Koschorke best serve to conceptualize this broad and diverse phenomenon for two reasons. First, those depictions that Weigandt calls docetism are expressions in which the problem of the details of the Christ's appearance are "glossed over," while those Weigandt calls not docetistic simply attempt a more detailed explanation of the impassibility of Christ.[29] Second, Slusser objects to the tendency of Weigandt and others to disregard the perceptions of the early heresiologists, such as Irenaeus, when they categorize a scheme of thought as docetistic.[30] Especially now that the Nag Hammadi documents may contribute to the discussion, Slusser argues, we can see that the "appearance" of Christ that for docetists was an illusion is useful if "we are careful to refer the word 'appearance' not to the

---

[26]Michael Slusser, "Docetism: A Historical Definition," *The Second Century* 1 (1981): 163-172.

[27]Baur, *Die christliche Gnosis oder die christliche Religions-Philosophie in ihrer geschichtlichen Entwicklung* (Tübingen, 1835), 258-59, cited in Slusser, "Docetism," 171.

[28]Klaus Koschorke, *Die Polemik der Gnostiker gegen das kirchliche Christentum* (Leiden: Brill, 1978); cited in Slusser, "Docetism," 171.

[29]Slusser, "Docetism," 167-68.

[30]Slusser, "Docetism," 168-69.

phenomenon considered statically, nor to the means by which the Savior appeared on earth but to his *act of appearing*."[31] The early heresiologists, then, knew whereof they spoke when they grouped together as docetists those who denied that the divine Christ was the actual subject of the human experiences of the earthly Jesus.[32]

Let us now consider several major opinions concerning how the opponents depicted in the Johannine Epistles may be related to docetism.[33] In his commentary on the Epistles, Raymond Brown surveys the history of scholarship on the problem of identifying the opponents with known heresies in the general time period of the Epistles. After a brief discussion of those who would draw parallels with other groups condemned in the New Testament, especially the churches in Revelation,[34] Brown spends the lion's share of the section on the groups with whom the epistolary opponents are most often identified: (1) the docetic opponents of Ignatius of Antioch; (2) second century gnostics, and (3) Cerinthians.[35] Brown concludes that, due to differences in nuance of belief, or of different time frames, or both, one cannot make an exact identification of the opponents in the Johannine Epistles with any of these groups.[36] The opponents, rather, "admitted the reality of Jesus' humanity, but refused to acknowledge that his being in the flesh was essential to the picture of Jesus *as the Christ*," and this belief puts them in a trajectory that would develop into full-blown gnostic thought.[37]

---

[31]Slusser, "Docetism," 172.

[32]Slusser, "Docetism," 172.

[33]It should be noted that not all commentators subscribe the opinions of the opponents to any recognizable form of docetism. A number of commentators describe the opponents as "pneumatics" without necessarily implying a connection to the historical movements of gnosticsm or docetism. See, for example, Johannes Beutler, *Die Johannesbriefe* (Regensburg: Pustet, 2000), 23-24; Pierre Bonnard, *Les épitres johanniques* (CNTN 13c; Geneva: Labor et Fides, 1983), 20-25; Hans-Josef Klauck, *Die Erste Johannesbrief* (EKK 23.1; Zürich: Benziger and Neukirchen-Vluyn: Neukirchener, 1991), 34-42.

[34]Brown, *Epistles*, 56-57.

[35]Under each topic, Brown (*Epistles*, 56-60) cites in footnotes those commentators who have argued for each identification.

[36]Brown, *Epistles*, 67.

[37]Brown, *Epistles*, 60; 76. Before Brown, Schnackenburg had concluded similarly that, while the opponents in 1 and 2 John could not be identified precisely with any known heresy at the time, they show several significant points of contact with those like Cerinthus and the opponents of Ignatius, and therefore the opponents show (to quote Schnackenburg's 1992 English edition, p. 23) "one example of that pseudo-Christian tendency which manifested itself in gnosticism and was such a threat to the church." K. Weiss as well compares the opponents' lack of interest in the human person Jesus, as well as any ethical implications of his life and atoning effects of his death, as related to gnostic ideas but without fully developed gnostic features. K. Weiss, "Die 'Gnosis' im Hintergrund und im Spiegel der Johannesbriefe," *Gnosis und Neues Testament* (ed. K.-W. Tröger; Gütersloh: Gütersloher, 1973), 341-56.

More recently, Georg Strecker suggests that docetic thought can be divided into three systems.[38] The first system includes those who suggested that the person crucified was another human being rather than Jesus. According to Irenaeus (*Adv. Haer.* 1.24.4), for example, Basilides claimed that the Christ stood by during the crucifixion "in the form of Simon" and watched, laughing. Second, some sources, including the *Acts of John* and the information about Cerinthus' thought, suggest that the Christ departed from Jesus before the passion commenced. Strecker suggests that this belief is a variant of the adoptionist idea that the Christ united with Jesus at the baptism, but the divine and human natures remained separate. The third category contains those who maintained that while a personal unity exists in Jesus Christ, he is of a pneumatic substance and could not suffer; here Strecker includes Ignatius' opponents, Valentinus, Pseudo-Tertullian, Marcion, Saturnius and Cerdon. Concerning the opponents in 1 John, the strongest case can be made for a connection with the docetism of Asia Minor, such as Cerinthus, though 1 John does not yield enough evidence for certainty.

Udo Schnelle closely follows Weigandt's description of docetism. Schnelle is particularly impressed by the parallels between the opponents in 1 John and those against whom Ignatius and Polycarp contended, and he also cautions, in agreement with Strecker, against too close an identification with Cerinthus.[39] He concludes that the opponents in 1 John "also taught a docetic christology;"[40] that is, the opponents taught that there was no corporeality to the Son of God, so he was incapable of suffering, and that the divine Christ, not the human Jesus, is the only one relevant for salvation.[41]

Stephen S. Smalley sees two groups troubling the author of 1 John, one that veered away from the author's Christology due to its Jewish beliefs, and the other that diverged based on Greek thought. The Fourth Gospel, according to Smalley, attempted to balance these tendencies of the two groups, the first who thought Jesus to be human, and the second who thought of him as God.[42] By the time of 1 John, these tendencies "had crystallized into recognizable error," so that the epistolary author

---

[38]Strecker, *Johannine Letters*, 69-76. The three-part delineation found in Walter Bauer and H. Paulsen, *Die Briefe des Ignatius von Antiochia und der Polykarpbrief* (HNT 18/2; Tübingen: Mohr, 1985) differs from Strecker's only in the conception of the third type, which they describe as the "perfect docetism" of those who "completely [dissolve] the earthly existence of the Lord into appearance." Cited in Schnelle, *Antidocetic*, 65 n. 150.

[39]Schnelle, *Antidocetic*, 69-70.

[40]Schnelle, *Antidocetic*, 67-68.

[41]Schnelle, *Antidocetic*, 68.

[42]Stephen S. Smalley, "What about 1 John?" *Stud Bib* (1978): 337-343. Cf. *1, 2, 3 John*, esp. xxiv-xxvi.

combats both of these heresies, adoptionism and docetism.[43] We can see this struggle in the Epistles when some passages seem clearly anti-adoptionistic, others seem clearly anti-docetistic, and still others are, "to say the least, ambivalent in their purport."[44]

John Painter, on the other hand, is generally persuaded by the reconstruction of Brown. He argues, however, that the opponents in 1 John are Gentiles who distorted the tradition inherited from the Fourth Gospel because they lacked the appropriate context of the synagogue conflict.[45] The use of "Son of God" as a pre-existent manifestation of God (see 1 John 4:9) rather than in a messianic sense "is an indication of the movement from the Jewish world to the Gentile world."[46] Painter argues as well, however, that for the opponents this divine manifestation descended upon the human Jesus at his baptism, and, hence, he was the model of this initatory pattern for all believers.[47]

Finally, two scholars should be mentioned who have argued for similarities between the Christology of the opponents and that of later docetic works. Pieter J. Lalleman builds on Painter's suggestion of a Gentile background of the opponents to argue that the opponents have the same docetic Christology (Jesus Christ had no real human body) as is found in the Acts of John; therefore, the assertion that the opponents' Christology was similar to Cerinthus is in error.[48] James Brownson lists several significant parallels between the Odes of Solomon and the opponents in 1 John.[49] In the realm of Christology, Brownson equates 1 John 4:2, that the opponents "do not confess Jesus Christ come in the flesh," with passages in the Odes suggesting that the incarnation is "more a matter of appearance, a condescension for the ignorant, than a salvific event in its own right."[50] Brownson concludes that "the writer of the Odes of Solomon looks very much like one of the 'secessionists' of 1 John."[51]

We see, therefore, disagreement concerning whether docetism should be defined in a narrow or broad manner, but general agreement that the opponents in the Epistles can be placed at least in the realm of docetic thought. The analyses of the opponents, however, tend to throw us back

---

[43]Smalley, "What about 1 John?" 338.

[44]Smalley, "What about 1 John?" 338-40.

[45]John Painter, "The 'Opponents' in 1 John," NTS 32 (1986): 48-71.

[46]Painter, "Opponents," 64-65.

[47]Painter, "Opponents," 67.

[48]Pieter J. Lalleman, "The Adversaries Envisaged in the Johannine Epistles," NedTT 53 (1999): 17-24.

[49]Brownson, "Odes," 54-60.

[50]Brownson, "Odes," 54-55. The Odes do, Brownson points out (61), reveal a familiarity with more christological traditions than does 1 John.

[51]Brownson, "Odes," 60.

into the conception of docetism question. Is the relationship, for example, between the "adoptionists" and "docetists" of Smalley's reconstruction one of ethnic association? Or are there more general christological patterns from the ancient Mediterranean environment at work here? To find an answer, we now turn to an examination of docetism in the context of the models described in the previous two chapters: metamorphosis and possession.

DOCETISM IN THE LIGHT OF METAMORPHOSIS AND POSSESSION MODELS

One obvious conclusion from this brief tour is that a manner of conceptualizing the overall phenomenon of docetism is needed, one that will also explain the diversity within it. When we consider the primary evidence for docetic thought in light of our metamorphosis and possession models, the reasons for the diversity of this christological schema become clear: while the majority of docetists applied a metamorphosis Christology to the Jesus event,[52] enough of these theologians employed the temporary possession model to throw into confusion any attempt at a narrow definition of docetic thought. I suggest a three-part division as well, but one that begins with those Mediterranean models. Thus, my three categories are: (1) the metamorphosis model; (2) the possession model and (3) blends of (1) and (2). I will first examine some primary evidence for those theologians who employed the metamorphosis pattern model to describe the appearance of the Christ on earth, then we will consider those who employ a possession pattern, and, finally, those who blend the patterns, before examining the Johannine Epistles to discern into which pattern the opponents best fit.[53]

To understand the appearance of Christ on earth as metamorphosis, let us recall our conclusions from Chapter Two concerning the metamorphosis phenomenon. The metamorphosis pattern entails a change in form and, therefore, in appearance, not a change in substance. While the vocabulary varies, none of the terms connote a change in essence—there is a continuity of mind and of identity. The most common description of metamorphosis, we saw, revealed simply the change in the actual physical form. An emphasis on the appearance as a nonmaterial one was present at times. Again, I would like to stress that these are not rigid *types* of metamorphosis as much as different tendencies of depicting the phenomenon which employed somewhat different vocabulary; in fact,

---

[52]Gregory J. Riley, in "'I Was Thought to Be What I Am Not:' Docetic Jesus and the Johannine Tradition," Occasional Papers for the Institute for Antiquity and Christianity Occasional Series 31 (Claremont Graduate School): 1-24, also suggests Greco-Roman models for docetism. I will discuss his contribution more directly in relation to the Fourth Gospel.

[53]My intention is not to survey every piece of evidence for docetic thought, or ultimately to solve the problem of docetism, but only to show the use of these Mediterranean patterns, which will provide a context for the Johannine pattern/s.

it will be clear especially in the realm of Christology that the boundaries between these emphases are permeable. In both tendencies, a polymorphic capability was sometimes emphasized.

Irenaeus is the great combatant of metamorphosis Christologies. In *Against Heresies* 2.22.4, we find an example of straightforward metamorphosis: "He [Jesus Christ] did not seem one thing while being another, as those affirm who describe him as being man only in appearance; but what he is, that he also appeared to be" (*non enim aliud videbatur et aliud erat, sicut inquiunt qui putativum introducunt; sed quod erat, hoc et videbatur*).[54] To Irenaeus, the outward appearance was not something altered; it could be trusted. For those thinkers he opposed, the essence of the savior remained the same, but a metamorphosis allowed him to appear as a human. This passage, however, does not reveal enough information to suggest either a nonmaterial or polymorphic emphasis.

A nonmaterial emphasis of the appearance is often, we have seen, indicated by a term like *phantasm*. Irenaeus says that several heretical groups impress young boys "by exhibiting phantasms (*phantasmata*) that instantly end," and they seem to "maintain that the Lord also performed such works only in appearance" (*per phantasmata, Haer.* 2.32.4). In Rome, Cerdon is said by Pseudo-Tertullian (*Haer.* 6.1) to have taught that the Savior was not born at all, coming to earth as Son of God but not in the substance of flesh (*in substantia carnis*), but only as a phantasm (*in phantasmate*).

In early Christianity, Marcion might be considered the metamorphosis theologian *par excellence*, and, if we can trust Tertullian, Marcion was heavily invested in the nonmaterial emphasis. We see the basic metamorphosis pattern in Irenaeus' description of Marcion's belief. Irenaeus records Marcion as believing that Jesus Christ appeared from heaven in the form of a man (*in hominis forma manifestatutum*) during the 15th year of Tiberius (*Haer.* 1.27.2). Irenaeus later asks, "how, moreover, supposing he was not flesh but appeared as if a man, could he have been crucified, and could blood and water have come forth from his pierced side?" (*quomodo autem et cum caro non esset, sed pareret quasi homo, rucifixus est, et e latere eius puncto sanguis exiit et aqua, Haer.,* 4.33.2). These passages indicate a metamorphosis emphasizing the change of the external form; for the second to be consistent with the first, it must mean that the fact that his body was not actually human would have prevented the issuing

---

[54]Since we are dealing in semantic fields, it is unfortunate that little of Irenaeus survives in the original Greek. Since most commentators, however, date the Latin translation to the third or fourth century, and the Latin terms in which we are interested compare well with Tertullian's expressions for the same phenomena, we can assume that the translated terminology is fair to the original in these limited instances. Patristic texts, with the exception of Ignatius, are from J.-P. Migne, Patrologia latina (217 vols.; Paris, 1844-1864) and Patrologia graeca (162 vols.; Paris, 1857-1886).

of blood and water from the pierced side. In the text, however, we have the semantic indications only of metamorphosis (*forma*).

The case is clearer in the evidence cited by Tertullian. Tertullian describes Marcion's position as maintaining that the substance of Christ's body only appeared "by an image of human substance" (*per imaginem substantiae humanae; Marc.* 3.10.2). Though the term *imago* is generally used, as we saw in Chapter Two, for mere form, Tertullian's choice of the term *substantia* may hint that the body was nonmaterial. *Substantia* generally indicates the "quality of being real or having an actual existence; also, of having a corporeal existence;" or, it can indicate "the reality of a thing" distinct from a "mere outward appearance," as well as "the material of which a thing is made."[55] In fact, we see that this "nonmaterial" supposition is correct, since otherwise Tertullian cites Marcion as describing the body of Christ as well as his nativity with the term φάντασμα (*Marc.* 3.9.1; cf. *Carn. Chr.* 1.2).[56]

One of these quotations is particularly interesting, since it assists us with other metamorphosis vocabulary. In *Against Marcion* 3.9.1, Tertullian claims that Marcion compares Christ's body with that of the angels who visited Abraham and Lot, who were "in a phantasm, apparently of supposed flesh" (*in phantasmate, putativae utique carnis;* cf. 3.11.1). This verb *puto* appears in the descriptions of several docetists. Satornilius, as Irenaeus tells us, said that the Savior was "without birth, without body, and without figure, but was, by supposition, a visible human being" (*innatum demonstravit, et incorporalem, et sine figura, putative autem visum hominem, Haer.* 1.24.2).[57] Unlike the Valentinians, Irenaeus asserts that the Jesus Christ seen by the apostles "was not a supposed being, but the truth" (*non erat putativus, sed veritas, Haer.* 2.22.6). Unnamed heretics will be judged, according to Irenaeus, by thinking Jesus Christ to be "supposed" (*putativus fuit*) and "having manifested himself as a supposed being" (*semetipsum putativum ostendebat, Haer.* 4.33.5). Other false teachers say Jesus Christ "appeared in mere seeming" (*putative dicunt cum apparuisse*), but Irenaeus contends that those who maintain this belief are vain, for "these things do not seem but happened in actual reality" (οὐ γὰρ δοκήσει ταῦτα, ἀλλ' ἐν ὑποστάσει ἀληθείας ἐγίνετα, *non enim putative haec, sed in substantia veritatis fiebant, Haer.* 5.1.2; cf. 3.18.6). *Puto*, then, apparently serves as a verbal

---

[55]Glare, *OLD*, 1851.

[56]Cf. *Adv. Marc.* 3.8.1; 3.10.11; 4.7.1-5; 5.8.3; 5.20.3. For an insightful discussion of Marcion's theology and Christology, and how both of these influenced his *Euangelion*, see Peter Head, "The Foreign God and the Sudden Christ: Theology and Christology in Marcion's Gospel Redaction," *TynBul* 44 (1993): 307-21.

[57]The term "puto," which generally means "to think, suppose, consider, regard" (Glare, *OLD*, 1526), Schnelle (*Antidocetic*, 66) points out is used as the Latin equivalent of δοκέω. It is not at all clear, however, that it should be equated to *phantasm*.

indication of the nonmaterial emphasis. The meaning field of the verb also emphasizes a lack of change in essence.

Our first example of the polymorphic tendency in docetic Christology comes from Ireneaus. Basilides, according to Irenaeus, taught that the Father sent the deliverer, Christ, who

> appeared (*apparuisse*), then, on earth as a man. He himself did not suffer death, but Simon, a certain man of Cyrene, was forced to carry the cross in his place, so that the latter, being transfigured by him (*transfiguratum ab eo*) so that he might be thought to be Jesus, was crucified...while Jesus himself received the form (*accepisse formam*) of Simon and stood by and laughed at them. For because he was an incorporeal power and was the Nous of the unborn father, he transfigured himself as he wished (*transfiguratum quaemadmodum vellet*), and thus ascended to him who had sent him...It is not necessary for us to confess the one who was crucified, but the one who came in the form of a man (*in hominis forma venerit*) and was thought to be crucified, and was called Jesus, and was sent by the father. (*Haer.* 1.24.3-7)

Note the appearance of the familiar metamorphosis terms *transfigura* and *forma*, indicating the metamorphosis of external form only. The continuity of mind and identity is clearly apparent in the laughter and in the consistent definition of the being as "an incorporeal power" and "the Nous of the unborn father."

Irenaeus also describes the self-proclaimed polymorph Simon the Samaritan, who "was glorified by many as a god, and taught it was he himself who appeared among the Jews as the Son (*quasi Filius apparuerit*), descended in Samaria as the Father (*quasi Pater descenderit*), and came to other nations in the character of the Holy Spirit" (*quasi Spiritus sanctus adventaverit, Haer.* 1.23.1). Simon's use of the metamorphic model, according to Irenaeus, extended to Christ as well, who had "descended, transfigured (*transfiguratum*), and assimilated to powers and principalities and angels, so that he himself might appear to be a human, but his was not human, and appear to suffer, while not suffering" (*Haer.* 1.23.3). Metamorphosis Christology, with traditional metamorphosis vocabulary, was clearly available to early Christian theologians.

Some of the apocryphal Acts display a polymorphic Christology. David Cartlidge has described this metamorphic tendency in the *Acts of John, Acts of Thomas,* and *Acts of Peter*.[58] All of these Acts distinguish

---

[58]David Cartlidge, "Transfigurations of Metamorphosis Traditions in the Acts of John, Thomas, and Peter," *Semeia* 38 (1986): 53-66. Cartlidge's interest is to provide examples of a pattern that he believes precedes the gospel accounts of the Transfiguration (Mk 9:2-8 and parallels). The polymorphic Christ in the apocryphal Acts, especially in the *Acts of John*, has received a considerable amount of attention. See, for example, Weigandt, "Doketismus," 83-96; Davies, "Origins," 33-35; R. I. Pervo, "Johannine Trajectories in the *Acts of John*," *Apocrypha* 3 (1992): 47-68; Lalleman, "Adversaries," esp. 18-19, and Schnelle, *Antidocetic*, 67.

between Jesus' apparent form and his essence, which is at times revealed for what it is: divine (*AJ* 90-91; *AT* 143; *AP* 20). These texts also "proclaim a christology of the polymorphic Jesus (*AJ* 87-89; *AT* 153-54; *AP* 20-21)."[59] The *Acts of John*, moreover, contains both the material and nonmaterial emphases: "sometimes when I meant to touch him I encountered a material, solid body; but, at other times when I touched him, his substance was immaterial and incorporeal, as if it did not exist at all" (93).

In none of the above examples is a change in essence indicated; in fact, just the opposite is the case. The emphasis for the metamorphosis theologians is that this Jesus Christ was simply a god, despite any external appearance of being human. His identity is divine, his mind is divine. The tendencies toward a nonmaterial form and polymorphism are particularly strong. These emphases are not surprising given the charges of *their* opponents, such as Irenaeus: that sacred texts described a birth from a human woman and a very real and bloody death.[60]

Some docetists, on the other hand, face their "orthodox" opponents by utilizing the possession model to reject any thoroughgoing union of the Christ and Jesus. We should at this point recall the diversity of the possession phenomenon in the ancient Mediterranean. First, the tendency of an occasional possession that involves displacement of the human mind and is usually recognizable by frenzied behavior and lack of recall is the type of possession I have called "ecstasy." Second, the tendency of an occasional possession that does not involve displacement of the human mind and is less often accompanied by frenzied behavior is best termed "inspiration." Third, the tendency of a permanent possession that does not involve displacement of the human mind and is generally not accompanied by frenzied behavior is "indwelling."

Irenaeus again provides us with a great deal of evidence. He makes a division between writers: those for whom Jesus is the receptacle of Christ at the baptism, and those using the metamorphosis model:

> But there are some who say that Jesus was a receptacle (*receptaculum*) of Christ, upon whom (*in quem*) the Christ, as a dove, descended from above, and that when he had declared the unnamable Father, he entered into the Pleroma in an incomprehensible and invisible manner...while others say that he merely suffered in outward appearance (*vero putative eum passum*), being naturally impassible. The Valentinians, again, maintain that the

---

[59]Cartlidge, "Transfigurations," 60. According to my research, however, Cartlidge makes a mistake in considering the term μορφή as denoting "both a change of shape and of essence." The distinction between the two in the texts is, nonetheless, present.

[60]For example, Irenaeus claims that the birth stories were rejected by these theologians precisely to "cast away the inheritance of the flesh" ('ιν' ἐκβαλωσι τὴν τῆς σαρκὸς κληρονομίαν, *Haer.* 3.22.1).

dispensational Jesus was the same who passed through Mary, upon
whom (*in quem*) that Savior from the more exalted [region] descended (*in
quem illum de superiori Salvatorem descendisse, Haer.* 3.16.1).

Irenaeus describes the Sethian-Ophite view as follows: "Christ united with
Sophia descended into him, and so Jesus Christ was produced...When
he was led out to death, they say that the Christ himself, with Sophia,
departed from him...while Jesus was crucified" (1.30.12-13). Note the lack
of a permanent union, but no indication of ecstatic behavior, fitting best
into the inspiration tendency.

Cerinthus provides us with the most notable example of temporary
possession, and he is especially worth some extended attention because
a number of commentators have associated the opponents in the Epistles
with his thought. In his commentary on the Epistles, Brown helpfully
provides an appendix describing the paradoxical evidence about Cerinthus
from several early church writers.[61] The confusion stems from the fact that
the earlier witnesses identify Cerinthus as a gnostic, while the later ones
consider him a Jewish-Christian. The first witness is *Epistula Apostolorum*
(mid-2nd c. Greek, now extant in Ethiopic, with some Coptic and Latin
fragments), which only associates him with Simon Magus.[62] The earliest
witness concerning his Christology is Irenaeus, who says

> Jesus was the son of Mary and Joseph like other men. Jesus is thought
> to have outdistanced all others in righteousness, prudence and wisdom;
> and after his baptism, Christ descended upon him in the form of a dove
> (*post baptismum descendisse in eum...Christum figura columbae*) from the
> Supreme Ruler. Then he proclaimed the unknown Father and performed
> miracles. In the end, however, Christ withdrew again from Jesus — Jesus
> suffered and rose again, while Christ remained impassible, inasmuch as
> he was a spiritual being. (*Haer.* 1.26.1)

Note the emphasis on Jesus' virtue, an emphasis we saw in Greco-Roman
sources on possession, as well as in Philo and Josephus.

---

[61]Brown, *Epistles*, 766-71. For a briefer summary of Cerinthus' thought, see Klaus
Wengst, *Häresie und Orthodoxie im Spiegel des ersten Johannesbriefes* (Gütersloh: Mohn, 1976),
33-34. Wengst is cautious about identifying the opponents with Cerinthus, but he does
conclude that their views agreed with the christological speculation of Cerinthus and that
both Cerinthus and the opponents probably relied on the Fourth Gospel, and that the most
likely reconstruction is that the views of the opponents were part of a trajectory that led to
Cerinthus (34). Grayston, on the other hand (15-19), concludes that the opponents share
little with Cerinthus, and are best depicted as lacking a Christology; that is, that Jesus'
anointing is a model followed by each person who, through baptism and anointing, also has
"unmediated access to God."

[62]Brown, *Epistles*, 766.

Hippolytus (*Ref.* 7.21) adds no new information,[63] but places Cerinthus in the same context as the Ebionites, whom he describes as similar to Cerinthus, but who lived like Jews and say anyone can be Christs who keep the law perfectly (7.22). He continues with a description of Theodotus, who, according to Hippolytus, appropriated his ideas of Christ from the gnostics, and of Cerinthus and Ebion:

> Jesus was a man, born of a virgin, according to the counsel of the Father, and that after he had lived promiscuously with all men, and had become preeminently religious, he subsequently at his baptism in Jordan received Christ, who came from above and descended in form of a dove. And this was the reason why powers did not operate within him prior to the manifestation in him of that Spirit which descended, which proclaims him to be the Christ. But some are disposed that never was this man made God at the descent of the Spirit; whereas others (maintain that he was made God) after the resurrection from the dead. (7.23)

Notice again the emphasis on the merit of Jesus before his possession.

Brown notes that Pseudo-Tertullian, Epiphanius and a medieval work citing Hippolytus all associate Cerinthus with the Jewish-Christian Ebionites.[64] Pseudo-Tertullian (*Haer.* 3.2-3) records Cerinthus as teaching that the world was created by angels who also gave the Law, and that the Ebionites were successors of Cerinthus in some of their ideas. Dionysius Bar Salibi (d. 1171) cites Hippolytus' claim that Cerinthus "taught the necessity of circumcision, that the creator was an angel, and Jesus was not born of a virgin, and that eating and drinking certain things were forbidden."[65] Epiphanius in *Panarion* "has Cerinthus identifying Christ with the Holy Spirit, a teaching similar to that of the Ebionites" (30.14) and makes him, in Brown's word, "a Judaizer of NT times."[66] Brown concludes that Cerinthus' thought as depicted in Irenaeus most closely resembles a "gnostic type of Christology" that we can now see in some of the Nag

---

[63]"He thought that Jesus was not generated from a virgin, but that he was born son of Joseph and Mary, just in a manner similar with the rest of men, and that he was more just and more wise. And he [Cerinthus] claims that after the baptism, Christ in form of a dove came down upon him, from that absolute sovereignty which is above all things. And then, Jesus proceeded to preach the unknown Father, and in attestation to work miracles. It was, however, (the opinion of Cerinthus) that ultimately Christ departed from Jesus, and that Jesus suffered and rose again; whereas that Christ, being spiritual, remained beyond the possibility of suffering" (*Ref.* 7.21).

[64]Brown, *Epistles*, 768.

[65]The information is from his commentary on Revelation (CSEO, Syri, Series II, 101.1.30ff). Cited in Brown, *Epistles*, 768.

[66]Brown, *Epistles*, 769.

Hammadi documents, and that it was a development of the position of the opponents in 1 John.[67]

Charles E. Hill reaches a comparable but more nuanced conclusion concerning Cerinthus.[68] He argues that the information in the *Epistula Apoistolorum* and in Irenaeus can basically be trusted, but that Cerinthus made what were apparent concessions to Jewish apologetics that he then transformed into arguments of supercession. Specifically, Cerinthus "conceded a purely human Jesus, but saddled him with a purely nonhuman Christ," and perhaps allowed for a type of chiliasm, then relegated it, like Marcion's, "to a time when the lower Creator would fulfill the earthly predictions of his prophets for his earthbound people."[69] What later looked Judaistic, then, was actually the opposite, a part of "a system which abhored every trace of 'Judaizing' in the Church."[70]

The application of the metamorphosis and possession models to early Christology, I suggest, helps us understand the paradoxical evidence about Cerinthus. The manner by which he described the union of human and divine in Jesus Christ was a temporary possession which began at the baptism. When, however, Cerinthus described exactly who the Christ was, he turned to a speculative system more typical of gnostic thought. Due to his use of the possession model, he later appeared to have the most in common with the Christology that by that time was known as adoptionism, a mode of thought more typical to those maintaining the strongest link with a Jewish background, like the Ebionites.

The problem of Cerinthus is a good introduction to the fluidity of some of this speculation as creative theologians sought solutions by blending the patterns. A gnostic text also gives us our first clear example of displacement. The *Second Treatise of Seth* (7.51.24-52.3; *NHD* 363-64) has Christ reveal: "I visited a bodily dwelling. I cast out the one who was in it first, and I went in…and I am the one who was in it, not resembling him who was in it first. For he was an earthly man, but I, I am from above the heavens." Here again we see the possessionist Christology with the early departure: "They struck me with the reed; it was another, Simon, who bore the cross on his shoulder" (7.56.8-11; *NHD* 365). This being departs and lurks above, laughing, then comes back down unrecognized, "for I was altering my shapes, changing from form to form" (7.55.25; *NHD* 365). Here the polymorphic ability comes to the fore. The *Second Treatise of Seth*,

---

[67]Brown, *Epistles*, 770. For comparison, he cites the *Second Treatise of Seth* 7:51.20-52.3), discussed below.

[68]Charles E. Hill, "Cerinthus, Gnostic or Chiliast? A New Solution to an Old Problem," *JECS* 8 (2000): 135-72.

[69]Hill, "Cerinthus," 171-72.

[70]Hill, "Cerinthus," 172.

indeed, depicts this savior as possessing every ability to interact on earth that the Mediterranean environment would allow.

Valentinus as well showed admirable flexibility in solving the problem of connecting divine impassibility with someone apparently human by employing both models. First, Valentinus attempts to explain the birth narrative by means of a metamorphosis model. Jesus, he claimed "was not in the substance of our flesh, but brought down from heaven some pneumatic body, passed through the Virgin Mary like water through a pipe, neither receiving nor borrowing anything from her" (Pseudo-Tertullian, *Haer.* 4). The Christ or Spirit descended upon this pneumatic Jesus during the baptism and departed at the passion (*Extr. De Théodote* 26.1),[71] a clear example of the possession pattern, but one whose metamorphic precursor protects the divine from any contact with the perishable.

So far, we have seen the patterns examined in Chapters Two and Three reappear in early Christology. We see clearly the problem of sorting out the Christologies in Irenaeus, who does an admirable job in *Against Heresies* 3.11.3:

> For if anyone studies the systems of all of [the heretics], he will see that the Word of God is brought in by all as without flesh and impassible, as is also the Christ from above. Some consider [Jesus Christ] to have been manifested as a transfigured human (*hominem transfiguratum*), but they maintain that he was neither born nor became incarnate; others, that he did not assume a human form (*figuram*) at all, but that as a dove he desended upon that Jesus (*descendisse in eum Jesum*) who was born of Mary.

Metamorphosis argues that a heavenly being was transfigured to appear human on earth. This metamorphosis usually emphasized the nonmaterial aspect of the metamorphosed body, and often the being exercised a polymorphic capacity. Possession appears as well, more specifically, a tendency we have called inspiration, which displays no ecstatic behavior, nor displacement of the human mind. The one clear indication of displacement shifts our continua somewhat, since there is no indication of ecstatic behavior, to something between ecstasy and inspiration. In each case, although the possession is of a temporary nature, it pushes to that right end of the continuum, since, like many OT figures, it lasts for the duration of the assigned task. Some thinkers in the realms of Christology, moreover, attempt to blend the patterns to answer all objections. The evidence from one last author, however, remains to be examined before we consider the Epistles.

Like the Johannine author/s, Ignatius provides evidence in his letters that he differed with other thinkers in the realm of Christology. I have

---

[71]Cited in Davies, "Origins," 23. Cf. Irenaeus, *Haer.* 3.11.3.

reserved the discussion of the opponents of Ignatius to the end of this
section for two reasons: (1) this evidence is exceptionally important
for the Johannine literature, due to its comparable time frame, and is
often cited by commentators in reference to 1 John, and (2) I prefer the
reader already to have in mind evidence of both the metamorphosis and
possession christological patterns while we review the evidence from
Ignatius at some length.

Commentators have long struggled to discern whether Ignatius faced
one, two, or three groups of opponents.[72] One of the most novel suggestions
has been that of Michael Goulder, who suggests that there is one group of
opponents and they should be identified with the Ebionites discussed in
Irenaeus and Epiphanius.[73] Goulder outlines the assertions that Ignatius
makes in counter to his opponents and associates those assertions with
elements of the Ebionite system, such as the human paternity by the lineage
of David, his birth by the Virgin, his baptism, crucifixion and passion,
and his death and resurrection, offering physical proof particularly of the
resurrection from Luke 24.[74] Goulder concludes that both Ignatius' Jewish
Christian opponents and the Ebionites share "a prophetic, possessionist"
Christology, which is most reminiscent of OT prophets "possessed by a
divine power for a period."[75] Goulder's argument is particulary strong
when he points out that Ignatius cites nothing in a confessional sense
of Jesus' life between the baptism and the passion in passages intended
to contradict opponents; therefore, Goulder suggests, this silence exists
because there was in fact no real contention between the Ignatius and the
opponents about that portion of Jesus' life.[76]

My reading of Ignatius will lend some support to Goulder's general
hypothesis that most opponents of Ignatius share a possessionist
Christology, the one we earlier termed "inspiration" due to its temporary
nature, though the letter to the Trallians shows some evidence of
combatting a metamorphosis (usually termed "docetist") Christology. An
examination of the crucial passages in Ignatius' letters *Philadelphians* and
Magnesians, which are generally agreed to be directed against a "Judaizing"
movement, shows Ignatius' emphasis on the coming and especially the
passion and resurrection of Jesus Christ. Like Goulder, however, I see

---

[72]For more lengthy summaries of the academic discussion, see Daniel L. Hoffman,
"Ignatius and Early Anti-Docetic Realism in the Eucharist," *Fides et Historia* 30 (1998): 75-77;
Christine Trevett, *A Study of Ignatius of Antioch in Syria and Asia* (Lewiston: Mellen, 1992),
194-99 and "Prophecy and Anti-Episcopal Activity: A Third Error Combated by Ignatius?"
JEH 34 (1983): 1-18.

[73]Michael Goulder, "Ignatius' 'Docetists,'" *VigChrist* 53 (1999): 16-30. Goulder (p. 24)
points out that he is proposing "a revised form of a 17th century hypothesis."

[74]Goulder, "Docetists," 26.

[75]Goulder, "Docetists," 25.

[76]Goulder, "Docetists," 26.

similar patterns in *Smyrnaeans*, a letter usually used to demonstrate the existence of "docetists," and I also will argue that the evidence used to support the idea of Jesus as a phantasm is at best inconclusive.

Christians who emphasize the Jewish law fail, according to Ignatius, to place enough emphasis on the gospel; that is, on the coming, passion and resurrection of Jesus Christ. The prologue of *Philadelphians* stresses already the importance of believing in the blood, passion and resurrection of Jesus Christ, and these are regularly emphasized in the letter (3.3, 8.2, and 9.2). *Magnesians* adds an important emphasis: the "union of flesh and spirit" in Christ and, therefore, in the churches. In the first section of the letter, Ignatius emphasizes his desire that in the churches there will be "a union of the flesh and spirit of Jesus Christ," as well as unions of faith and love, and of Jesus and the Father. If we, the believers, endure (ὑπομένοντες) in all these, we will reach God (1.2). While sections 8-10 clearly warn against the Jewish challenge,[77] the section immediately following (11.1) is often seen as anti-docetic: "be convinced of the birth and passion and resurrection that happened during the procuratorship of Pontius Pilate, because these things were truly and certainly done by Jesus Christ."[78] Logic, however, suggests that this section actually concludes and summarizes Ignatius' warning against those Christians who are still too focused on Judaism. The believer, Ignatius insists, should rather "be convinced of the birth and passion and resurrection that happened at the time of the procuratorship of Pontius Pilate, because these things were truly and definitely done by Jesus Christ" (11). The conclusion of the letter includes a prayer resumptive of the union of flesh and spirit emphasis (13.1-2).[79] So far, then, we have seen that the "true" death and resurrection are emphasized against a Jewish threat.

Commentators have seen evidence of a docetic opposition in Ignatius' letters *Ephesians*, *Trallians*, and especially *Smyrnaeans*. *Ephesians* 7.2 emphasizes against heretical "wild beasts" that "there is one physician, both flesh and spirit, born and not born, God in man, true life in death, both from Mary and from God, first passible and then impassible, Jesus Christ our Lord." In the letter to Polycarp, Ignatius asserts in a similar vein that

---

[77]Goulder ("Docetists," 29-30) argues that 8.2 in particular relates to the Ebionites as portrayed in Irenaeus, who held that the Christ descended into Jesus from the highest Power, as distinguished from the "unknown Father." Ignatius' statement on the one God manifesting himself as Jesus Christ the Word, which proceeded from silence, seems to stress the one God and no other "intervening power."

[78]Hoffman ("Ignatius," 80) suggests that we do find two heresies combatted in this book because "the scandal of a crucified Messiah for Jews could have led to a docetic Christology among some Jewish Christians," citing Davies, "Origins," 117-19.

[79]Goulder ("Docetists," 21) points out that fleshly union might be a "dangerous concept" for a pastor to pray for in his flock, but "it would be easy to understand the saint's language if, as so often, he had in mind the fleshly and spiritual union *of Jesus Christ*" as in the first paragraph of the letter.

while God is invisible, he became visible for us, and while he cannot suffer, accepted suffering for us (3.2). These passages are inconclusive, since they could argue as well for against the idea of no permanent union between the flesh and spirit of Christ as well as against a nonmaterial body.

In the prologue to the *Trallians*, Ignatius addresses the church having peace "in flesh and spirit by the passion of Jesus Christ, our hope through our resurrection to him." Again, though it applies to the believer, the union of flesh and spirit made possible through passion and resurrection is notable. The true bodily nature of Jesus Christ is emphasized in 8.1, where faith is called "the flesh of the Lord," and love "is the blood of Jesus Christ." The confession in 9.1-10.1 has garnered the most attention and provides the best evidence in this letter that the opponents are docetists.

> Be deaf, then, when anyone speaks to you apart from Jesus Christ, who was from the lineage of David, and of Mary, who was truly (ἀληθῶς) born, both ate and drank, was truly (ἀληθῶς) persecuted by Pontius Pilate, truly (ἀληθῶς) crucified and died, in the sight of those in heaven and on earth and under the earth. He was also truly (ἀληθῶς) raised from the dead, when his Father raised him, as likewise his Father will raise in Christ Jesus us who believe in him, apart from whom we have no true life. But if, as certain ones say who are without God, unbelievers, his suffering was a semblance (τὸ δοκεῖν), though it is they who are a semblance (τὸ δοκεῖν), why am I a prisoner...?

The terms on which commentators have focused are ἀληθῶς and τὸ δοκεῖ ν. Hoffman agrees with J. B. Lightfoot that ἀληθῶς was "the watchword against docetism."[80] These terms are in themselves, however, inconclusive, since they could also suggest an argument against those who asserted a temporary posssession. The key to the passage, it seems to me, is the "truly ate and drank." We saw in Chapter Two that not eating and drinking is a characteristic of a body whose essence is nonmaterial, and, since Ignatius puts this during the earthly life of Jesus, he seems to emphasize it against those who maintain the body of Jesus during his life was the result of a metamorphosis with a nonmaterial emphasis. This piece of evidence is the one that defines what is meant in this context by "semblance."

Ignatius' letter *Smyrnaeans*, however, cannot be assumed to make the same argument. Near the beginning of the letter (1.1-2), Ignatius compliments the recipients for being of immovable faith,

> as if nailed to the cross of the Lord Jesus Christ, both in flesh and spirit, and confirmed in love by the blood of Christ, being fully persuaded as touching our Lord, that he is in truth of the family of David according to the flesh, God's son by the will and power of God, truly born of a virgin,

---

[80]Hoffman, "Ignatius," 78.

baptized by John that "all righteousness might be fulfilled by him," truly nailed in the flesh for us under Pontius Pilate and Herod the Tetrarch, by which fruit are we from his divinely blessed passion, that he might fix a sign for all ages through his resurrection.

The passage is not conclusive, but the "flesh and spirit" combination without any pattern or semantic field of metamorphosis leans toward the use of a possession model.

Next, Ignatius launches into another assurance that Jesus Christ "truly suffered even as he also truly raised himself," opposing those who say that "his passion was only in semblance – but it is they who are merely in semblance, and even according to their opinions it will happen to them, and they will be without bodies and διαμονικοῖς" (2.1). In the *Loeb Classical Library* edition, K. Lake translates the term διαμονικοις as "phantasmal." Though a rare term,[81] it is, of course, from the common term δαίμων. Ignatius immediately asserts that "I know he was in flesh even after the resurrection," citing the apostles being able to touch him and claiming Jesus said "Take, handle me and see that I am not a *daimon* without a body" (διαμόνιον ἀσώματον, 3.1-2). Ignatius continues that after the resurrection, Jesus ate and drank with them "as a being of flesh (σαρκικός), though he was united in spirit to the Father" (3.3).

The question is: does the use of the term *daimon* as a nonmaterial appearance ensure that we are talking about (metamorphic) docetism? We recall from the possession chapter that Dionysus was called a *daimon* in Euripides play in which he possessed his followers, and that by Plutarch and Cicero, *daimons* were sometimes seen to be the specific possessing entities. In the Jewish realm, the LXX uses the terms for evil beings, sometimes for the pagan gods.[82] In early Christian and patristic evidence, they are generally evil spirits who can and do possess humans.[83]

---

[81] Liddell-Scott (*Lexicon*) cites only one occurrence, and *BAG* only five occurrences.

[82] Most often, these are beings that actually appear and interfere in the work of God and humans; for example, in Tobit, an evil demon by the name of Asmodeus had to be defeated by Raphael (Tob 3:8, 17 etc.). Psalm 95:5 describes the gods of the Gentiles as δαίμονες, while Psalm 105:7 charges Israel with having sacrificed its sons and daughters to δαίμονες (cf. Isa 65:3, 11). Baruch also indicts Israel with having provoked God by sacrificing to those beings rather than to him, but also insists that those afflicting Jerusalem will be inhabited by δαίμονες (Bar 4:7, 35). We see, therefore, that the "other gods" of the Hebrew Scriptures have, in the Greek understanding, become those intermediate beings the Greco-Roman world knew as *daimones*. The only indication that these beings do not truly exist comes in Isa 65:3, that Israel burned incense on bricks to the *daimones*, "which do not exist."

[83] The *Testament of Solomon* records the stories and ways of conquering the various spirits, called *daimons*, who afflict humans; for example, "I ordered another δαίμονα to appear before me. There came a δαίμονα having the shadowy form of a man and gleaming eyes" (15:1). A

Does this passage, then, support the hypothesis that the theologians against whom Ignatius warned this community believed Jesus Christ appeared, metamorphosed, with a nonmaterial body? While a *daimon* does not have a material body,[84] it is not necessarily the same as a phantasm, that is, a metamorphosed body that has no material substance. A *daimon*, we saw, is a heavenly being that can and does possess a human body. In his *Hermeneia* commentary, moreover, Schoedel argues that since this term is otherwise foreign to Ignatius' writings, he is probably quoting a tradition about the resurrection.[85] This passage, then, is not nearly so conclusive concerning a "docetic" body as it appears on first glance. It could also indicate that the union of spirit and flesh in Jesus Christ endures after the resurrection, rather than the flesh having been discarded and only the possessing *daimon* remaining.

In the remainder of the letter, the possession model better expresses the Christology Ignatius opposes. Ignatius asserts that "if it is only in semblance (τὸ δοκεῖν) that these things were done by our Lord I am also handed over in semblance;" but instead, he insists, he is suffering with Christ (4.2). We have seen, however, that δοκεῖν requires other elements to clearly define its implicaton. In 5.2, Ignatius asks what anyone profits who "do not confess that he [Jesus Christ] bore flesh?" (μὴ ὁμολογῶν αὐτὸν σαρκοφόρον). The one who says this "has denied him completely, bearing a corpse" (ὢν νεκροφόρος). He insists he will not even remember them "until they repent concerning the passion, which is our resurrection" (5.3). They "do not believe on the blood of Christ" (6.1), nor do they "confess the Eucharist is the flesh of our savior Jesus Christ who suffered for our sins, whom the Father raised up by his goodness" (7.1).[86] The bishop ends the letter by saluting the recipients "in the name of Jesus Christ, and in his flesh and blood, by his passion and resurrection both of flesh and spirit (σαρκικῇ τε καὶ πνευματικῇ), in union with God and with you" (12.2). This is the final, definitive statement that it is the permanent union of the flesh and spirit, the Jesus and the Christ, that is the definitive statement of faith.

---

giant who died in age of giants says at one point, "I seat myself near dead men in the tombs and at midnight I assume the form of the dead" and if he seizes anyone, he immediately kills him, sometimes because he is possessed by a *daimon*. For patristic evidence on the possession of humans by *daimons*, see, for example, Origen, *Princ.* 3.3.5, *Clem. Hom.* 9.10.

[84]Tatian, for example, says "none of the demons possess flesh; their structure is spiritual, like fire or air" (*Orat.* 15).

[85]William R. Schoedel, *Ignatius of Antioch* (Hermeneia; Philadelphia: Fortress, 1985), 226-27.

[86]The denial of the Eucharist is a theme of the opponents throughout the letters. Cf. *Phld.* 3.3, 4.1; *Mag.* 7.1-2; *Trall.* 2.2-3; *Smyr.* 7.1, 8.1-2, 9.1; *Eph.* 20.1-2. In itself, it is inconclusive, since the opponents could deny the union of the human and divine in Christ in the crucifixion as well as a nonmaterial metamorphosed body.

I conclude, therefore, that the term "docetism" is indeed an umbrella term and is best understood as referring to a diversity of phenomena. The common thread is that the appearance of or connection to a physical presence on earth is temporary; hence, the confusion and/or overlap between the two. Slusser is correct, then, that the broader definitions are more useful to describe the phenomenon as a whole. When we look at the *ways*, however, that docetists went about explaining this lack of a meaningful unity between the human and divine, we see that the majority found the metamorphosis model most helpful, but a crucial minority opted for the inspiration model. Baur, in fact, already discerned this basic pattern: "Either objectivity is denied to the human in Christ," a formulation that is close to the point of the metamorphosis pattern, "or at least the human is so separated from the divine that there is no personal unity between the two," a formulation that encompasses a possession (inspiration) Christology. The picture is complicated, of course, by those later theologians who sought to blend the models. We are now ready to read the Johannine Epistles within this conceptual framework to discern between the Christology of the authors and opponents in that literature. I emphasize that rather than trying to identify particular individuals (e.g. Cerinthus) as opponents, we will try to identify the models being used.

2 JOHN

We have seen that in the ancient Mediterranean environment there were two basic understandings of how a divine being appears on earth to interact with humans, and that early Christian writers took advantage of both of these models, and permutations of them, to explain the Christ event. The argument of this chapter is that the author and his opponents in the Johannine Epistles believed in a heavenly being who possessed the human Jesus during his baptism; that is, both author and opponents chose to build upon a possession model. The author, however, argues that the permanence of the salvific system depends on the permanence of the association of the Christ with the human Jesus, so that his tendency is, more specifically, what in Chapter Three I called "indwelling." The opponents, it will appear, did not find the permanent association necessary; therefore, their christological pattern is best described as "inspiration." We will now turn to the Epistles to explore the theme of permanence versus impermanence and how this theme affects christological and community issues, beginning with 2 John.

This short letter contains one brief but important reference specifically to the christological controversy. The first obvious sign of trouble in the community comes in verses 5-6: "But now, dear lady, I ask you, not as though I were writing you a new commandment, but one we have had from the beginning, let us love one another. And this is love, that we walk according to his commandments; this is the commandment just as you have heard it from the beginning—you must walk in it." The insistence of the author suggests the importance of three themes: (1) trust in the original witness/teachings is a foundational belief of the community; (2) loving one another is a foundational belief of the community, and (3) an implication that there are those who are following neither.

Our suspicions concerning the third point are confirmed in the next verse: "For many deceivers have gone out into the world, those not confessing Jesus Christ coming in the flesh (Ἰησοῦν Χριστὸν ἐρχόμενον ἐν σαρκί); this one is the deceiver and the antichrist" (v. 7).[87] The interpretation of this verse turns on the form of the verb ἔρχομαι. The present form of the participle can technically have a present or a future sense. In a minority position, Strecker, with Schnelle following him, argues for the future and takes it as a reference to the parousia, an interpretation that makes the opponents chiliasts. Strecker and Schnelle conclude, therefore, that 2 John does not reflect the same christological struggle as does 1 John.[88] Schnackenburg, however, discounts Strecker's option, arguing that in Christian usage the parousia is generally expressed not as coming "in the flesh" but "in glory."[89] While he concedes that the formula is probably influenced by the Gospel passages that describe Jesus as "the one [who is] to come" (1:15, 27; 12:13), Schnackenburg applies the phrase to Christ's death and also to the period after the resurrection, "the supratemporal significance of the incarnation."[90] Brown says that while syntax slightly favors a future meaning of the participle, "it does not demand it," and that scholarly opinion overwhelmingly favors a perfect or imperfect meaning, reading the participle in light of the perfect participle of the verb in 1 John 4:2 (in a similar context).[91] Brown decides on a third option, a stereotyped formula, for which he argues on

---

[87]Verse 7, P. Bonnard points out, gives the cause for the preceding section, that because of those who left the community there is a obvious need to emphasize the original instruction of the community. Pierre Bonnard, *Les Epitres Johanniques* (CNT 2.13c; Geneva: Labor et Fides, 1983), 124.

[88]Strecker, *Johannine Letters*, 232-43; Schnelle, *Antidocetic*, 50.

[89]Schnackenburg, *Johannine Epistles*, 284.

[90]Schnackenburg, *Johannine Epistles*, 284. Smalley (*1, 2, 3 John*, 327-38) concurs with the use of the present to express the "timelessness of the Christ event" and argues that the formula is useful both against those opponents who consider Jesus only human as well as those who consider him only God.

[91]Brown, *Epistles*, 669-70. I assume Brown is referring to the fact that ἔρχομαι is one of the verbs whose present tense commonly carries a future force (BDF, 323; Wallace, 536-37; Smyth par. 1881). This force, however, usually applies to the indicative rather than to the participle, as Smyth makes clear. This interpretation continued to dominate after Brown; see, for example, Beutler, *Johannesbriefe*, 159 and Bonnard, *Epitres*, 124.

the basis that the First Epistle uses the term "to come" for both Christ (4:2; 5:6) and the Antichrist (2:18b; 4:3).[92]

If we consider the participle, however, without benefit of the text in 1 John, what could it mean about the Christology of the authors and opponents? First, in the case of indirect discourse, the participle generally maintains the sense of the direct discourse.[93] Brown points out that one must wonder why the author moved from a perfect participle in 1 John 4:2 "to a less exact present tense," an element that leads him to believe that the author is simply repeating a stereotyped formula.[94] If we try reading 2 John as the first document in the series, however, the picture improves: the present participle could refer to a continuing state, that Jesus Christ *abides*, one might say, in the flesh, with the vagueness of the present participle being completely appropriate for an early expression of the conflict, when all that is being asserted is the continuity of Jesus' abiding. The author in 2 John 7, therefore, states that his opponents, in a way that he is not clearly specifying, deny the continuing fleshly existence of Jesus Christ.[95] More precise explanation of the correct christological confession will be necessary, which the audience will receive in 1 John.

While the evidence for our interpretation is admittedly limited at this point, we find some support for this interpretation in verse nine, which refers, for the first time, directly to the opponents: "anyone who goes ahead (προάγων) and does not abide (μένων) in the doctrine of Christ does not have God; he who abides (μένων) in the doctrine has both the Father and the Son." Here the author clearly presents the dichotomy of permanence/ impermanence with respect to the believer in the immediate context of the christological debate. We should note that the verb προάγω means not only to "go ahead" oneself but also has connotations of "to induce, persuade" and "to lead or bring out;"[96] thus, the author hints that the concern is most serious since the progressives also seek to lead others onto their path. This danger becomes apparent in the following verses, which encourage the community to be careful of these "progressives" to the point of refusing them hospitality (vv. 8, 10-11).

Also in verse nine is the first appearance of the crucial verb μένω. In the New Testament, one might think of this verb as the "property" of the

---

[92]Brown, *Epistles*, 670. Klauck suggests that the connection to a stereotypical messianic formula (cf. Mal 3:1; John 11:27; 12:13) strengthens the interpretation of the participle as expressing the timelessness of the incarnation; Hans-Josef Klauck, *Der Zeite und Dritte Johannesbrief* (EKK 23/2; Zürich: Benziger and Neukirchen-Vluyn: Neukirchener, 1992), 53-55.

[93]Daniel B. Wallace, *Greek Grammar Beyond the Basics* (Grand Rapids: Zondervan, 1996), 646.

[94]Brown, *Epistles*, 669-70.

[95]Cf. Schnackenburg, *Johannine Epistles*, 285; Smalley, *1, 2, 3 John*, 329.

[96]Liddell-Scott, *Lexicon*, 1466; BAG, 702.

Johannine corpus.[97] The verb occurs 118 times in the New Testament, with sixty-seven of these occurring in the Johannine writings: forty in the Gospel, twenty-seven in 1 John, 3 in 2 John. The range of classical meanings is: to stand fast (as in battle); to stay at home or where one is; to lodge; to be lasting, stable, or permanent, and to abide by a conviction or opinion.[98] The verb, then, can be applied with respect both to space (to dwell) and to state (to remain).

In the LXX, μένω is most often used to translate עמד and קום, and the term is relatively often concerned "with the existence or continuing validity of something" such as a vow.[99] It is particularly used of God: "his relationship with man is not severed by him (Ps 112/111:3, 9), and hence his word (Isa 40:8) and truth (Ps 117/116:2) endure…God is the living one who endures forever (Dan 6:26; Ps 102/101:12). His people (Isa 66:22), his plan (Ps 33/32:11; Isa 14:24), his righteousness (Ps 111/110:3), and his praise (Ps 111/110:10) remain forever."[100] Later Jewish literature uses μένω in similar fashion: of abiding truth (1 Esdr 4:38); or instructively, to abide in truth (T. Jos. 1:3), or to remain in Judaism (2 Macc 8:1).

In the New Testament, the classical usages are all found; also, the unchanging character of God and his aspects are also expressed with μένω.[101] Not surprisingly, then, the aspect of abiding permanently is transferred to Jesus. In Hebrews 7:24, Christ holds the priesthood forever because he abides forever (διὰ τὸ μένειν αὐτὸν εἰς τὸν αἰῶνα), so the believer has an abiding possession (μένουσαν) in heaven (Heb 10:34). For Paul, the ministry of the Spirit, through its permanence (τὸ μένον), transcends in glory the temporary ministry of the law (2 Cor 3:11).[102]

Brown recognizes the emphasis on permanence contained in the word, and correctly points out that "the Johannine writings use *menein* and its synonyms not only for the indwelling of the Father and the Son in the Christian, but also for the indwelling of divine attributes, gifts, and powers."[103] I suggest, however, that it is the permanence of the union

---

[97]See Strecker, *Johannine Epistles*, 44-45; Schnackenburg, *Johannine Letters*, 103-04; Brown, *Gospel*, 510-12, who cites extensively G. Pecorara, "De verbo 'manere' apud Joannem," *Divus Thomas* 40 (1937), 159-71. For a general survey, see Jürgen Heise, *Bleiben: Menein in den Johanneischen Schriften* (Tübingen: Mohr [Siebeck], 1967).

[98]Liddell-Scott, *Lexicon*, 1103.

[99]K. Munzer, "μένω," *TDNT* 3.224.

[100]Munzer, *TDNT* 3.224.

[101]Munzer, *TDNT* 3.224-225.

[102]The New Testament writers other than John also use the terms ἐνοικέω or κατοικέω for similar meanings: ἐνοικέω occurs five times; κατοικέω, 44 times, including in the Apocalypse (in which μένω does not appear). Cf. Lawrence O. Richards, *Expository Dictionary of Bible Words* (Grand Rapids: Zondervan, 1985), 55.

[103]Brown, *Gospel*, 511; cf. Heise, *Bleiben*, 169.

between Christ and Jesus that, for the Johannine writings, enables all the other "indwellings." We will be testing this hypothesis through our continuing analysis of these writings, beginning with 2 John 9.

Now, to return to this verse: "any one who goes ahead (προάγων) and does not abide (μένων) in the teaching about Christ does not have God; he who abides (μένων) in the teaching has both the Father and the Son." The audience is cautioned about those who do not remain permanently in the teaching of Christ. Here, the debate concerns whether "of Christ" is an objective or subjective genitive.[104] The best argument for the subjective sense is the parallel with the "teaching of Jesus" found in the Fourth Gospel (7:16, 17; 18:19). But, as B. Weiss points out, the teaching of *Jesus* is not necessarily equivalent to the teaching of *Christ*.[105] While Brown dismisses this argument on the basis of the close association of the names of Jesus with Christ,[106] Weiss's comment, along with the immediate context of correct christological confession, seems to me persuasive.[107]

The author insists, therefore, that the progressives have not abided permanently in the teaching that has existed from the beginning (the implication of the description of opponents as "going ahead") that the savior is consistently human, but if the believers will abide permanently in the doctrine, they will "have" (ἔχει) both Father and Son." The progressives have shown that abiding permanently requires that the believer correctly position himself christologically, that the position is otherwise not secure.[108] The expression of "having" the Father and the Son is enigmatic, but an "ontological relationship" drawing on covenant language is possible.[109] It certainly, however, is part of the indication of permanence: that a permanent confession of an enduring state with respect to the savior results in a permanent status for the believer.[110]

We can now see that the author gave indications of the unfolding drama at the beginning of the Epistle: "The elder to the elect lady and her children, whom I love in the truth, and not only I but also all who know the truth, because of the truth which abides (μένουσαν) in us and will be with us forever" (vv. 1-2). The community foundations of love, knowledge, and

---

[104]For a complete summary, see Brown, *Epistles*, 674-75;

[105]Bernhard Weiss, *Die drei Briefe des Apostel Johannes* (MeyerK 14; 6th ed.; Göttingen: Vandenhoeck & Ruprecht, 1899), 182; cited in Brown, *Epistles*, 675. Schnackenburg (*Johannine Epistles*, 286) offers an innovative solution, though it has not gained significant support: that the subjective genitive refers literally to Christ; that is, the language of faith.

[106]Brown, *Epistles*, 675.

[107]Cf. Painter, *1, 2, and 3 John*, 354 and Smalley, *1, 2, 3, John*, 332.

[108]Schnackenburg, *Johannine Epistles*, 103.

[109]Brown, *Epistles*, 353-54.

[110]Or, as Talbert summarily expresses it, "The need is for a continuing commitment to a correct Christology" (*Reading John*, 10).

permanence are already here, and we now know why: there are those who are challenging the foundations.

Unfortunately, this work gives us limited assistance in discerning to which pattern, metamorphosis or possession, the opponents subscribe. They could be insisting that the Christ simply metamorphosed outwardly and so was never truly fleshly, or, that the Christ possessed Jesus temporarily, so that the union with the flesh was neither complete nor permanent. We might lean, however, toward the possession model because of the use of the vocabulary "come," which fits better with the vocabulary of the the possession pattern as described earlier, along with the fact that there is no evidence of the semantic field related to metamorphosis. One verb, however, is in actuality less than conclusive.

3 JOHN

Concerning the chronological order of the Epistles, 3 John presents a difficult problem, since there is no direct reference to the christological controversy that is so crucial in 1 and 2 John.[111] Given, however, that the arguments for the single authorship of these two letters is persuasive, and including the reference in 3 John 10 to a previous writing,[112] I lean toward Talbert's suggestion that we are seeing in 3 John "a glimpse of an institutional side effect of the larger conflict."[113] Third John provides no new information on the actual christological controversy, and the place of 3 John is not crucial to the thesis argued here.

1 JOHN

First John provides a fuller understanding of the Christology of the author and opponents than does 2 John. Again, my thesis is that the author and his opponents shared a belief in a divine figure who possessed the human Jesus during his baptism. The author, however, argues that the permanence of the salvific system – involving community, ethics, and eternal life – depends on the permanence of the association of the Christ with the human Jesus. The opponents, it appears, did not find such a thorough and permanent association necessary. I will examine the passages that reveal the author's Christology while considering what we can know of that of the opponents at the appropriate points, remaining particularly attentive to patterns encouraging permanence or cautioning against impermanence, as well as to the vocabulary associated with these patterns.

---

[111]See esp. Thomas, "Order," 70-71.

[112]Painter (1, 2, and 3 John, 375-76) provides a thorough discussion of the question. He argues persuasively that, while there is now a general agreement that 3 John 10 refers to a lost work, the arguments are ultimately unconvincing.

[113]Talbert, Reading John, 13.

One of the difficulties in understanding 1 John is that it does not provide the thorough information of a systematic treatise, since the author initially addressed an audience who presumably had familiarity with the themes and the situation. I suggest, however, that there is a persuasive movement in the letter as the author attempts to relate Christology and community. To accomplish this task, the author begins with attention to the identification of Jesus Christ as the Son of God and to the salvific significance of this being. Then, he reaches the christological crux as he insists specifically upon the necessity of the identification with the human Jesus with the divine Christ/Son of God, reaffirms the salvific significance of this being, and wraps up the letter, *inclusio* fashion, by asserting again that the Son has come and it is not only Christ/Son of God, nor only Jesus, but *Jesus Christ*. In this letter, we will see, titles matter: the only instances in which the name Jesus is separated from the titles "Christ" or "Son" are those in which the author his highlighting the fact that the Christ/Son must be identified with the human Jesus. Otherwise, the emphasis falls on the permanent union between the divine and human and what belief in that union entails for the community.

The first verse of 1 John casts an intriguing lure to the audience in its proclamation of "that which was from the beginning, which we have heard, which we have seen with our own eyes, which we have looked at and touched with our hands" (1 John 1:1). The phrase "touched with our hands" has engendered much discussion concerning to which point of the life of Jesus Christ it refers, whether his pre-resurrection or post-resurrection life. The primary arguments for the post-resurrection perspective are the story of Thomas in John 20 and the Lukan resurrection tradition, "Touch me and see" (Lk 24:39). The lack of another direct mention of the resurrection in the Epistle may argue for the pre-resurrection reference. If the Epistle shows itself to be focused on showing Jesus Christ was no phantasm (metamorphosis) or was temporarily possessed (inspiration), it will add evidence to the pre-resurrection interpretation; conversely, if the emphasis of the letter supports an indwelling pattern, the post-resurrection interpretation will be strengthened. While the issue cannot be judged until we work through the Epistle, at least the door is open to a focus on the continuing identity of the divine and human in Christ even after the resurrection.

The audience is introduced at the beginning as well to a salvific figure who enables community. The identity of the "eternal life which was with the Father and was made manifest to us" and who enables the fellowship of the community is the Father's "Son Jesus Christ" (1:2-3). As Smalley points out, "John's use of the full title, 'his Son Jesus Christ,' nevertheless points to the human as well as the divine status of the Lord."[114] This

---

[114]Smalley, *1, 2, 3 John*, 13.

passage identifies this life, this union, but says nothing about how the identity between the Son/Christ and Jesus occurred. The figure, however, is salvific: the blood of Jesus Christ cleanses, so that this Jesus Christ is an expiation for sin (1:7-2:2).

The critical impetus for the letter does not appear until 2:19: the schism in the community, or, we might say, the *impermanence* of the community's unity. "They went out from us, but they did not belong to us, for if they had belonged to us, they would have remained (μεμενήκεισαν) with us;" in other words, they would have "abided permanently" with us.[115] Note the metaphorical interplay between the spatial and the existential aspects of μένω: the opponents *go out* and do not *abide* enduringly. Here we see the thematic continuation and the intensification from 2 John. The Epistle must explain how this impermanence on the part of the progressives could have happened.

The primary christological problem is that the progressives somehow did not confess the association between the pre-existent redeemer figure Christ and the human Jesus: "Who is the liar but the one who denies that Jesus is the Christ (εἰ μὴ ὁ ἀρνούμενος ὅτι ʼΙησοῦς οὐκ ἔστιν ὁ χριστός)? This is the antichrist, the one who denies the Father and the Son" (2:22-23). Note that this is the first instance of the intentional separation of the name "Jesus" from "Christ" or the "Son." As several commentators have made clear, the articular noun suggests the subject of the sentence is properly "Christ," so that a more specific translation would be "the Christ is Jesus."[116] It cannot be that the progressives denied that it was this particular human and not another with whom Christ became associated, since had that been the case, they would presumably not have been part of the community at any point.[117] To see the problem with the identification between Christ and Jesus, we must continue to move through the Epistle.

The salvific significance, introduced early in the Epistle, is revisted in the third chapter. This being appeared to destroy work of the devil (3:4), and he laid down his life for us (3:16). The title for this united being is reaffirmed: the community must believe in the name of "his Son Jesus Christ" (3:23). The foundation for this very human ability to give up one's life, laid in 1 John 2, is also reaffirmed.

---

[115]For how μένειν ἐν and εἶναι ἐν express interiority and the new covenant relationship in 1 John, see Edward Maletesta, *Interiority and Covenant: A Study of einai en and menein en in the First Letter of St. John* (AB 69; Rome: Biblical Institute, 1978).

[116]See, for example, Brownson ("Odes," 66, n. 25); E. V. N. Goetchius, *JBL* 95 (1976): 147-49 reviewing L. C. McGaught, *Toward a Decriptive Analysis of EINAI as a Linking Verb in New Testament Greek* (SBLDS 6; Missoula: Scholars Press, 1972); Bonnard, *Epitres*, 58-59 and Painter, *1, 2, and 3 John*, 200.

[117]Cf. Bonnard, *Epitres*, 58-59.

In 1 John 4, we acquire more evidence by which to reconstruct the opponents' view: "By this you know the Spirit of God: every spirit that confesses that Jesus Christ has come in the flesh (πᾶν πνεῦμα ὃ ὁμολογεῖ Ἰησοῦν Χριστὸν ἐν σαρκὶ ἐληλυθότα) is from God, and every spirit that does not confess Jesus is not from God" (4:2-3). Four elements require mention: (1) the title Jesus Christ; (2) the expressing "has come," in relation to both its tense and its meaning; (3) the meaning of "flesh," and (4) the use of the name "Jesus." First, the use of the name "Jesus Christ," given the use of titles we observed in 1 John 1, emphasizes the union of the being of which we speak. The implication would not be that merely the "Christ" came in flesh (metamorphosis or possession with complete displacement), or that only Jesus was flesh, but that the union is the crucial confession.

The perfect participle of ἔρχομαι has inspired considerable discussion. For example, Strecker takes this past tense as an "obvious reference to the incarnation;" Talbert prefers the literal sense of the perfect, "Jesus having come and remaining in flesh," and Brown asserts that "such tense value is probably foreign to the Epistles," since 2 John 7, 1 John 4:2, and 1 John 5:6 all use different tenses.[118] Again, the tense values are understandable if the Epistles are read in an order different from the current critical orthodoxy. In 1 John 4:2, the christological conflict has developed further than that in 2 John, and the author, therefore, develops his argument more carefully and is understandably more specific. The perfect tense here, since the participle in indirect discourse "retains the sense of the direct discourse," expresses completion with permanent result.[119]

What exactly is the meaning of "coming?" In other words, Jesus Christ has come and permanently remains in the flesh. Denying "the Christ is Jesus" is shorthand for denying that Jesus and the Christ are permanently associated.[120] Since the confession is christological, we look to the patterns of how a god was expected to appear on earth. Metamorphosis, we have seen, entails very specific vocabulary: transfigura, φαντάσμα, and so on. The semantic field for possession, however, is more generalized, though it often involves the movement of the possessor on or into the possessed: placing, filling, leaping, giving, resting on, coming, etc. This instance clearly fits more neatly into the possession pattern of heavenly being entering into the fleshly human.

---

[118]Talbert, *Reading John*, 35; Brown, *Epistles*, 493; Strecker, *Johannine Letters*, 134-135.

[119]Wallace, *Greek Grammar*, 646; 573.

[120]As Marshall (*Epistles*, 70-71; cf. 205) expresses it, "The use of the present [2 John 7] and perfect tenses becomes significant if the point is that Jesus Christ had come *and still existed* 'in flesh.'" He goes on to say that the author appears here to be carefully excluding the interpretations of thinkers like Cerinthus and Basilides.

DeBoer, building on Brown,[121] points out that in the Fourth Gospel the verb ἔρχεσθαι not only occurs frequently, but there is "pregnant with already traditional messianic associations of effective and intentional saving action."[122] He concludes that this coming of Jesus Christ/Son of God into the world "does not merely denote his visible appearance on the world stage. His 'coming' *as such* includes saving action."[123] He argues that the primary reference in this verse, then, including the "coming," is the specific salvific action of Jesus' death.[124]

To my mind, De Boer's analysis serves only to strengthen the author's connection between the permanent union and the salvific nature of that union. De Boer simply brings out the ramifications of what in the text, I would argue, is the *primary* meaning (notice DeBoer's statement "does not merely denote his visible appearance"). The Gospel of John, we will see in the next chapter, carefully expands exactly *how* the entering the world, career, and death are salvific. Those references cannot be used to "pad" this verse, which is fundamentally christological.

Third is the question of the meaning of "flesh" in 1 John 4:2. M. M. Thompson argues that in the Johannine literature, the basic meaning of σάρξ is "humanity, creatureliness, what is natural and earthly" and always "connotes what is material or bodily."[125] De Boer extends this insight to insist that the mention of flesh "figuratively emphasizes the *concreteness* or *tangibility* of Jesus Christ's effective saving action, of his 'coming.'"[126] Again, I would argue that this is an integral but secondary meaning. To put it quite simply, there is no salvific action of the death if there is no real death, and there is no real death if there is no real flesh or real union. This point does not decide in itself, however, whether the "flesh" counters a metamorphosis or inspiration model.

Finally, the emphasis on the name Jesus, "every spirit that does not confess Jesus is not from God," adds the final piece. The shift from the union "Jesus Christ" to the confessing of Jesus highlights, again, that "the Christ is Jesus," and that the Christ is one with the human Jesus is the correct christological confession.[127] What would such a confession mean if it opposed a metamorphosis pattern? The name of the specific human *forma* would not in any way be relevant. Rather, the emphasis better fits a real union with the particular human, and that this identity between the

---

[121]Esp. *Epistles*, 576.

[122]DeBoer, "Death," 336; cf. Bonnard, *Epitres*, 86.

[123]De Boer, "Death," 336-37.

[124]Cf. Beutler, *Johannesbriefe*, 103; Klauck, *Erste*, 293.

[125]Marianne Meye Thompson, *The Humanity of Jesus in the Fourth Gospel* (Philadelphia: Fortress, 1988), 49-50.

[126]DeBoer, "Death," 344-45.

[127]Cf. Bonnard, *Epitres*, 86.

two was salvific because it endured. The cumulative evidence of the four aspects highlighted in this passage, then, best fits an argument intended to counter an inspiration rather than a possession model.

Lest we doubt that the author is interested in delineating the union of these two formerly separate beings, 1 John 4:9-11 gives another view into the author's view of the Son/Christ, tracing the cause of his appearance in the world to God's desire to manifest his love for humanity: "In this the love of God was manifested, that God sent his only Son into the world...to be the expiation for our sins" (cf. v. 14). As Painter points out, this verse shows that "Jesus was the name of the human figure while Christ, Son of God, indicated the pre-existent, divine manifestation of God."[128]

In another crucial christological passage, we again see the separation of titles to emphasize it is Jesus, specifically, who is the Christ: "Every one who believes that Jesus is the Christ [the Christ is Jesus] is a child of God" (5:1). Jesus, specifically, is the son of God, indicating clearly that Christ and Son of God are interchangeable titles, as in 5:5: "Who is it that overcomes the world but the one who believes that Jesus is the Son of God?" Immediately following the christological confession of 5:1 and 5:5, the author plays his trump card: "This is the one who came by water and blood (ὁ ἐλθὼν δι' ὕδατος καὶ αἵματος), Jesus Christ, not with the water only but with the water and the blood" (5:6). The use of ἔρχομαι connects this statement to the previous christological confessions[129] and is much more compatible with the semantic field of possession than of metamorphosis. We might rephrase, then, that one must confess that this Christ is Jesus, with respect both to water and to blood.

To what the "water" and "blood" refer have been discussed by commentators at length. Brown surveys four primary categories of possibilities for "water and blood:" (1) they refer to the sacraments of baptism and eucharist; (2) both refer to the incarnation, since they are the bodily elements; (3) the water refers to the baptism and the blood refers to the death, and (4) both refer to the death, with reference to the water and the blood that came out of Jesus' side (John 19:34).[130] Though Brown reluctantly supports the fourth option, most commentators agree that the third is the most obvious choice.[131]

---

[128]Painter, "Opponents," 64.

[129]Bonnard (*Epitres*, 107) in particular stresses the christological connections between the uses of this verb, and adds that the aorist participle is significant here in emphasizing the historical coming of Jesus of Nazareth.

[130]Brown, *Epistles*, 575-578. For a briefer but thorough discussion of opinions, see Smalley, *1, 2, 3, John*, 277-79 or Martinus de Boer, "Jesus the Baptizer: 1 John 5:5-8 and the Gospel of John," *JBL* 107 (1988): 90-92.

[131]Marshall (*Epistles*, 231-32) is typical when he makes this association, but does not see the author as suggesting that the incarnation began at the baptism; rather, against the

The water in this case interpreted as the water of baptism, symbolizing the event at which time the Spirit descended upon Jesus, fits quite well into the ancient Mediterranean possession pattern and is a reasonable choice in the context of the letter.[132] The sacramental aspect, if present, is surely secondary, since there are no other sacramental references in the Epistle, and "the use of αἷμα to stand for the eucharist is without parallel."[133] The term "coming" in water and blood is less convincing with reference exclusively to the death on the cross, especially since the reference in John 19:34-35 is in reverse order, "blood and water." DeBoer makes an interesting argument for the "coming in the flesh" (1 John 4:2) referring primarily to the salvific action of Jesus' death being passed on through Jesus' act of baptizing which is continued in the community ("the water").[134] I suggest, however, that these implications are, again, secondary, for two reasons. First, this reconstruction overlooks the issue of permanence in the letter. Second, any reference to the sacramental activity of baptism surely follows on Jesus' baptism, and not only because his baptism effected the sacramental action. Placing it in the context of the possession pattern provides the foundation from which the salvific actions stem. The primary issue is inspiration versus indwelling, and though indwelling no doubt enabled by baptism. Identity precedes and provides for activity.

Interestingly, here we find agreement between the author and his opponents; concerning the blood, however, they do not concur. Recall that those who employ either inspiration or metamorphosis models cannot admit the suffering of the preexistent savior. When we combine the lack of willingness to confess that the Christ is Jesus, come in flesh, with the author's emphasis on confessing Jesus Christ in blood as well as in baptism, a unified picture emerges of opponents for whom the typical

---

Cerinthian-type heresy, "John emphasized that it was Jesus Christ—not simply a human Jesus—who experienced both baptism and crucifixion. John thus understood the baptism of Jesus in a different way from his opponents." In a similar fashion, Klauck (*Erste*, 296-97) suggests that the reference to Jesus' baptism is expanded for the author by means of John 19:34 to connect to the death of Jesus. Cf. Bonnard, *Epitres*, 106.

[132]Bonnard (*Epitres*, 107) points out that "water" appears generally to be an allusion to baptism among the Johannine community, citing John 3:5, 8; 4:10, 11, as it is in Acts 8:36-39.

[133]Smalley, *1, 2, 3 John*, 282; cf. Beutler, *Johannesbriefe*, 121-22 and Bonnard, *Epitres*, 107. Those who support the sacramental interpretation often point to the existence of an unction by the Spirit preceding baptism and Eucharist in the early Church. See esp. T. W. Manson, "Entry into Membership of the Early Church," *JTS* 48 (1947): 25-33; W. Nauck, *Die Tradition und der Carakter des ersten Johannesbriefes* (Tübingen: Mohr, 1957), 153-79; Frédéric Manns, *Le Symbole Eau-Esprit dans le Judaisme Ancien* (Studium Biblicum Franciscanum 19; Jerusalem: Franciscan, 1983), 293-95, and Ignace de la Potterie, *La vérité dans Saint Jean* (2 vols; AB 73; Rome: Pontifical, 1999), 1.319-20.

[134]Martinus C. de Boer, "The Death of Jesus Christ and His Coming in the Flesh," *NovTest* 33 (1991): 326-46, esp. 330-38. Cf. Colin Kruse, *The Letters of John* (Grand Rapids: Eerdmans, 2000), 174-80.

Mediterranean pattern of temporary possession fits. The opponents, I suggest, are the traditionalists with respect to the Mediterranean environment compared to the author, who supports a less common form of the pattern: only permanent possession, Christ and Jesus permanently joined, will result in the permanent spiritual status all desire.

The passage 1 John 5:7-8 only strengthens this intepretation: "There are three witnesses, the Spirit and the water and the blood, and the three agree." As Smalley suggests, the "most natural" way of understanding these references is historically: that is, they refer to events in the salvific life of Jesus Christ.[135] The Spirit is the one who descended on Jesus at his baptism, the same one Jesus gave to his disciples after the resurrection (John 20:22).[136] Blood and water express the "terminal points" of Jesus' ministry on earth: the water refers to the baptism, which Smalley interprets as the time when "Jesus 'came' into his power and authority by the 'water' of his baptism," and the blood signifies the cross.[137]

The results of the progressives' incorrect Christology, in the author's opinion, we can now clearly discern as we step back and watch the movement of the Epistle: "Whoever says, 'I have come to know him,' but does not obey his commandments, is a liar, and in such a person the truth does not exist...whoever says, 'I abide in him (ἐν αὐτῷ μένειν),' ought to walk just as he walked" (2:4, 6). The author challenges this boast by the progressives, that they abide permanently in God, by insisting that they do not obey God's commandments, which are clear: to "believe in the name of his Son Jesus Christ and love one another" (2:23). These opponents do not abide, however, because they hate their brothers, and only the one who loves his brother "lives (μένει) in the light" (2:9-11), since "God is love" (4:8). Those who do not love are murderers who "do not have eternal life abiding in them" (ἐν αὐτῷ μένουσαν) but rather "abide in death" (μένει ἐν τῷ θανάτῳ; 3:14-15). Not loving one's brother is a clear sign of not abiding permanently in God, which occurs because of the christological error of refusing to acknowledge the incarnation: in the author's solution, and especially in the Gospel of John, we shall see exactly what this incarnation entails. Lack of christological permanence results in lack of ethical permanence, all of which leads inevitably to schism.

The author offers *permanence* as the solution to such problems. First, the believer must trust the witness he has received. Immediately following the accusation toward the progressives in 2:22-23, the author

---

[135]Smalley, *1, 2, 3 John*, 282-83.

[136]Smalley, *1, 2, 3 John*, 282.

[137]Smalley, *1, 2, 3 John*, 278. Smalley objects, however, to the attempt to read an antidocetic emphasis in this interpretation (278-79). See also Painter (*1, 2, and 3 John*, 305): "rather than seeing the Christ dscending on Jesus at his baptism, 1 John sees Jesus Christ revealed at his baptism."

insists on the authority of the witness: "Let what you have heard from
the beginning abide in you (ἐν ὑμῖν μενέτω). If what you heard from the
beginning abides in you (ἐν ὑμῖν μείνῃ), then you will abide in the Son
and in the Father" (ὑμεῖς ἐν τῷ υἱῷ καὶ ἐν τῷ πατρὶ μενεῖτε, 2:24); this
is what "having both the Father and the Son" means (2 John 9). At the
beginning of the Epistle we meet the essential content of the witness, the
Christ event: "the eternal life which was with the Father and was made
manifest (ἐφανερώθη) to us" (1:2). This "life" was heard, seen and touched,
and is now proclaimed for the purpose of having community, just as is
the fellowship that exists between the community and the Father and
his Son Jesus Christ (1:1, 3). This passage establishes the authority of the
original witnesses and those who have received the testimony from them.
Verses 1-3 refer to the entire Christ event, making no distinction between
individual events of Jesus' life. This lack of distinction is crucial: it is the
entire life through crucifixion and resurrection that is the content of the
witness and the subject of the incarnation. Trusting in the witness leads
to a correct and continuing christological confession, that Jesus is the
Christ (2:22; 5:1), that Jesus is the Son of God (5:5), and that he has come
in the flesh (4:2)—all of the language implies a complete and enduring
identification between the Christ and Jesus.

The preexistent Christ is to be identified fully in the flesh with the
human Jesus, through the blood of the crucifixion and death. What gives
the believer this assurance? "There are three that testify: the Spirit and the
water and the blood, and these three agree" (5:7-8). Which Spirit is this?
Only the Spirit that confesses Jesus Christ having come in the flesh (4:2).
The Spirit of God witnesses to the correct christological confession, and
that Spirit testifies to the identification of Christ and Jesus through the
crucifixion. This Spirit, moreover, witnesses to and enables the state of the
believer with the correct confession to become permanent: "By this we
know that we abide in him and he in us (ἐν αὐτῷ μένομεν καὶ αὐτὸς ἐν ἡμῖν),
because he has given us of his Spirit...God abides in those (ὁ θεὸς ἐν αὐτῷ
μένει) who confess that Jesus is the Son of God, and they abide in God (καὶ
αὐτὸς ἐν τῷ θεῷ)" (4:13, 15; cf. 3:24). Note the building upon the promise
of God's spirit given to the people from Ezekiel, Isaiah and Joel that we
discussed in the last chapter, which has been extended by this author to a
mutual indwelling.[138] What are the results of abiding in God? The believer
does not regularly sin because God's seed abides in him (ἐν αὐτῷ μένει;
3:9), loves his brothers and sisters (3:24), and has eternal life (3:25), since
God is love, shown by the fact that he sent his Son as the atoning sacrifice
(revisited) (4:7-10; cf. 1:7; 2:2; 3:16), as Savior (4:14).

---

[138]We will have more cause to examine this extension of the possession pattern to a
mutual sense by the Johannine authors in the next chapter.

In the fifth and final chapter, we see the emphatic repeat of the Son's relation to God as well as the implications of that relationship for believers. The title "Son" or "Son of God" is stressed in 5:10, 11, 12 and 13, with the emphasis on the connection with God and God's testimony for the Son, and the life for the believer who "has" (ὁ ἔχων) the Son. In the next to last verse, the author concludes his christological argument: "And we know that the Son of God has come and has given us understanding to know him who is true; and we are in him who is true, in his son Jesus Christ." Through christological explorations and the implications of the union of human and divine for the believer, we have returned to the initial title of the Epistle, which now so clearly identifies the divine Christ with the specific human Jesus.

So we have come full circle, to the accurate confession that the Christ in the flesh is Jesus and remained so through the crucifixion and resurrection, to enable the believer to abide permanently in God and God in him. As the author concludes: "And we know that the Son of God has come (ἥκει)…and we are in him who is true, in his Son Jesus Christ. He is the true God and eternal life" (5:20).

CONCLUSION

We can now see the bases of the various interpretations that interpreters have made of the Christology of the author and opponents in the Epistles. For example, Smalley can see two groups of opponents, one adoptionist and one docetist, because the broader phenomenon "docetism" can encompass no real unity between the human and divine, whereas later the possession model became adoptionism. His list of passages can serve either because of the broad nature of docetism, encompassing both metamorphosis and possession patterns. We can now see, moreover, that it is not the material nature of Jesus Christ's body that should be the focus, but the overwhelming emphasis of permanence in the letter, which makes sense only in the context of the question as to the temporary or permanent nature of possession. A question of material or nonmaterial nature simply makes no sense of the implications of the permanence.

In summary, the Johannine Epistles revolve around a christological dispute between the author and his opponents concerning the nature of the Savior by which the author explains how the schism was possible. The opponents hold to a temporary possession model. The author maintains a full and permanent identity between the Christ and the human Jesus through the crucifixion and resurrection. Only through this permanence, and by confessing its truth, can the believer abide permanently in God, and God abide permanently in the believer. This abiding enables and is revealed by the constant love within and unity of the community. By going ahead into a widely employed Mediterranean pattern of temporary possession rather than abiding in the original witness to a permanent association between the Christ and Jesus, the opponents are bound to impermanence in all aspects of the life of faith.

If the Fourth Gospel was written at approximately the same time as 1 John, we should expect to see similar issues addressed but explored more fully. Would the audience of the Gospel of John understand it to be building on a possession pattern? Would they hear it explore the ramifications of a possession that remains permanent, or spell out the implications of such a union between human and divine for the community drawn into that union? Does that Gospel reveal the existence of others who build upon different models? It is finally time to listen to how the Fourth Gospel portrays the appearance of a divine being on earth.

CHAPTER 5
THE GOSPEL OF JOHN

INTRODUCTION

If the Gospel of John is closely related to 1 John and composed at approximately the same time, and my analysis about the christological issue faced in the Epistles is correct, then in the Fourth Gospel we should see an emphasis on the tendency I have called "indwelling." This emphasis, moreover, we would expect to be shaped to counteract the inspiration tendency; that is, it should fall on the permanence of the union between the human and divine, with no tendencies toward ecstatic behavior and none toward displacement of the human mind. One would also expect consequences of this investment in permanence that extend past an abstract theological point.

We have also seen in the Mediterranean environment, however, the use of a different docetic pattern, one that was built upon the metamorphosis model with a nonmaterial emphasis and, at times, a polymorphic tendency. It is not impossible, then, especially given that both are a "seeming" (one seems a union between divine and human but ultimately is not, and the other seems a physical existence but is not) that we would see protections against that interpretation of the Jesus event as well. As I pointed out in the Introduction, most commentators who think the Gospel was composed with a docetic opponent in mind consider it docetism narrowly defined; that is, a docetic Christology based on the metamorphosis model with a nonmaterial emphasis. The controls that the Gospel gives the audience to shape the hearing of the narrative, then, must be carefully discerned.

If the foregoing analysis is correct, that the primary christological emphasis is based on the possession pattern I am calling "indwelling," and if the Gospel of John was written with a division in the community at least partly based on the use of the possession pattern I call "inspiration" in view, we should see several elements appear in the Gospel: (1) a statement of the identities of the divine being as well as the human; (2) a description of how the union of the two took place, one that would make sense to the audience given the patterns to which they are accustomed in the culture, that will provide a control through which to hear the rest of the narrative; (3) an emphasis throughout the narrative on the permanence of the unity between the divine being and human possessed by that being, with no signs of ecstatic behavior in the human nor evidence of the lack of understanding or recollection that we saw in the ecstasy tendency, but with evidence of the continuing conscious identity of both the human and divine; (4) an emphasis on the union playing the major role in making his death and resurrection salvific, and finally (5a) an emphasis that this permanence in the correct christological confession leads to unity in the community, accompanied by (5b) warnings against succumbing to impermanence, that is, not believing that the Christ and Jesus are fully and permanently united, is a mistake that leads to division (impermanence) in the community as well. The case will be strengthened if vocabulary familiar from the particularly christological passages in the Epistles appears.

I suggest that all of the above is exactly what we see in the Gospel of John. The identity of the divine being (Logos) is defined in the prologue, and that of the human (Jesus) somewhat at the end of the prologue and more clearly soon after the prologue, as well as throughout the Gospel. The role of the baptism has generally been insufficiently appreciated both as the event that describes *how* the divine being became flesh and also as a control through which the remainder of the Gospel would have been heard. It is not only the prologue that controls the audience's understanding of the Gospel but also the account of the events at Jesus' baptism: that is, the *how* of the *who* and *what* placed before the audience in the prologue. Previous commentators have been tripped up by defining the phenomenon of docetism too narrowly (only a metamorphosis model) and by presuming that the "conception Christologies" in the Gospels of Luke and Matthew that became orthodoxy must be present in the Gospel of John.

In the narrative that follows the baptism event, the permanence of this union between the divine Christ and the human Jesus is repeatedly emphasized, and it is particularly explored both existentially and spatially through the use of the term μένω. Spatially, the christological question revolves around where the savior is from, where he is at the present time, and where he is going. Existentially, the issue revolves around exactly who this figure is: Jesus of Nazareth, or the Christ/Son of God. The spatial and existential aspects intertwine in questions of when and how Jesus Christ is "with," "sees," and "hears" the Father, and in the chronological aspect; that is, for how long are the two united? Given the patterns in the cultural environment, the lack of evidence of ecstatic behavior or of displacement is notable, as seen in the alternating expressions of the divinity of Jesus Christ as well as his humanity.

The consequence of this investment in the permanent unity of the divine and human is no less than the means of salvation offered to humanity. The key vocabulary of permanence, μένω, is also transferable to the unity of the community, since the indwelling of the divine and human in this being, and his indwelling with the Father, enables the mutual indwelling with the community. This mutual indwelling is enabled in particular by the continuing identity of this being, which must, therefore, be emphasized throughout the salvific death and the resurrection, that "how" that gives witness to the permanence. Throughout, the theme of *witness* to this identity is crucial. To choose impermanence in the community despite the witness, like the schism we saw in the Epistles, is decried in the narrative as a christological offense.

The procedure in this chapter continues the audience-oriented methodological perspective. I have in previous chapters demonstrated the patterns of a divine being appearing on earth that I think the audience would bring to a hearing of this narrative. I will ask here not only which pattern the audience would assume upon hearing the first chapter of John, but also what the audience would hear as the narrative progresses. Are there concepts whose meanings can be said to expand as the audience builds its knowledge during the progression of the narrative?[1] Do the

---

[1]In *Rhythm in the Novel* (Lincoln, Neb.: University of Nebraska Press, 1950), E. K. Brown describes rhythm as "repetition with variation," repetition being a powerful force "to order, unify, reinforce, and evoke associations not explicitly stated" (113). The repetition may be "simple," combinations of words and phrases, sequences of incidents, or groupings of characters, which function to unify and order the narrative, adding greater force to what it communicates (9, 28). The repetition, however, may also be that of a symbol, and that symbol may be either *recurrent* or *expanding*. While a recurrent symbol reveals its full meaning early in the narrative and serves more as a reminder than as a development, an expanding symbol grows "as it accretes meaning from a succession of contexts" (9; cf. 57). Brown states that the expanding symbol is particularly useful "when the idea or feeling the novelist is rendering is subtle or otherwise elusive," and it well serves the novelist who is "prophetic," who struggles "to communicate an emotion about something that lies behind his story and his people and his setting, about something much more general, much less definite than any of these" (55, 57-58). With the expanding symbol, the author impels and persuades his readers towards two beliefs. First, that beyond the verge of what he can express, there is an area which can be glimpsed, never surveyed. Second, that this area has an order of its own which we should greatly care to know…[it] is an expression of belief in things hoped for, an index if not an evidence of things not seen (59). For other discussions of Brown, see J. C. Anderson, *Matthew's Narrative Web: Over, and Over, and Over Again* (JSNTSS 91; Sheffield: JSOT Press, 1994), 197-202; Warren Carter and J. P. Heil, *Matthew's Parables: Audience-Oriented Perspectives* (CBQMS 30; Washington, D. C.: Catholic Biblical Association, 1998), 37-38, and Larry Paul Jones, *The Symbol of Water in the Gospel of John* (JSNTSS 145; Sheffield: Sheffield Academic Press, 1997), 19.

concepts expand in a way that supports indwelling rather than inspiration? Since this work is not a commentary, it is not possible, of course, to examine each piece of the Gospel to see how it fits into the development of the audience's picture of this divine and human being. I will, however, generally move through the narrative as it comes, discussing the sections that particularly add to the audience's knowledge of the christological themes I have highlighted. By arranging the material in this way, I am hoping to avoid an artificial separation of motifs from narrative in favor of highlighting the persuasive intertwining of themes that provides a cumulative argument for the audience.

FROM PROLOGUE THROUGH BAPTISM: IDENTITY ESTABLISHED

Since the identity of the savior figure is established as one of the primary guides to the listening audience in the first chapter of John, it is necessary for us to spend some extended time on this one chapter. I suggest that this chapter introduces the audience to the divine being known to the audience from the culture potentially by many names (e.g. Logos, Spirit, Son, *Memra*), and that it also provides the "why" and "what" of the union between this divine entity and a human being (the incarnation). Following the prologue, the narrative of John 1 then explains the "how:" the possession that occurs at the baptism. Witnessing and the salvific results of the maintenance of the union through the death and resurrection of this being are emphasized as well.

The Prologue

The prologue of the Gospel of John is replete with themes that are expanded throughout the Gospel and are related to our topic; hence, examining these motifs with care will prove fruitful when we watch how they play out in the narrative. The primary emphasis is our first theme listed above: a statement of the identities of the divine and the human beings involved. Among the many issues that have been addressed in the prologue in Johannine scholarship, four require our attention to discern these existential identities: (1) a review of some persuasive arguments that the entire prologue is an integral part of the Gospel; (2) what the prologue indicates, both existentially and spatially, to the audience concerning the divine being it calls "Logos;" (3) the reason why witnessing to the incarnation is a crucial motif, which is bound together with the description of the incarnation in the prologue, and (4) the results of that incarnation. Remember: the larger goal is to discern into which pattern the audience would understand the appearance of this divine figure to fit.

Since the work of Adolf von Harnack the dominant trend has been to understand the prologue as a separate composition from the following narrative of the Fourth Gospel, though the role of the verses in that prologue describing John the Baptist (1:6-8, 15) have constantly been debated.[2] The separation between the prologue and the narrative has only been underlined by the general consensus that the prologue is best described as a wisdom hymn. Already in 1917, J. Rendell Harris connects certain themes in the prologue with those of Jewish wisdom literature.[3] Although Bultmann emphasizes "eastern gnostic" thought as the background to the Logos,[4] by the time of Schnackenburg's 1965 and Brown's 1966 commentaries, the path of wisdom speculation as the primary guide to understanding the symbol had generally been settled upon.[5] Eldon J. Epp concluded in 1974 that the prologue's Logos hymn was based on wisdom hymns both in content and in form.[6]

Though this hypothesis became critical orthodoxy, parts of it have been impressively challenged. Elizabeth Harris suggests that the prologue in the Gospel functions like the prologues of Greek dramas: it announces past events, summarizes the present situation along with the cosmic implications of that situation, and introduces primary and secondary characters who are necessary to the fulfillment of the divine plan to be described in the body of the work.[7] In fact, she argues, the characters introduced in the prologue, Moses, John and Jesus, as well as their functions, are described fully in the "drama" of the Gospel, with the role of Jesus described especially in the Gospel through the uses of the christological expressions Son of Man, ἐγώ εἰμι(and the Son (of God).[8] She concludes that "the prologue's carefully constructed cryptic unity" prepares the audience for the presentations of

---

[2]See, to cite only formative examples: Bultmann, *Gospel*, 13-15; J. A. Robinson, "The Relation of the Prologue to the Gospel of St. John," *NTS* 9 (1962-63): 120-29; Ernst Käsemann, "The Structure and Purpose of the Prologue to John's Gospel," in *New Testament Questions of Today* (Philadelphia: Fortress, 1969), 162-63; Rudolf Schnackenburg, *The Gospel According to St. John* (3 vols; trans. Kevin Smyth; New York: Crossroad, 1982), 1.224-29. A good discussion of the issues may be found in Gail R. O'Day, *The Gospel of John* (NIB 9; Nashville: Abingdon, 1995), 516-18. By the time Schnackenburg's commentary, however, it was generally accepted that "in its present form, [the prologue] is indissolubly linked with the Gospel itself, and it only remains to ask what is its point as the opening section" (221).

[3]J. Rendell Harris, *The Origin of the Prologue to St. John's Gospel* (Cambridge: Cambridge University Press, 1917).

[4]Bultmann, "History of Religions," 43-46.

[5]Schnackenburg, *Gospel*, 1.481-93 and Brown, *Gospel*, 519-24. The best initial work was done by Dodd, *Interpretation*, 263-85.

[6]Eldon J. Epp, "Wisdom, Torah, Word: The Johannine Prologue and the Purpose of the Fourth Gospel," in *Current Issues in Biblical and Patristic Interpretations* (ed. G. F. Hawthorne; Grand Rapids: Eerdmans, 1974), 130.

[7]Elizabeth Harris, *Prologue and Gospel: The Theology of the Fourth Evangelist* (JSNTSS 107; Sheffield: Sheffield Academic Press, 1994), 1-25; 189.

[8]Harris, *Prologue*, 26-194.

the Gospel and that "there is no clause, no phrase, no noun, no verb which does not play its part in this preparation."[9]

Warren Carter also argues that "the claim that [the prologue] was an addition faces the problem of the similarities of content between the prologue and the gospel," such as the consistent presentation of John the Baptist in both the prologue and the remainder of the narrative as well as "the presentation of Jesus in terms of origin, revelation, and response."[10] Carter discusses how four interrelated themes in the prologue play an important role in the Gospel.[11] He sees one theme in particular, Jesus as the only revealer, in conflict with "a synagogue interested in traditions concerning the heavenly visions of Moses, Abraham and Isaiah," as seen in contemporary texts such as 2 Baruch, 1 Enoch and 4 Ezra.[12] The presentation of Jesus as Wisdom would also be intended to transcend the Torah as "the dwelling place and embodiment of wisdom," and the prologue with its religious symbols serves the function of emphasizing the uniqueness of the community.[13] The prologue, then, Carter reads as fitting into the struggle with the synagogue on a social level.[14] While I differ from Carter's close following of the Martyn/Brown schema in reconstructing the community, his work is extremely helpful in highlighting the continuity between the entire prologue and the Gospel.

As we see in Carter's analysis, the prologue's close connection with the subsequent narrative does not mitigate its ties (or that of the entire Gospel) to the Jewish wisdom tradition.[15] In Reading John, Charles Talbert conveniently summarizes twelve parallels between the prologue and the Jewish wisdom myth.[16] For our purposes, four parallels are particularly instructive. First, both Logos and Wisdom are described as divine (cf. John 1:1 and Wis 7:25-26).[17] Second, both "continually come into the world"

[9]Harris, Prologue, 195.

[10]Warren Carter, "The Prologue and John's Gospel: Function, Symbol and the Definitive Word," JSNT 39 (1990): 35-36.

[11]Carter, "Prologue," 37-43.

[12]Carter, "Prologue," 44-48.

[13]Carter, "Prologue," 49-50.

[14]Carter, "Prologue," 47-49.

[15]Most recently, see Walter Grundmann, Der Zeuge der Wahrheit: Grundzüge der Christologie des Johannesevangeliums (ed. W. Wiefel; Berlin: Evangelisch Verlagsanstalt, 1985); Scott, Sophia and the Johannine Jesus; Ringe, Wisdom's Friends; Willett, Wisdom Christology in the Fourth Gospel; Fiorenza, Jesus: Miriam's Child, Sophia's Prophet, and Witherington, John's Wisdom. An earlier work should be mentioned for its influence: A. Feuillet, Le prologue du quatrième évangile: Etude de la théologie johannique (Brussels: Desclée de Brouwer, 1968).

[16]Talbert, Reading John, 68-69.

[17]Talbert, Reading John, 68.

(cf. John 1:9 and Wis 6:13-16; 7:27; Sir 24:6-7; 1 Enoch 42:1).[18] Third, both "create a relation with God among those who are receptive" (John 1:12-13 and Wis 7:27; 9:18).[19] Fourth, both appear on earth and "tabernacle" among humans (cf. John 1:14a with Bar 3:37 and Sir 24:8, 11-12).[20]

In a modification of this hypothesis, however, Thomas Tobin concentrates on the ways the Logos in the prologue goes beyond the figure of Wisdom in Jewish speculation.[21] He highlights three elements of this extension: (1) the functions and attributes of the Logos, such as the ability to make people children of God; (2) the contrast between light and darkness, including the association of light with life, and (3) the incarnation of the Logos in Jesus of Nazareth.[22] Tobin finds parallel "structures of thought" in the role of Logos in the biblical interpretation of Philo of Alexandria, and he concludes that the type of speculation in which the author of the hymn in John 1 engages is part of "the larger world of Hellenistic Jewish speculative interpretations of biblical texts."[23]

If the prologue is an integral part of the gospel, Tobin's article in particular allows us to see the talent of the author in creatively adapting the traditions or models received from the surrounding culture. Two other expectations follow from this integral nature of the prologue: (1) the audience would use it as a guide for listening, to set up expectations, and (2) the Gospel narrative would explain and expand upon what it has already asserted. The prologue is crucial as, to repeat Heitmüller's familiar phrase, "an overture to the Gospel that follows. The principal themes are sounded here, and will be more fully developed in the Gospel itself."[24] I suggest that we take this assertion with the utmost seriousness, as does Schnelle: "for the evangelist, the prologue functions as a programmatic introductory text."[25]

---

[18]Talbert, *Reading John*, 69.

[19]Talbert, *Reading John*, 69.

[20]Talbert, *Reading John*, 69.

[21]Thomas H. Tobin, "The Prologue of John and Hellenistic Jewish Speculation," *CBQ* 52 (1990): 252-69.

[22]Tobin, "Prologue," 254-55.

[23]Tobin, "Prologue," 268. Tobin concurs with most commentators in seeing the hymn (excluding the John the Baptist passages, following the reconstruction of Brown, *Gospel*, 3-37) as a separate work incorporated into the Gospel. Cf. John Ashton, "The Transfiguration of Wisdom: A Study of the Prologue of John's Gospel," *NTS* 32 (1986): 161-86.

[24]Wilhelm Heitmüller, *Das Johannes-Evangelium* (SNT 4; 3rd ed.; Göttingen, 1920), 37; translation from Schnelle, *Antidocetic*, 211.

[25]Schnelle, *Antidocetic*, 226; cf. 212: "If the prologue represents the opening of the Gospel both in time and in content, it has an introductory function. It leads us into the theme of the Gospel by treating central features of the content of what is to come, and thus it prepares us to understand the Gospel and gives a substantial direction to that understanding. This is clear from the terminological and material agreements between the prologue and the rest of the Gospel." Schnelle goes on to provide a convenient summary of those agreements (212-13).

The most persuasive explanation for the arrangement of the prologue to my mind has recently been made by Daniel Boyarin,[26] and the discussion of his article leads us into a discussion of the second point listed above: what exactly does the prologue indicate by the term "Logos," which confronts the audience already in John 1:1? While Boyarin does not doubt the identification of themes in the prologue with Jewish wisdom literature, he points out how the assumption that this was a separate Logos *hymn*, parallel to so-called wisdom hymns, has hindered seeing not only the entire prologue as a unity but also led to identifying it by the wrong *Gattung*. A study of Logos and *Memra* in Jewish literature of the time reveals, according to Boyarin, that "until v. 14 what we have before us is a piece of perfectly unexceptional non-Christian Jewish thought that has been seamlessly woven into the Christological narrative of the Johannine community."[27]

Boyarin demonstrates the parallel usages of Logos, Sophia and *Memra* in Jewish texts of the Hellenistic period. The personifications of each are treated as separate gods, whether the Logos in Philo, Sophia in Philo and in the wisdom literature, and *Memra* in the Palestinian Targum.[28] Boyarin particularly highlights the parallel functions of the Logos with those of *Memra* in the Palestinian Targum: (1) creating; (2) speaking to humans; (3) revealing himself; (4) punishing the wicked; (5) saving, and (6) redeeming.[29] The Palestinian Targum also "reveals close connections between the *Memra* and the figure of Wisdom."[30] The prologue, then, only departs from typical Jewish speculation involving the divine being (variously called Son, Wisdom, angel, God, Lord and Logos) at 1:14, when it describes the incarnation of this divine being.[31]

Boyarin then moves to argue for a different reconstruction of the prologue, first identifying its *Gattung* not as hymn but as a midrash on creation ("in the beginning") in the first five verses, one that is transformed in the following verses by means of a particular wisdom myth, "the well-attested myth of Wisdom's frustration in her desire (and God's) that she

---

[26]Daniel Boyarin, "The Gospel of the *Memra*: Jewish Binitarianism and the Prologue to John," *HTR* 94 (2001): 243-84.

[27]Boyarin, "*Memra*," 265.

[28]Interest in Israel's so-called "second god" has increased since the publication of Alan F. Segal's *Two Powers in Heaven: Early Rabbinic Reports about Christianity and Gnosticism* (Studies in Judaism and Late Antiquity; Leiden: Brill, 1977). The most comprehensive collection of texts that give evidence of this concept is Margaret Barker, *The Great Angel: A Study of Israel's Second God* (Louisville, Ky.: Westminster/John Knox, 1992). Barker sees Jesus as a "manifestation of Yahweh" (*Angel*, 3) without addressing his human identity.

[29]Boyarin, "*Memra*," 256-57.

[30]Boyarin, "*Memra*," 261.

[31]Boyarin, "*Memra*," 268.

find a home in the world."[32] This frustration described in the prologue (reading κατέλαβεν in 1:5 as "received" rather than "overcome") is logically followed by the witness of the Baptist (1:6).[33] That analysis makes 1:6 a transition from the pre-existent targumic midrash to the "narrative gloss on it that follows" and verses 10-11 as a "Sophialogical gloss on the midrash of the first five verses."[34] Verses 11-13 refer not to the lack of reception narrated in the Gospel narrative, but to the myth of Wisdom's previous visits to earth when it was received by only a few, such as Abraham.[35] This lack of reception explains the need for the Logos incarnate as well as the witness who precedes him, with 1:6 referring to the John the Baptist's pre-incarnation witness, with 1:15 as "his testimony to the fulfillment of his testimony after that event."[36]

One might add to Boyarin the tantalizing *Prayer of Joseph* fragment, in which the descending Israel is called "first born," "archangel," "a man seeing God." Also, as J. Z. Smith points out, "his role as 'the Beginning' and his 'eldership' is clearly implied."[37]

> I, Jacob, who is speaking to you, am also Israel, an angel of God and a ruling spirit. Abraham and Isaac were created before any work. But I, Jacob, who men call Jacob but whose name is Israel am he who God called Israel which means, a man seeing God, because I am the firstborn of every living thing to whom God gives life. And when I was coming up from Syrian Mesopotamia, Uriel, the angel of God, came forth and said that "I had descended to earth and I had tabernacled among men and that I had been called by the name of Jacob (*Prayer of Joseph* Fragment A, 1-4).

Smith compares (as, he notes, have many others) the entire fragment with a passage from Philo on the Logos: "God's firstborn, the Logos, who holds the eldership among the angels, an archangel as it were. And many names are his for he is called the Beginning, and the Name of God, and His Word, and the Man after His Image and He that Sees, that is to say, Israel."[38] Smith, in fact, impressively lists a parallel in Philo for each of these terms in the *Prayer of Joseph*.[39]

---

[32]Boyarin, "*Memra*," 271.

[33]Boyarin, "*Memra*," 272.

[34]Boyarin, "*Memra*," 273.

[35]Boyarin, "*Memra*," 275.

[36]Boyarin, "*Memra*," 274.

[37]"The Prayer of Joseph," trans. J. Z. Smith, in Charlesworth, *Pseudepigrapha* 2.701; cf. "The Prayer of Joseph," in *Religions in Antiquity: Essays in Memory of E. R. Goodenough* (Studies in the History of Religions 4; ed. Jacob Neusner; Leiden: Brill, 1968), 253-94.

[38]Smith, "Prayer," in Charlesworth, 701 and n. 11.

[39]Smith, "Prayer," in Charlesworth, 701, n. 11. On the possible influence of the *Prayer of Joseph*, a descending angel tradition in 11Q Melch on a Johannine Jesus interpreted as

The connections between the Logos of John and of Philo, both also characterized at times as the Son and spoken of as divine, are also highlighted by Peder Borgen.[40] In his discussion of agency in the Fourth Gospel and contemporary Judaism, Borgen draws attention to the use of the names Logos, Son, and Israel to depict heavenly figures who see, and therefore know, God.[41] This figure also descends and ascends as God's agent.[42] The evidence is extensive, therefore, that the multi-named mediator or second power concept was widespread in the Judaisms of the Hellenistic period.

In light of this recognition, what does the prologue indicate, both existentially and spatially, to the audience concerning the divine being it names "Logos?" The lofty first verse of the Gospel introduces the existential question concerning the Logos, who was with God and who was, as Schnelle phrases it, "of the nature of" God.[43] If we accept especially the insights of Boyarin, the audience expectations would extend past the Logos to include those conceptions in the Jewish world of binitarianism of which Logos, Wisdom and *Memra* in particular are only the most common expressions in the texts left to us. The first five verses would remind the audience that this divine being has attempted to dwell among humans before and been rejected.

Our third concern in the prologue is the reason for the importance of witnessing to the incarnation, which involves how that incarnation is described in the prologue. John 1:6-8 shifts to "a man sent from God," John the Baptist. Moloney correctly emphasizes that John is the only person other than Jesus who is said in the Gospel to be sent by the Father (the disciples are later sent by Jesus), showing that "John was part of the divine plan."[44] To be "sent" then is part of the salvific pattern, rather than identifying the redeemer specifically. John is introduced for the purpose

---

an angelic Son of Man, see J.-A. Bühner, *Der Gesandte und sein Weg im 4. Evangelium: Die kultur- und religionsgeschichtlichen Grundlagen der johanneischen Sendungschristologie sowie ihre traditionsgeschichtlich Entwicklung* (WUNT 2; ser. 2; Tübingen: Mohr, 1977). Bühner's two-stage reconstruction of Johannine Christology, in which he sees the Johannine Jesus portrayed initially as a human who is caught up into heaven and is transformed into an *angelic* Son of Man who becomes incarnate, has not won wide acceptance.

[40]Borgen, "Agent," 144-48.

[41]Borgen, "Agent," 146-47.

[42]Borgen, "Agent," 147.

[43]Schnelle, *Antidocetic*, 214. For our purposes, the debate over whether or not this verse *grammatically* describes the Logos as God himself is secondary, since I am suggesting that actually none of the concepts of the prologue can be fully defined without the narrative that follows. It is enough for us to look to the debate to understand that the audience could have brought to the text several possibilities at this point. For a summary of the grammatical problem, see Wallace, *Greek Grammar*, 256-90.

[44]Francis Moloney, *The Gospel of John* (SP 4; Collegeville, Minn.: Liturgical Press, 1998), 38

of witnessing (recall 1 John and the importance of the believable witness). This passage continues as well the existential question, as John is clearly identified as a witness to the light rather than the light itself (1:8).[45]

Verses 9-13 expand the existential identity of the savior figure into a spatial one, as well as expanding the implications for those who receive him and those who do not. Verse nine contains the important statement that the light "was coming into the world" (ἐρχόμενον εἰς τὸν κόσμον). This appearance of the divine on earth gives the audience their first clue concerning the pattern involved. Recall 2 John 7 about the opponents who denied "the coming of Jesus Christ in the flesh." No metamorphosis language is present, but language more adaptable to the possession semantic field. While "the world," "his own home," and "his own people" have already been defined as unpleasant places of rejection, it is also asserted that the savior will make into children of God those born "not of blood, nor of the will of the flesh, nor of the will of man, but of God" (1:13). This three-part formula refers to the natural birth,[46] so that the theme of birth is seen as negative or useless when referring to the biological but salvific when referring to the spiritual, an important distinction which will eventually fall into the indwelling pattern. Note that "water" is not used for natural birth, a point that will become useful and important in later interpretations of certain Gospel passages that are directly related to Christology.[47]

The importance of witnessing grows as the description of the divine entering the world continues. In the history of Johannine scholarship, the verse of towering influence has been 1:14: "and the Word became flesh and tabernacled among us (ὁ λόγος σάρξ ἐγένετο καὶ ἐσκήνωσεν ἐν ἡμῖν), and we have seen his glory, the glory as of a father's only son, full of grace and truth." In the crucial verse 1:14, there are three elements with which to grapple at some length: "became," "flesh," and "tabernacled among us."

First, the preexistent Logos "became" (ἐγένετο). This is the fourth appearance of this precise verbal form in the prologue (1:2, 6, 10, 14). Much of the discussion in the past century centered around whether "became" indicated a substantial change or merely an appearance; in other words, was it deliberately anti-docetic or somewhat docetic in itself? While Bultmann identifies the entire phrase as intentionally

[45]For more on the emphasis of the Baptist as witness and the results of his witnessing in leading others to meet and follow Jesus, see D. G. van der Merwe, "The Historical and Theological Significance of John the Baptist As He Is Portrayed in John 1," Neot. 33 (1999): 267-92.

[46]See, for example, Brown, Gospel, 12-13; Schnackenburg, Gospel, 263, and Moloney, Gospel, 44-45.

[47]For the argument that water symbolizes birth, see esp. Witherington, Wisdom, 97 and "The Waters of Birth: John 3:5 and 1 John 5:6-8," NTS 35 (1989): 155-60.

antidocetic,[48] Käsemann, similar to Baur before him, calls it "a manner of appearance," an element of the portrait of Jesus in the Fourth Gospel that is naively docetic.[49]

J. C. O'Neill argues that ἐγένετο should be translated as "born" on the basis of parallels in Justin and Athanasius.[50] It cannot mean "become," he maintains, since that translation would entail a change in the nature of the Logos.[51] Jey Kanagaraj effectively refutes O'Neill by pointing out that passages O'Neill cites are not parallels at all, since the complement used in those passage is ἄνθρωπος rather than σάρξ.[52] On the other hand, Luke 24:19, which says that Jesus of Nazareth became (ἐγένετο) a prophet, and 3 John 8, "we became (γινώμεθα) fellow-workers," provide true parallels, in which the complements describe what the subject became without in any way suggesting that the subject ceased to be what it previously was.[53] Someone can be described with γίνομαι as "becoming" something else, Kanagaraj demonstrates, without necessarily changing his/her nature.

This reconstruction also fits with the christological issues reflected in the Epistles. The author of 2 John 7 states that his opponents, in a way that he does not clearly specify, deny the fleshly existence of Jesus Christ. In 1 John 4:2, the conflict is more specifically defined, since the perfect tense of the participle expresses completion with permanent result: Jesus Christ completed his coming and permanently remains in the flesh. First John 2:22, using the present indicative to state that the Christ is (ἐστιν) Jesus, fits the letter's current thought of a permanent union. John 1:14, the "Word became (ἐγένετο, aorist) flesh and dwelt among us" makes an even more definitive statement with an aorist indicative.[54] This usage is best interpreted as an ingressive aorist, which "occurs with *stative* verbs in

---

[48]Rudolf Bultmann, *Johannes*, 41-43. Cf. Georg Richter, "Die Fleischwerdung des Logos im Johannesevangelium," *Studien zum Johannesevangelium* (BU 13; Regensburg: Pustet, 1977), 157-58.

[49]Ernst Käsemann, *The Testament of Jesus* (London: SCM, 1969), 24. F. C. Baur (*Kritische Untersuchungen über die kanonischen Evangelien* [Tübingen: Fues, 1847], 233) suggested that since the author could have used ἄνθρωπος instead of σάρξ, σάρξ here indicates a "covering." There are no other instances in the Gospel, however, where σάρξ could be understood to have that meaning. Baur as well as others before Käsemann understood the depiction as the Johannine Jesus as god rather than a human, with the flesh just serving as the mode of communication (metamorphosis model, in my terms).

[50]J. C. O'Neill, "The Word Did Not 'Become' Flesh," *ZNW* (1991): 126-127.

[51]O'Neill, "Word," 125-26.

[52]Jey J. Kanagaraj, "Did the Word Not 'Become' Flesh? A Response to J. C. O'Neill," *ExpTim* 110 (1999): 80-81.

[53]Kanagaraj, "Word," 81.

[54]Talbert, *Reading John*, 74.

which the stress is on *entrance into the state.*[55] In the New Testament, the aorist of γίνομαι is commonly used with nouns (as are other past tenses) to indicate entering into a new state or condition.[56]

Schnelle points out that the verb generally signals a genuine change of nature, "to indicate their entering into a new condition."[57] The Logos, Schnelle asserts, "now is what it previously was not, namely, a real, genuine human being. The incarnation of the preexistent Logos contains both a statement of identity and a statement of essence, since the identity of subjects in v. 14 and v. 1 produces an affirmation about the essence and the true humanity of Jesus."[58] This interpretation glosses over the same verb form used in creation of the world and in the appearance of John (1:3, 6, 10). One could argue that the presence of a direct object, however, is determinative in leaning toward Schnelle's reading.[59] We may at least suspect at this point, therefore, that the Gospel is making a statement about permanence.

Is what the Logos became, "flesh" (σάρξ), decisive? "Flesh" in the Gospel of John is described by Schnackenburg as "that which is earth-bound (3:6), transient and perishable (6:63), the typically human mode of being, as it were, in contrast to all that is divine and spiritual" and "linked up with the cosmic dualism of 'above-below' (cf. 3:3; 8:23) and 'earth-heaven'" (3:31).[60] Some commentators, however, argue that when applied to Jesus, his "flesh" signifies "his very self" given for salvation, emphasizing that his incarnation occurred for the purpose of his death.[61] Does "the flesh," however, already have soteriological significance for the audience in 1:14?

M. M. Thompson surveys the uses of σάρξ in the Fourth Gospel and concludes that it denotes "the human and natural sphere" as well as "what is material or bodily. Thus, 'the Word made flesh' cannot mean simply that revelation occurred in the earthly sphere or in the 'realm of createdness';

---

[55]Wallace, *Greek Grammar*, 558. Σάρξ "expresses that *state* into which the Divine Word entered by a definite act" (268).

[56]BAGD, 159.

[57]Schnelle, *Antidocetic*, 221 quoting BAGD, 159.

[58]Schnelle, *Antidocetic*, 222.

[59]Schnackenburg (*Gospel*, 266) argues that "it is a different γίνεσθαι from the "appearance" of John the Baptist (v. 6) and the "coming to be" of creation (vv. 3, 10b)," then states unconvincingly that "the context alone provides the key."

[60]Schnackenburg, *Gospel*, 267.

[61]DeBoer, "Death," 342-44, citing Schnackenburg, *Gospel* (2nd German edition, 1963), 221. Schnackenburg, however, more precisely describes 1:14, "the flesh assumed by the Logos in the Incarnation is the presupposition of the death on the Cross" and that the idea was "probably already in the mind of the Evangelist, who then brings it out clearly in the discourse on the bread of life" (268).

rather, it must mean that such revelation (1:18) occurred through and in the 'flesh' of Jesus."[62] I suggest, therefore, that soteriological significance is a necessary but chronologically secondary expansion of the concept in the narrative, based of necessity on the primary requirement that there is real union with real flesh with which to act (as I argued in 1 John). At this point, the "flesh" is best seen as some type of real union with humanity, "union" being preferable to "transformation" because we have seen the possession pattern to be indicative of a real change, while transfiguration usually expresses complete continuity with the previous identity.

What is the cumulative effect of the verb in the prologue (vv. 3, 6, 10, 14)? All of the meanings can be summarized as "come into being" in the sense of "as part of God's plan." The details are not described. We do not need the description of the world, since the "midrash" already refers the audience to Genesis 1. John came into being as part of God's plan that he witness to the Logos in the world. The Logos came into being as flesh as part of God's intention.

But, how? Does our investigation into the metamorphosis and possession patterns support the assertion of Schnelle? The metamorphosis semantic field tends to be a very specific one, involving terms with the specific denotations of "transfiguring" a "form."[63] "Became" generally fits better in the possession pattern. Recall that metamorphosis maintains continuity of mind and identity, whereas possession can, but certainly does not necessarily, involve displacement. It is, however, a definite change, whether temporary or permanent. The Word did not have the appearance, or the image, or the form of flesh, but it *became* flesh; therefore, there is little evidence of the metamorphosis pattern. Admittedly, the verb "became" here is not particularly helpful in discerning a pattern; we must wait until the author recounts Jesus' baptism to elucidate *how* the Word became flesh.[64]

The other crucial verb of this verse is ἐσκήνωσεν, "to tabernacle." The verb σκηνόω draws on LXX usage in which God dwells with Israel, first in the tent of meeting (from which he would come and go), then permanently in the temple. Chronicles, for example, records the words of Solomon at the dedication of Temple: "The Lord has said that he would reside (κατασκηνῶ σαι) in thick darkness. I have built you an exalted house, a place for you to reside in forever" (τοῦ κατασκηνῶσαι εἰς τοὺς αἰῶνας(6:1-2). This dwelling is

---

[62]Thompson, *Humanity*, 50.

[63]Only in metamorphosis pattern in *Homeric Hymn to Dionysus* did we see the use of "became" in the metamorphosis pattern.

[64]As Loader correctly insists, the interpretation of 1:14a "has suffered far too much by people treating it as a key to the gospel, but not reading it first within the wider context to which it belongs." William Loader, *The Christology of the Fourth Gospel: Structure and Issues* (BET 23; 2d ed.; Frankfurt: Peter Lang, 1992), 179.

also connected in the LXX with wisdom motifs. *Sirach* describes Wisdom's living on earth using the same verb (24:3-24:12), as does the *Prayer of Joseph*, already cited. Moloney points out that this verb may be connected to the Hebrew verb שׁכן that in Exod 25:8, 29:46 and Zech 2:14 is used to describe Yahweh's dwelling in Israel.[65] In the attribution of this aspect of the wisdom myth to the Christ, the audience receives another hint of the magnitude of the theme of permanence.

This verb is used, however, only five times in the New Testament, once in the Gospel of John and four times in the Apocalypse; the use here, then, is striking. Why draw the parallel to God dwelling among Israel in the tent of meeting, to Wisdom living with Israel in the Law, and not continue to use it in the rest of the Gospel for the presence of the Christ? Like Logos, the term is one of introduction to something that will be clarified only by hearing the entire Gospel. For the permanence of the incarnation and the resultant enduring state between God/Christ and the believer, the author chooses the verb μένω.

For our purposes, we can see the similarities with those possession model passages in which Wisdom is pictured as a divine element that descended from heaven and possessed a person or an entire people. Also, recall the angel-as-possessor pattern that Levison detects in Hellenistic Judaism, an apparent parallel to the daimon-as-possessor move in some Greco-Roman thought. Such patterns, we assume, could be part of the expectations the audience would bring to this verse. The broad disagreements show that this statement is not as decisive as we might have hoped. While the verb can indicate a change that does not erase the previous identity, it is not included in the semantic field of metamorphosis, so that the interpretation of Baur and Käsemann does not seem justified. While the general nature of the vocabulary leans toward possession, the audience must wait for the narrative to understand the *how* of the process. We will have to wait to see how the narrative explicates this "becoming" to be certain.[66]

The audience can discern, however, that the "tabernacling" binds the existential and the spatial: the Logos not only existentially became flesh, but he also made his dwelling among humanity.[67] It also provides the context for understanding the additional existential and spatial expansions

---

[65]Moloney, *Gospel*, 39. For speculation on the connection of this usage with the later *shekinah*, see Brown, *Gospel*, 33-34.

[66]Schnelle does save his analysis of the prologue until the end of his book, though he seems to arrange his material in that way to lay first his foundation for redactional analysis of the Gospel before applying that method to the prologue.

[67]Schnelle, however, asserts that skhnou/n "refers to the mortal human body (cf. Wis 9:15; 2 Cor 5:1, 4; 2 Pet 1:13, 14), so that v. 14b represents an intensification of the statement about the incarnation in v. 14a" (*Antidocetic*, 222).

in the verse: that he is "full of grace and truth" and that "we have seen his glory, the glory as of the only Son from the Father." Δόξα in John combines elements from the OT to depict Jesus as representing "the visible divine presence exercising itself in mighty acts,"[68] though Schnelle finds the passages of the δόξα of Sophia most telling (Wis 7:25; 9:11).[69] This full existential meaning will only be accomplished, of course, in the depictions in the Gospel of the ways Jesus manifested his δόξα through signs, though the audience familiar with OT descriptions may already perceive that this incarnation equals "the revelation of the divine in the human story."[70]

Tied closely to the compact existential and spatial statement of 1:14 is the theme of witnessing. Most interestingly, here we find an intersection of vocabulary with that used in the christological conflict of the Epistles. John's witness is emphasized in 1:15: "The one coming (ἐρχόμενος) after me is before me." Notice the verbal form ἐρχόμενος, the same we saw in 1 John 7, and soon after the first naming of this Logos who became flesh, the product of this union, "Jesus Christ" (1:17). Like 1 John, the double name is significant, given the depiction in 1:14 of the being as a union of preexistent heavenly being, of the same nature as God but distinct,[71] with the flesh of a man.

We have finally reached our fourth point of interest in the prologue: the results of that incarnation. Reading chronologically like Boyarin, the results of the incarnation in 1:14 are: seeing his glory (1:14); receiving grace upon grace (1:16) and truth (1:17), and knowing the Father (1:18). Clearly, this list is not explicated immediately, but the audience must wait for the narrative to reveal exactly what these elements mean, especially for the "knowing" of the Father. The structure of the last verse, though, highlights the importance of the theme "making the Father known," as Herman Waetjen notes: "That story [that follows the prologue] will also provide the direct object of the verb ἐξηγήσατο (which appropriately stands at the very end of the prologue, pointing forward to what follows."[72]

Verse 18 concludes the prologue with another statement intertwining the spatial with the existential: "in the bosom of the Father." Moloney argues that the word κόλπον indicates "an external part of the body (cf. 13:23)," so that the passage should be interpreted, "Jesus Christ is turned

---

[68]Brown, *Gospel*, 503.

[69]Schnelle, *Antidocetic*, 223.

[70]Moloney, *Gospel*, 39.

[71]See 1:14d, where the relationship of Word and God is first distinguished as Son and Father (Moloney, *Gospel*, 39).

[72]Herman Waetjen, "Logos pro.j to.n qeo,n and the Objectification of Truth in the Prologue of the Fourth Gospel," *CBQ* 63 (2001): 286. Cf. Harris (*Prologue*, 91-115), who examines several issues in 1:18; with regard to this particular verb, she argues for a translation in context of "communicate divine things."

toward the Father at all times during the story that is about to be told."[73] I would say, however, that Schnackenburg points us closer to the mark when he notes the uses of the word in various aspects of family life in the OT[74] and says that the phrase "renders the 'with God' of v. 1 in another way."[75] The "with God" and "was divine" of 1:1, then, is revisited in 1:18 with a clarification: that the intimacy is, by analogy, as of family: of the same type, yet with some distinction of persons.[76]

To this point, we have seen our first concern, a statement of the identities of the divine and human beings involved in the union, partially answered in the prologue. The prologue as it stands is a unified piece, with the first five verses based on or incorporated from a Genesis midrash, and an integral part of the Gospel, that indicates to the audience that the divine being with various names in the culture has now become flesh. The radical nature of this entry into the human sphere makes it necessary for witnessing to be a major theme of the depiction. The results of this incarnation will be salvific. While the entry into time and space of the divine being is described with utmost brevity, we see no indication of the semantic field usually associated with metamorphosis.

We see in the prologue, therefore, the introduction of many tantalizing elements. Taken by itself, however, it intrigues more than resolves. If the prologue is truly an introduction to the narrative, it can only be fully understood in terms of the narrative that follows and depicts the ideas. In Moloney's words, "the reader has been told *who* Jesus is and *what* he has done, but an important question remains unanswered: *how* did this action of God in the human story take place? Only a Johannine story of Jesus can answer this question."[77] The narrative now moves to a fuller description of the human being involved as well as to the depiction of how the incarnation actually occurred.

---

[73] Moloney, *Gospel*, 47.

[74] Schnackenburg, *Gospel*, 280. Cf. B. Lataire, "The Son on the Father's Lap. The Meaning of εἰς τὸν κόλπον in John 1:18," *SNTSU* 22 (1997): 125-38, who highlights the NT and Septuagint meanings and comes to the conclusion that the family connotations are of care, love, tenderness and affection of the Father toward the Son.

[75] Schnackenburg, *Gospel*, 280. Brown (*Gospel*, 36) also highlights the echoes of 1:1 present in 1:18.

[76] Kugler has recently argued for the translation "womb," but he still places the image within the cultural understanding of the relationship between father and son. This interpretation still plays out for Kügler as the Son having a share in divinity without being the same as the Father. Joachim Kügler, *Der andere König: Religionsgeschichtlich Perspektiven auf die Christologie des Johannesevangeliums* (SBS 178; Stuttgart: Katholisches Bibelwerk, 1999), 23-71; 149-50.

[77] Moloney, *Gospel*, 34.

John, the Baptism, and the Existential "How"

If the Gospel is asserting a permanent possession model (indwelling) over against a temporary model (inspiration), it is possible that adherents of both models could easily agree on the initiatory event of the possession. We may hope, nonetheless, that some indication would be given to the audience of the permanence in the very event upon which the opponents agree. I suggest that the audience is given that key in the baptism narrative through both the emphasis on identity and the introduction of the term μένω.

The witnessing theme of the Baptist intertwines with the definitive theme of identity as "the Jews"[78] send questioners to inquire about John's identity. They suggest several of the expected titles of this period of Judaism: the Christ, Elijah, the prophet (1:19-23), but they receive no positive statement from John other than a quotation from Isaiah 40:3 that indicates that the Baptist considers his role to be a preparatory one.[79] Questioned concerning his baptismal activities, John gives only slightly more information, that there is one already present in the world who is more important than he is (1:24-28). John clarifies the next day with his statement that it is Jesus who is the Lamb of God and who was "before" him (1:29-32). Note the identification of Jesus as "the one coming," ἐρχόμενον (1:29; 2 John 7). Having already witnessed to Jesus, that is, having claimed to know that this person is present, he then recounts the proof of all he has claimed about this man: his recollection of what happened during the man's baptism. The narrator is not retreating from an emphasis on the baptism for sectarian reasons by "merely" having John recall the event for the audience; rather, he is using the technique to place the narrative weight

---

[78]The use of the collective term "the Jews" in the Fourth Gospel has, of course, been the subject of much attention. The best review of the recent evidence is by Urban C. von Wahlde, who, in light of the research of the past fifteen years, discerns three intentions of the term: (1) as an "outsider" term; (2) to designate the "official" leadership position of the author's opponents, those in charge of the synagogue who were responsible for the community's expulsion, and (3) that Judea was the primary site of the hostility. None of these referents are "based on political or ethnic considerations. This is all but universally agreed to." Urban C. von Wahlde, "'The Jews' in the Gospel of John: Fifteen Years of Research (1983-1998)," *ETL* 76 (2000): 53-55. One interesting question, it seems to me, is whether or not the previous rejection of Wisdom as described in that myth and, according to Boyarin, in the prologue, affects any of the uses of "the Jews" in the Fourth Gospel; that is, does the term ever designate those who rejected Wisdom and continue to reject Wisdom/Logos/*Memra* incarnate?

[79]Moloney (*Gospel*, 52) points out that the use of Isa 40:3 in verse 23 "maintains this author's concentration on the Baptist as a witness." Arguments that the Baptist's role is diminished in the Fourth Gospel in comparison with the synoptics pale when we recognize exactly *to what* the Baptist was a witness. For an expression of the supposed reduced role of the Baptist, see, for example, S. S. Smalley, *John: Evangelist & Interpreter* (New Testament Profiles; Downer's Grove, Ill: InterVarsity Press, 1978), 24.

on the Spirit remaining on Jesus, as well as the "seeing" and "witnessing" (1:32, 34), all foundational claims of the Johannine community, the importance of which in the face of christological mistakes and schism we have already encountered in 1 John.

To begin the process of fully understanding the terms of the prologue, and to continue the shaping of the terms by which the audience hears the remainder of the Gospel, the baptism of Jesus is decisive. The existential and spatial overlap introduced in the prologue, in fact, can only be placed on a narrative level, and hence, of assistance to the reader, when laid out in the event of the baptism. Also, only the baptism can introduce the foundation by which the mutual indwelling of the Father and Jesus Christ as well as the mutual indwelling of the Father, Jesus Christ and the believer can be achieved.

John the Baptist recalls the event:

> I have seen the Spirit descending (καταβαῖνον) from heaven like a dove, and it remained on him (ἔμεινεν ἐπ' αὐτόν). I myself did not know him, but the one who sent me to baptize with water said to me, 'He on whom you see the Spirit descend and remain (καταβαῖνον καὶ μένον) is the one who baptizes with the Holy Spirit.' And I myself have seen and have testified that this is the Son of God. (1:32-34)

These verses describe how the Word becoming flesh actually occurred. There are four issues to discuss in this passage: (1) the baptism as the point of incarnation; (2) the Spirit as possessor; (3) the importance of μένω, and (4) the witness to the Son of God. Recall 1 John 5:5-6, that Jesus came through water and blood, and that the resistance to understanding the mention of water there as the water of baptism is the charge of adoptionism. If, however, the incarnation did occur at the baptism, 1 John 5:6 ("not with the water only but with the water and the blood") makes perfect sense: the Christ came for salvation at the baptism (water), and he necessarily remained to complete the salvific activity that extended through the death (blood). First John and the Gospel reflect a common christological issue.

The majority opinion, reaching as far back as Baur and Holtzmann, has maintained that the descent of the Spirit at the baptism of Jesus is a sign for the Baptist and/or others,[80] or, at most, a prophetic commissioning

---

[80]See, for example, F. C. Baur, *Vorlesungen über neutestamentliche Theologie* (Darmstadt: Wiss. Buchgesellschaft, 1973), 107-108, 366; H. J. Holtzmann, *Lehrbuch der neutestamentlichen Theologie II* (2nd edit.; Tübingen: Mohr, 1911), 451, 508-09; F. Porsch, *Pneuma und Wort: Ein exegetischer Beitrag zur Pneumatologie des Johannesevangeliums* (FTS 16; Frankfurt: Knecht, 1974), 104; F.-M. Braun, *Jean Le Théologien* (3 vols; Etudes bibliques; Paris: Gabalda, 1966), 3.68ff; Ernst Haenchen, *John: A Commentary on the Gospel of John* (2 vols; Hermeneia; Philadelphia: Fortress, 1983), 1.156; Brown, *Gospel*, 66.

by the Spirit,[81] though the commentators admit to a tension between the preexistent Logos tradition and the prophetic possession tradition.[82] A few scholars, however, have challenged that interpretation as it concerns the Gospel of John. Early in the twentieth century, speculation about Jesus' baptism was somewhat diverse. While W. Lütgert, for example, thinks that Jesus' awareness of his identity was awakened at the baptism, he identifies Spirit and Logos, and F. Büchsel sees receiving the Spirit as a stage of the process of incarnation.[83] I will survey four more recent opinions concerning the baptism as the point of incarnation before adding evidence to support this interpretation.

In their 1953 book *The Gospel of the Spirit*, E. C. Colwell and E. L. Titus examine the Spirit's descent upon Jesus at the baptism to understand the "method of transition from the pre-existent status with the Father to that of the earthly situation."[84] The passage John 1:29-34 is crucial in pointing out that the descent of the Spirit onto Jesus did not just identify him for the Baptist's sake, as earlier commentators had argued; rather, the fact that the Spirit is described as having *remained* on Jesus indicates that an actual change took place in Jesus himself: "I saw the Spirit descend as a dove from heaven, and it *remained* on him," a detail not necessary for simple identification.[85] The Fourth Evangelist is stressing that Jesus became the Son of God at this time and that John the Baptist was the witness.[86] Similar themes, moreover, in a passage describing Jesus' baptism from the so-called Gospel to the Hebrews (quoted in Jerome) suggest that the idea of the Spirit descending on Jesus and remaining is "current in the general period of our gospel."[87] They call this "incarnationism" rather than adoptionism.[88] Colwell and Titus then point out that one finds other evidence in the Gospel that this change took place at the baptism; primarily, the Gospel author nowhere acknowledges Davidic descent or a supernatural birth as evidence of Jesus' messiahship; rather, the Jews continue to insist upon the

---

[81]See, for example, Schnackenburg, *Gospel*, 1.304-05; J. P. Miranda, *Die Sendung Jesu im vierten Evangelium* (SBS 87; Stuttgart, 1977), 54; Bühner, *Gesandte*, 304.

[82]Brown, *Gospel*, 66; Schnackenburg, *Gospel*, 1.304-05; Haenchen, *John*, 1.156; G. W. H. Lampe, "The Holy Spirit and the Pre-existence of Christ," in *Christ, Faith, and History: Cambridge Studies in Christology* (ed. S. W. Sykes and J. P. Clayton; Cambridge: Cambridge University Press, 1972), 117; Burge, *Anointed*, 72-73, 87.

[83]W. Lütgert, *Die Johanneische Christologie* (2nd ed.; Gütersloh: Bertelsmann, 1916), 25; Friedrich Büchsel, *Das Evangelium nach Johannes* (NTD 4; Göttingen: Vandenhoeck & Ruprecht, 1934), 40.

[84]E. C. Colwell and Eric Titus, *The Gospel of the Spirit* (New York, Harper), 107.

[85]Colwell and Titus, 108-109.

[86]Colwell and Titus, 109.

[87]Colwell and Titus, 109, n. 4.

[88]Colwell and Titus, 110-111.

obvious facts of Jesus' biography on the physical plane, without realizing that this plane is no longer relevant to the divine being he has become (1:45-46; 4:43-45; 6:41-42; 7:40-43, 50-52).[89]

In his essay "Christmas, Epiphany, and the Johannine Prologue," Reginald Fuller presents a form-critical argument to suggest that the incarnation occurred at the baptism. Fuller agrees with Bultmann and others that the prologue is a hymn in verse that was expanded at a later stage; he also believes that while the hymn grew out of the Hellenistic Jewish wisdom tradition, it was already a Christianized Wisdom-Logos hymn when taken over by the author of the Fourth Gospel.[90] Since the hymn originally stood independently, "the Logos became flesh" (1:14) originally concluded it and would have referred to Jesus' earthly life as a whole rather than to one specific moment, an interpretation bolstered by reading ἐγένετο as a complexive aorist, which is used for linear actions that are completed and, hence, are looked back on as a whole.[91] After engaging in an extensive rearrangement of the prologue, Fuller argues that this understanding of the incarnation occurring at the baptism is not adoptionism, because adoptionism denies the divine initiative; therefore, though the Christology of John differs from that of the Nicene Creed, that does not necessarily make it adoptionist.

Charles Talbert gives four reasons to support his argument that the incarnation occurred at the baptism in the Fourth Gospel in his essay "'And the Word Became Flesh': When?" First, reader-response criticism discerns that a hearer from the Hellenistic Jewish environment accustomed to multiple names for the descending-ascending redeemer figure would have heard phrases such as "the Word became flesh" (1:14), "the Spirit descended and remained on him"(1:32-34), and "it is not by measure that God has given the Spirit to him"(1:34) as "variant expressions of the same event." If it is the case that Wisdom, Word, Son and Holy Spirit would be heard interchangeably, then "the Word became flesh" would equal "the Spirit descended and remained on Jesus" and the incarnation would have been assumed to have taken place at Jesus' baptism.[92] Second, the Gospel makes clear the public perception that Jesus is the son of Joseph from Galilee (1:45; 6:42; 7:41-42, 50-52) and contains no inarguable indication that the author was aware of the conception Christology of Matthew and Luke. While John 8:41, in which the Jews say to Jesus, "We were not born of fornication; we have one Father, even God," has been

---

[89]Colwell and Titus, 116-120.

[90]R. H. Fuller, "Christmas, Epiphany, and the Johannine Prologue," *Spirit and Light* (ed. M. L'Engle & W. B. Green; New York: Crossroad, 1976), 64-65.

[91]Fuller, 66-67; 72 n. 7 citing Blass-Debrunner-Funk, 332.

[92]Talbert, "Word," 45-47.

read as a reference to the odd nature of Jesus' paternity according to the
birth traditions, Talbert shows that in its context the passage refers not to
Jesus' paternity but to the issue of Jewish faithfulness or unfaithfulness to
God, an interpretation supported by the fact that fornication is used as a
metaphor for unfaithfulness to God in Jewish tradition.[93]

Talbert's third point is that in 1 John 5:4b-12 the Johannine author does
not challenge the position of his opponents that Jesus Christ came "by
water"; the author merely adds that Jesus Christ also came "by blood."
The reference is most likely to the water of baptism; this passage, therefore,
supports the thesis that the merging of Jesus and Christ occurred at that time
for the Johannine community. Fourth and finally, both the Gospel of Mark
and the lost Gospel to the Hebrews have similar views of the incarnation
to that proposed for the Fourth Gospel, providing a context within early
Christianity for the Johannine view. Talbert argues that the Christology of
the Fourth Gospel does not fit the view later referred to as adoptionism
because that view presumed human merit, whereas in this Gospel, the act
is one of grace.[94] John's contribution, rather, is "his community's *explicit*
insistence on the continuing union of the divine and human in Jesus on
into the period after his death, resurrection, and ascension, as opposed to
the other two gospels' *implicit* assumption of it." [95]

Francis Watson in "Is John's Christology Adoptionist?" argues that
adoptionist is indeed the appropriate label because the union between
the Logos of God and Jesus of Nazareth occurs at the baptism. Watson's
primary evidence is 1 John 5; he suggests, like Talbert, that in the passage
concerning Jesus Christ having come by water and blood, the water refers
to that of baptism, and that this view is shared by the author and his
docetic opponents.[96] Watson then surveys early evidence of adoptionist
and docetic Christologies from Irenaeus and Ignatius to provide an
historical context to support the possibility of this reading. Having laid
this groundwork, Watson turns to the Gospel of John, arguing on two bases
that its Christology is adoptionist: (1) the portrayal of John the Baptist,
and (2) the Johannine Christ's claim to have come down from heaven.

First, the fact that the Gospel begins with the Baptist's witness about
the descent of the Spirit onto Jesus at the baptism suggests the same kind
of adoptionism described by Irenaeus in the beliefs of Cerinthus and some
Jewish-Christians; moreover, the Baptist's witness is unique and superior
to that of the apostles. Watson sees this reading as supported by two other

[93]Talbert, "Word", 47-48.

[94]Talbert, "Word," 50-52; e.g. Hippolytus, *Haer.* 7.35.2; Eusebius, *Hist. eccl.* 7.30-35.

[95]Talbert, "Word," 52.

[96]Francis Watson, "Is John's Christology Adoptionist?" in *The Glory of Christ in the New
Testament*, ed. L. D. Hurst & N. T. Wright (Oxford: Clarendon, 1987), 114-20.

points: (i) similar terminology is used for the descent of the Spirit in 1:32 as is used for the descent of the Son from heaven in 3:13 and 6:33 (he also cites for comparison 6:38, 41, 42, 50, 51, 58), and (ii) the Testimony of Truth from Nag Hammadi portrays the Baptist in the same way and also espouses an adoptionist Christology; if its portrayal of John's witness was derived from the Gospel, it would show that some read the gospel as adoptionist.[97]

Second, the Christ's claim to have come down from heaven is similar to the adoptionist view of *The Second Treatise of the Great Seth*, in which Jesus is an ordinary man whose human mind is suppressed when the divine Christ comes to live in his body and speaks through him. This view is also similar to "a widespread contemporary view of inspiration: man in his natural state consists of body and mind, but when inspiration occurs, the mind is banished and the Divine Spirit becomes united with a human body."[98]

In the work of these commentators, it seems apparent that the incarnation is depicted as having occurred at Jesus' baptism for the following reasons: (1) the prologue discusses the incarnation both as "entangled with" and as an introduction to the Baptist's witness to Jesus as the Christ — no form-critical division and rearranging of the text is necessary to see this; (2) there is no compelling evidence in the Gospel for the incarnation having occurred at birth; (3) other early Christian evidence shows that it was one contemporary belief, and (4) the descending-ascending redeemer myth of Hellenistic Judaism in particular shows that the terms used to refer to the redeemer cannot be used out of context to say, for example, that references to the Word must refer to conception. Adoptionism is not an issue because of its traditional association with merit; the inclusion of some statement on the merits of the human Jesus prior to the descent of the Spirit at the baptism would have been important for the audience to hear that model.

Three issues concerning the baptism remain for consideration at this point: (1) the Spirit as the possessor; (2) the implications of the term μένω, and (3) the theme of witnessing to the Son of God. First, concerning the Spirit as the possessor, the interchangeability of names for a secondary divine being expected by the audience of this time has already been highlighted. Boyarin points out that "an ambiguity between God and the Logos is to be found wherever Logos theology is to be found."[99] Not only

---

[97]Watson, "Adoptionist," 121-122.

[98]Watson, "Adoptionist," 122. Watson cites one example from Philo in n.35.

[99]Boyarin, "*Memra*," 255 n. 44; *contra* Martin McNamara, "Logos of the Fourth Gospel and *Memra* of the Palestinian Targum," *ExpTim* 79 (1968): 115, who argues that *Memra*, in a more traditional fashion, is another name for God, since the Targums vary the names "God" and "*Memra*" in the same contexts. Martin Scott (*Sophia*, 56) makes the same point about God and Sophia in Proverbs and Sirach: "the two are so closely related that they may almost be seen as one."

that, but in Justin, Boyarin identifies the many names that this second power is called by the Holy Spirit (that is, in scripture):

> God has begotten as a Beginning before all His creatures a kind of Reasonable Power from Himself, which is also called by the Holy Spirit the Glory of the Lord, and sometimes Son, and sometimes Wisdom, and sometimes Angel, and sometimes God, and sometimes Lord and Word. (*Dial.* 61.1)[100]

While Justin identifies the Spirit as the entity speaking through the Scriptures, earlier Jewish sources also equate Holy Spirit as another of the names (along with Wisdom, Angel and Logos). Already in the Wisdom of Solomon, not only are Wisdom and Word equated (9:1-2; cf. Sir 24:3), but "in 9:17 the parallelism links Wisdom and Holy Spirit; in 18:15 Logos and angel are identified."[101] Philo as well identifies Spirit and Wisdom (*Creation* 135; *Giants* 22, 27).[102] In the *Prayer of Joseph*, angel, Son and Spirit are merged but are separate from Logos and Wisdom.[103] C. H. Dodd clearly delineates how closely Philo's Logos parallels the Spirit in the Fourth Gospel.[104]

We have already seen (Chapter Three) John Levison's conclusions that the spirit is sometimes in the Judaism of the Hellenistic period transformed by means of Greco-Roman influence into an invading angel. By making this transformation, Levison argues that Philo, Josephus and Pseudo-Philo are able to distance God from the oracles of Balaam. Josephus in particular alters the vocabulary of Daniel and describes John Hyrcanus to suggest that a spirit/angelic presence *accompanied* rather than possessed these humans.[105] This tendency in Josephus, I suggest, shows by his discomfort the existence of another interpretation, the interpretation that the angelic spirit/*daimon*, which is too close to God, possesses the person.

The question then becomes how the audience would hear the move from Logos as divine being in the prologue to Spirit as possessor in the baptism scene. I suggest that just as Logos (Word) is the more appropriate appellation in a prologue built upon a midrash on Genesis,[106] Spirit is the most expected title in possession context, and the title that will be expanded throughout the narrative. "Jesus originated as the Logos (1:1ff.), he returns as the Spirit (14:18; etc.), and therefore Logos and

---

[100]Translation from Boyarin, "*Memra*," 282; cited also by Talbert, *Reading John* 275 to serve a similar point.

[101]Talbert, *Reading John*, 272; cf. Barker, *Angel*, 114-32.

[102]Talbert, *Reading John*, 272.

[103]Talbert, *Reading John*, 274; on *Prayer of Joseph* fragment, see my pp. 12-13.

[104]Dodd, *Interpretation*, 65-72.

[105]Levison, *Spirit*, 187-89.

[106]Boyarin, "*Memra*," 275.

Spirit are virtually two ways of expressing a similar thought."[107] This interpretation is strengthened in the Fourth Gospel, because the Spirit is identified with the Word:

> That is, the Spirit Jesus possesses and the Spirit he can offer are the words he speaks. Jesus as the Logos (the Word) becomes one with his mission and presents himself in the words he offers. This striking suggestion follows from John's metaphor for the Spirit, living water...John's interest in word and Spirit follows from a christology developing the motif of the eschatological prophet.[108]

The indwelling model make the clearest sense of this motif.

G. W. H. Lampe, though he is not willing to see the baptism as the point of incarnation,[109] explains theologically why Spirit is a better concept than Logos to denote God's immanence: "the Logos concept lent itself least readily" to the "immanent relationship of Christ to believers," though it "was well suited to express Christ's relationship to God."[110] "Although the very title 'Christ' signified the 'anointing' of Jesus with the Spirit, this tended to be forgotten and 'Christ' became either simply a name or, in later theology, a way of emphasizing that in the incarnation human nature was 'anointed' with deity."[111] Lampe sees the potential for a Christology based on spirit possession, like that of the Old Testament prophets, in the baptism scenes of the canonical gospels, especially in John's description of the Spirit's "coming down" and "resting upon" him (his translation; John 1:32), but says that the Fourth Gospel "does not develop this theme."[112]

The indwelling model is supported by our analysis of the Spirit here and in Chapter Three. In that previous chapter, we saw that possession was the typical understanding both of divinely appointed prophets and leaders in the OT. While prophecy in and of itself tends to employ an inspiration model, leadership, especially of David and of the expected Davidic messiah, falls within the indwelling tendency. W. J. Bittner recognizes as well the close connection between the Spirit and (1) the anointing of David (1 Sam 16:15), (2) the messianic expectation of Isaiah 11, especially verse 1, and (3)

---

[107]Burge, *The Anointed Community: The Holy Spirit in the Johannine Tradition* (Grand Rapids: Eerdmans, 1987), 113.

[108]Burge, *Anointed*, 102; 109.

[109]Lampe, "Holy Spirit," 125.

[110]Lampe, "Holy Spirit," 114.

[111]Lampe, "Holy Spirit," 118.

[112]Lampe, "Holy Spirit," 117. Lampe makes an intriguing doctrinal argument for the potential superiority of a possessionist Christology, an "inspirational" rather than an "incarnational" Christology (see esp. 122-30).

the baptism of Jesus as described in the Fourth Gospel.[113] In fact, the Spirit will be the element that will unite the emphasis on the permanence of the divine/human union in Jesus Christ, the necessity of that union through the crucifixion and resurrection to provide salvation, and the potentiality for permanence (avoidance of schism) in the community.

The third issue in the passage on Jesus' baptism concerns the first appearance in the Gospel of the term μένω. Discussing this verb in the context of the Epistles, we saw that it connotes not only a physical dwelling place, as does σκηνόω, but that it also carries strong connotations of permanence, used often in the LXX for "abiding" of the Lord forever. The special presence in the tent of meeting and the Temple, then found in Wisdom, is now through the term σκηνόω said to be in the "word became flesh," the term μένω emphasizes the permanence of that situation.

Others have recognized the connection between the prophetic possession model, messianic speculation and the Wisdom figure. Scott notes that μένω is often used to depict the relationship between the teacher Jesus and his disciples, "which is something dynamic between the Father and Son and between Father-Son-Disciple."[114] He also points out the connection to Wisdom, especially in Wisdom 7:27, which describes Wisdom's "'abiding' [μέουσα] nature and her indwelling of her disciples, again based on her relationship with God."[115]

Burge has explored the use of μένω and its connection to anointing, and he highlights many of the messianic expectations of the spirit resting upon someone.[116] He recognizes the permanence of mutual indwelling implied as well, quoting favorably "the unity of Spirit and Son was as permanent and comprehensive as the unity between Father and Son."[117] He continues as follows:

> It appears then that John has deliberately moulded the idea of the Son of God in the first instance upon the prophetic model...The human mould, so to speak, into which the divine sonship is poured is a personality of the prophetic type. Upon this plane, the difference between prophet and Son is that the latter possesses in an absolute sense that which the prophets possess ideally but not in full actuality, and possesses permanently what

---

[113]Wolfgang J. Bittner, *Jesu Zeichen im Johannesevangelium: Die Messias-Erkenntnis im Johannesevangelium vor ihrem jüdischen Hintergrund* (WUNT 2.26; Tübingen: Mohr, 1987), 139; 245-46.

[114]Scott, *Sophia*, 157.

[115]Scott, *Sophia*, 158.

[116]Burge, *Anointed*, 54-56; cf. Heise, *Bleiben*, 62.

[117]A. Wurzinger, "Der Heilige Geist bei Johannes," *Bibel et Liturgie* 36 (1962-63): 289-90; cited in Burge, *Anointed*, 55.

they perhaps possess intermittently and *ad hoc* (cf. 8:35 ὁ υἱος μένει [ἐν τῇ οἰκίᾳ] εἰς τὸν αἰῶνα).[118]

The prophetic model, as we saw in Chapter Three, *is* a possession model. What will follow that compares to these narratives if the author of the Gospel is trying to extend the pattern?

Our fourth concern was the witnessing to the Son of God: "I have seen and bear witness that this is the son of God" (1:34).[119] There are two elements to point out. First, the importance in this passage of witnessing to the identity of this divine and human being ties the baptism to the prologue. The witnessing of John the Baptist here completes the "who" and "why" of the prologue with the "how" described in the baptism. Second, as Schnelle points out, "It is striking that directly in the context of the bestowal of the Spirit on Jesus the central christological title of the Fourth Evangelist appears for the first time in the full revelatory-theological sense: ὁ υἱὸς τοῦ θεοῦ. As bearer of the Spirit is Jesus of Nazareth the Son of God."[120] The intimate connection between identity and witness is seen immediately in 1:34 with the addition of the title Son.

Let us pause to take stock of how we have progressed through the five elements we expect to see in a work emphasizing an indwelling over an inspiration christological pattern. The narrative has (1) revealed the identities of both the divine and the human beings, and it has (2) described the union between them by a pattern understandable in the cultural context, a description that provides a lens through which to view the remainder of the Gospel. To complete the pattern, the narrative should now emphasize: (3) the permanence of the union, without evidence of ecstatic behavior or displacement; (4) the permanent union as necessary for the salvific death and resurrection, and (5) the permanence in the community that will result from correct christological confession, along with warnings against succumbing to an impermanence that will lead to schism. The argument for indwelling will be most strongly made by the expansion of the Spirit/Paraclete until it becomes virtually identical with Jesus Christ, who is still the Jesus of the narrative.

FROM FOLLOWERS TO THE FAREWELL DISCOURSE: IDENTITY EXPLORED

If the preceding suggestions are correct, one would expect the audience to be guided through the narrative with signposts indicating the

---

[118]Dodd, *Interpretation*, 255.

[119]Brown (*Gospel*, 56) points out that 1:32 uses the perfect tense teqe,amai, which "indicates that the action, which took place presumably at Jesus' baptism, is still having its effect, namely, the Spirit is still with Jesus."

[120]Udo Schnelle, "Johannes als Geisttheologie," *NovTest* 40 (1998): 23.

permanent effects of the union that occurred during Jesus' possession by the Spirit. If the Gospel only emphasized elements that indicate Christ's preexistent status, we might suspect a typical metamorphosis pattern, or a temporary possession pattern in which the divine mind and identity have supplanted that of the human. The recurring emphasis on the humanity underlines the indwelling pattern, demonstrating how far we are from the supplanting of human identity by the divine mind. I suggest that the narrative of Jesus' life gives the audience that direction through the exploration of the intertwining of the identity of this human and divine being and the implications of the possession event not only for Jesus, but also for the community. What is implicit in the OT is explicit and expanded by the Fourth Evangelist.

In the narrative preceding the passion, the audience hears the development of our third through fifth themes variously emphasized in John 1-12, then intertwining dramatically in John 13-17. The gathering of disciples and the Cana pericope stress the indwelling identity of the divine and human in Jesus Christ. The Temple incident brings to the fore the importance of Jesus Christ himself as the key to salvation through his salvific death and resurrection, which is only possible through his enduring unity. The episodes involving Nicodemus and the Samaritan woman focus on the importance of the permanent unity of the divine and human in providing for a permanent community, while the debates of John 5 highlight the schism that can result from an inadequate Christology. These emphases interlace and expand in the Bread of Life discourse, as well as in the Lazarus episode and its surrounding material. In addition, the role of the Spirit, for which the audience was prepared in the baptismal account, expands until that Spirit may be understood as that which binds together the five themes that reveal the focus of the Fourth Gospel on an indwelling Christology.

Followers in Space and Time

Immediately after John's narration of the baptism comes the next instance of μένω; it is hard to see this as coincidence. Upon seeing Jesus, John again proclaims that Jesus is the lamb of God, and two of John's disciples begin to follow Jesus. When Jesus asks them for what they are looking, they ask: "where are you staying (ποῦ μένεις)?" Jesus invites them to come and see (echoes of the prologue, 1:9, 18), and they stay (ἔμειναν) with him for that day (1:38-39). Note again the confluence of the spatial and existential meanings of the verb, a concurrence quite similar to that in 1 John 2:19 concerning those who had left the community: "if they had been of us, they would have remained (μεμενήκεισαν) with us." The existential and spatial aspects of the divine/human identity are intertwining in historical time and space, and those aspects are beginning to involve the believer as well. Upon finding his brother, Andrew states: "We have found the Messiah" (1:41). These disciples not only found out where Jesus was lodging, but they recognized who he is: truly seeing Jesus is the beginning of community. Only late in the Gospel will they see the full implications of the abiding of Jesus, and of their abiding with him.[121]

John 1:43-51 continues the characters' struggle to identify this person. Recall the emphasis that Colwell, Titus, and Talbert place on the assertions in the Gospel about Jesus' place of origin. Philip tells Nathanael: "We have found him about whom Moses in the law and also the prophets wrote, Jesus son of Joseph, from Nazareth" (1:45). "Jesus of Nazareth, son of Joseph," the human, is the one of whom Moses and the prophets wrote (1:45). The human is quickly recognized with a forceful echo of the vocabulary from the baptism as Nathanael proclaims that this Jesus from Nazareth is the Son of God (1:49). The human identity of Jesus is not denied and the incarnation is affirmed for the audience, though the characters in the Gospel are not yet fully aware of the implications of their confessions. Nathanael still equates the Son of God with the King of Israel, falling short of full realization,[122] as Jesus reveals in 1:50: "You will see greater things than these." The audience, however, may in this confession hear echoes of the Davidic kingship, which we have already identified (Ch. 3) as an OT example of permanent possession of the Spirit for leadership.

The explication of the "greater things" advances the theme of identity: "Very truly, I tell you, you will see heaven opened and the angels of God ascending and descending upon the Son of Man" (1:51), a reference to Jacob's experience in Genesis 28:12-17. The ambiguity of the בו in Genesis 28:12, which can be read as either "on it" (the ladder) or "on him" (Jacob), was debated in rabbinic circles,[123] but preference was given to the ladder, "on it," in the LXX.[124] While the interpretations of 1:51 are numerous and varied, Brown discerns the common element: "the vision means that Jesus as Son of Man has become the locus of divine glory, the point of contact between heaven and earth."[125] The possibility that there was an interpretation known to the audience that the angels descended and ascended on Jacob, however, opens up the potential to hear the change

---

[121]*Contra* Moloney (*Gospel*, 54), who says Jesus' invitation contains no symbolic value.

[122]Moloney, *Gospel*, 56. Cf. Schnackenburg (*Gospel* 1.319): "The titles used by Nathanael are meant as Messianic, but provide the reader with the possibility of a deeper understanding."

[123]Cf. *Gen. Rab.* 68.12, 18 (Talbert, *Reading John*, 84).

[124]There is also some question concerning the appropriate translation of evpi,, but the case for "upon" has been carefully made by H. Maillet, "'Au-dessus de', ou 'sur'? (John 1, 51)," *ETR* 59 (1974): 207-13.

[125]Brown, *Gospel*, 91. Cf. Burge, *Anointed*, 86-87; Moloney, *The Johannine Son of Man* (2nd ed.; Bibloteca di Scienze Religiose 14; Rome: Las, 1976), 26-30 and McGrath, "Going Up and Coming Down," 107-18.

to "Son of Man," especially in the light of the descent of Jacob/Israel in the *Prayer of Joseph,* as an incorporation (or a transcending?) of the Jacob/Israel angelic motif by the human and divine Jesus Christ.

We should note here the audience's first encounter with another title, the "Son of Man." This generally messianic label from Jewish culture occurs thirteen times in the Fourth Gospel, beginning here and concluding in 13:31 with the "glorification" of the Son of Man. I will save the full discussion of this complex designation for the discussion of John 13, at which time the full implications can be seen through the cumulative argument of the narrative. Two points will suffice at this time: (1) the context here reveals both a spatial and existential aspect to the concept of the Son of Man, and (2) the context of the communication between the heavenly and earthly realms may alert the audience to a potential expansion of the title from its messianic denotations in the culture.[126]

To summarize, in John 1:35-51 the audience begins to hear the solidifying of the indwelling of the human by the divine savior. Hints are given, moreover, that the struggle for humans to accept or reject this Christology will determine the permanence of the believers' status as well as the potential for community, though this aspect is more promised than developed at this juncture. These themes will continue to crystallize in the Wedding at Cana pericope.

Human and Divine: The Wedding at Cana

As the Gospel continues, the narrative develops its emphasis on the first of our themes, the abiding humanity and divinity of Jesus Christ. The importance of the wedding at Cana as the first of Jesus' signs (σημεῖα) can only be fully appreciated when read in context of an extension of the possession that occurred at the baptism.[127] While the emphasis in interpreting this

---

[126]The literature on the Son of Man in the Fourth Gospel is copious. Some of the most helpful works are as follows: Moloney, *Son of Man;* J. Coppens, "Le Fils de l'homme dans l'évangile johannique," *ETL* 52 (1976): 28-81; Peder Borgen, "Some Jewish Exegetical Traditions as Background for Son of Man Sayings in John's Gospel (Jn 3:1-14 and context)," *L'Evangile de Jean: Sources, rédaction, théologie* (ed. M. de Jonge; BETL 44; Gembloux: Duculot and Leuven: Leuven University Press, 1977), 243-58; Wayne A. Meeks, "Man from Heaven;" Bühner, *Gesandte,* esp. 274-99; Robert Rhea, *The Johannine Son of Man* (ATANT 76; Zürich: Theologischer Verlag, 1990); Delbert Burkett, *The Son of THE Man in the Gospel of John* (JSNTSS 56; Sheffield: Sheffield Academic Press, 1991); S. S. Smalley, "The Johannine Son of Man Sayings," *NTS* 15 (1969): 278-301. For a recent summary on the state of the NT Son of Man question in general, see Burkett, *The Son of Man Debate: A History and Evaluation* (SNTSMS 107; Cambridge: Cambridge University Press, 1999).

[127]In the case of this and other pericopes, I am certainly not arguing that these are the *only* implications of the passage; John's symbolic world is too rich for that type of oversimplification. "As we shall often discover in the Johannine use of symbols, the evangelist shows many facets of his theology through one narrative" (Brown, *Gospel,* 103).

pericope has generally fallen on the revelation of Jesus' divinity, the stress on his humanity is also extraordinary and often overlooked.

The pericope begins with an apparently mundane description of those present at this typical celebration: Jesus, his mother, and his disciples (2:1-2). We are left to imagine most of the festivities, with the narrative resuming at the point (after much festivity, no doubt) that the wine ran out (2:3). While the interaction between Jesus and his mother is variously interpreted, C. H. Giblin has demonstrated that "What have you to do with me?" establishes some distance between the parties, a hesitation on Jesus' part to become engaged with the issues at hand in favor of his dominant concern for his "hour."[128] While that phrase indeed indicates a change that has taken place in Jesus, I suggest that what is easily overlooked here is that the human unity between them underlies their interaction; that is, the human relationship is not merely presupposed but is emphasized by two means: (1) that she is specifically called the "mother of Jesus" four times in 2:1-12, and (2) by the very existence of the dialogue in the narrative, a dialogue which continues the description of the celebration in 2:1-2. The ongoing intimacy of their relationship is demonstrated by his mother's reaction when she instructs the servants, "do whatever he tells you" (2:5).

While miracles in and of themselves do not necessarily indicate divinity in the ancient Mediterranean,[129] Schnelle is correct to point out that the "magnitude" of the miracle here (a quantity of approximately 700 liters) "underscores Jesus' divinity," but, at the same time, the emphasis on the materiality, "which is bound up with the earthly and subject to verification in space and time, points to Jesus' *humanity*. [The] conspicuous character confirms that the one who does such deeds has really entered into fleshly existence."[130] I suggest, however, that all that Schnelle here asserts is not clear in isolation but only in context of the indwelling announced in 1:14 and described in 1:32-34, which pushes the audience to be alert for evidence of the "remaining" of this union between divine and human. The sign is said to reveal the "glory" of Jesus (2:11), an example in space and time of the assertion of the prologue: "we have seen his glory, glory as of

---

I do, however, hope to highlight an overlooked stream that the audience steeped in the possession pattern would hear in the Gospel.

[128]Charles H. Giblin, "Suggestion, Negative Response, and Positive Action in St. John's Gospel (John 2:1-11; 4:46-54; 7:2-14; 11:1-44)," *NTS* 26 (1980): 203. Cf. J.-P. Michaud, "Le signe de Cana dans son contexte johannique," *Laval Théologie et Philosophique* 18 (1962): 247-52.

[129]See, for example, Loader, *Christology*, 180. Nock's maxim "miracle proved deity," however, was apt to the Greco-Roman situation in particular. See Versnel, *Ter Unus*, 190-94; A. D. Nock, *Conversion: The Old and the New in Religion from Alexander the Great to Augustine of Hippo* (Oxford: Clarendon, 1933, 1961), 91; Ramsey MacMullen, *Paganism in the Roman Empire* (New Haven: Yale University Press, 1981), esp. 95-96.

[130]Schnelle, *Antidocetic*, 165-66.

the only Son from the Father" (1:14cd). The Cana miracle demonstrates the
narrative technique of continuing to provide evidence of divinity within
an underscored emphasis on abiding humanity.

The miracle concludes with another statement of human identity. After
the miracle, the pericope closes by stating that Jesus went to Capernaum
with his mother and brothers and disciples, and "there they stayed (ἔμειναν)
for a few days" (2:12). The startlingly everyday quality of this description
is a narrative strategy. In other words, the human relationships noted
in 2:1-2 continue, with that humanity providing a narrative frame for a
revelation of divinity. In this closing verse, a reminder of the existential
change that has occurred is heard in the spatial aspect of μένω. I am not
arguing, of course, that each occurrence of this verb carries equal import.
I do suggest, however, that the more "mundane" occurrences of the verb
in the narrative serve as an echo or reminder of the crucial element of the
baptism scene, that the Spirit remained on Jesus. The audience is reminded
by these echoes to remain alert to the implications of that event the narrative
will develop. In the Cana pericope, the interweaving of the abiding human
relationships that frame the revelation of the glory Jesus now possesses
from God and that increases the belief of the disciples (enables permanent
community) is masterful. It will prove to be a foundation for subsequent
strategy in sections of the narrative that emphasize the permanence of the
human/divine union.

The Salvific Goal and the Cleansing of the Temple

Several elements separate the Temple incident in the Fourth Gospel
from the accounts in the synoptics. The story is dramatized with some
striking elements: oxen and sheep are present in the Temple area as well
as pigeons, and Jesus uses a whip to drive everyone out and pours out the
coins of the money-changers as well as overturning their tables (2:14-15).
Schnelle points out that these dramatic elements as well as the placement
of the Temple incident early in the Gospel shows without doubt that John
not only had a theology of the cross, but that he emphasizes its importance
from the beginning of the Gospel.[131] Allusions to the crucifixion have been
placed earlier in the narrative, according to Schnelle, at 1:29, 36 (Jesus as
the Lamb of God), and 2:4 (the "hour" not yet come and the address to
and presence of his mother, parallel to her presence and address at the
foot of the cross in 19:25-27).[132] The post-Easter perspective seen in the
remembrance of the disciples concerning the raising of the Temple (his
body) in three days (2:19-22) reveals that the community is to see the

[131]Udo Schnelle, "Die Tempelreinigung und die Christologie der Johannesevangeliums,"
NTS 42 (1996): 361.
[132]Schnelle, "Tempelreinigung," 365.

pericope as referring to the crucifixion/resurrection and Jesus as the place of salvation.[133] Already the audience hears the human emotion combined with an authority over the Temple precinct derived from the ultimate intimacy with the divine, which points forward to the conclusion of the union for the salvation of those who believe.

As we stated earlier, if the Gospel presents an indwelling Christology, the necessity of a true union between the human and divine should have a significant payoff. In the Temple incident the audience already is given clear evidence of the permanent identity of this person: "when he was raised from the dead, his disciples remembered that he had said this" (2:22). The fulfillment of Jesus' promise and the remembering, moreover, provides a basis by which enduring belief and permanent community are enabled. While the emphasis is most directly in this pericope on our fourth concern, the subsequent stories of Nicodemus and the Samaritan woman will reinforce this provision for community.

Identity and Baptism: Nicodemus and the Samaritan Woman

The implications of Jesus' baptism for humanity are most profoundly indicated so far in the narrative in the pericopes concerning Nicodemus and the Samaritan woman. Nicodemus' initial confession, "no one can do these signs you do unless God is with him," could fit any Mediterranean model: a god transfigured, or one who was possessed by a divine being either temporarily or permanently. Jesus' response, however, underlines the necessity of the birth from water and the spirit (3:5), a clear reference to baptism, especially if one reads ὕδατος καὶ πνεύματος as a hendiadys, in which "the significance of one [element] spills over into the other."[134] While Burge is correct in pointing out that for the Fourth Evangelist "the role of water in rebirth is wholly and exclusively defined in terms of Spirit,"[135] the appearance of both together ties the pericope to the baptism of Jesus, and it will provide a bridge as well to the crucifixion.

"That which is born from the flesh is flesh, and that which is born from the spirit is spirit" (3:6) is an existential statement about having to be born from a particular substance, or reborn, in the water/Spirit of baptism. Loader objects that "the earlier sections of ch. 3 should also not be seen as implying that Jesus was equipped or born of the Spirit at his baptism," since the tendency of the author to make statements that identify Jesus with the disciples can lead one to make the mistake of automatically applying what is said about the disciples to Jesus as well.[136] Given the emphasis on

---

[133]Schnelle, "Tempelreinigung," 361, 368-69.

[134]Burge, *Anointed*, 166.

[135]Burge, *Anointed*, 167.

[136]Loader, *Christology*, 176.

the indwelling between the Father and Jesus Christ that is expanded to the disciples, it seems that the audience is being led to hear this intertwining, that in fact a great deal of what originally applied to Jesus should in fact be applied to the disciples, since the baptism/possession of Jesus is the foundational act of indwelling.

The spatial intertwining comes with the earthly and heavenly, the above (already implied in ἄνωθεν) and below, the ascending and descending (3:12-13). One of the most dramatic expansions in the narrative comes with the raising of the serpent allusion to crucifixion (3:14). As Brown points out, the allusion to the serpent story is most clearly understood in the wisdom context, since Wisdom 16:6-7 interprets the Exodus story as follows: "They had a symbol of salvation to remind them of the precept of your Law. For he who turned toward it was saved, not by what he saw, but by you, the savior of all."[137] This interpretation fits the Johannine thought that Jesus lifted up becomes the source of salvation to all (12:32) and that whoever sees Jesus sees the Father (14:9). "The Targum, too, interprets the meaning of looking on the serpent: it means turning one's heart toward the *memra* of God (see Ap. II). Targum Ps-Jon. mentions *the name* of the *memra*, just as John 3:18 mentions *the name* of God's only Son."[138] This connection between Christ's death and his glory will be developed in the narrative as a *"leitmotif* of the passion narrative."[139]

Loader insists that the verse refers to the constant and complete giving of the Spirit from the Father to the Son, which did not occur in any way at the baptism.[140] Dodd sees it linking water and spirit to emphasize the baptism given by Jesus (the Church's baptism) rather than John's baptism of Jesus.[141] Although one stream of interpretation sees water as added to the pericope later by a sacramental community,[142] the controlling nature of the baptism pericope and the perspective on that event as indwelling make the presence of water perfectly understandable. Jesus' baptism enables the baptism of others as the first step of passing on the spirit and new life. This interpretation is supported in the pivotal passage 3:22-23, which focuses on baptism and continues the theme into the statement of the one who comes from above (3:31-36). These verses provide an interpretation of the Nicodemus pericope and also expand the spatial and existential prologue

---

[137]Brown, *Gospel*, 133.

[138]Brown, *Gospel*, 133.

[139]Moloney, *Gospel*, 101. The cross as exaltation in John is well-recognized. See, for example, Schnackenburg, *Gospel*, 1.396-97.

[140]Loader, *Christology*, 175-76. Loader sees "the Spirit as a constant gift of the Father to the Son and Jesus' baptism as a sign of this giving, of its permanence, and as a sign for the Baptist that Jesus is the expected one and the one whose pre-existent glory he affirms."

[141]Dodd, *Interpretation*, 311.

[142]Moloney, *Gospel*, 99. Haenchen uses it for sources as well (200).

and baptism assertions. Though he does not read the baptism as the point of incarnation, Schnelle well recognizes the connection between 3:34 and the baptism of Jesus, that the gift of the Spirit to Jesus by God is emphasized in both passages: "The Evangelist here formulates the fundamental conviction of his school: Jesus is the unique and authentic revealer of God."[143] Burge points out a later rabbinic parallel: "The Holy Spirit, who rests on the prophets, does so only by measure."[144] If this idea was current to the Fourth Gospel, "Jesus is being compared with the prophets in that his endowment with the Spirit is permanent, full, and eschatological. Thus οὐκ ἐκ μέτρου ties in with John's use of μένειν in 1:32, 33."[145]

The baptism theme is reemphasized in 4:1-2, as, I think, a controlling introduction to the Samaritan woman pericope that serves as a reminder of the indwelling that occurred in the context of Jesus' baptism. When the Samaritan woman enters the narrative, the baptism theme leads into the question of the living water that results in eternal life (4:10-14). Jesus' knowledge of her life leads the woman to the existential confession that he is a prophet (4:19; cf. Deut 18:15-19), an understandable conclusion, since in the Mediterranean tradition, prophetic possession of God's spirit led to such knowledge. Here, the audience should see by now that the naming of Jesus as a prophet is both correct (he possesses the Spirit) and incorrect (that is, incomplete, since he will possess it permanently).

The importance of worshipping in spirit and truth emphasized by Jesus (4:24) leads the woman to her statement of belief in the messiah (4:25), and to Jesus' identification of himself as that figure (4:26). Her witness opens the door for others to believe; some Samaritans ask Jesus to stay (μεῖναι) with them, "and he stayed (ἔμεινεν) for two days" (4:39-40). The progression of their belief ensues not through her witness, but because of what they have heard (compare hearing the Son and hearing the Father), as they proclaim him not messiah but "savior of the world" (4:41-42). This phrase occurs elsewhere only the NT in 1 John 4:14, also with μένω vocabulary: "we have seen and testify that the Father has sent his Son as the savior of the world. Whoever confesses that Jesus is the Son of God, God remains (μένει) in him, and he in God" (1 John 14:14-15). Moloney says it emphasizes the universal aspect of the salvation, appropriate in the Samaritan connection,[146] but it reveals more than that. The insiders have the correct confession, and they may not be whom you think; that is, those who in some sense believe in Jesus may nonetheless be christological opponents. His permanent identity,

---

[143]Schnelle, "Geisttheologie," 23.

[144]*Mid. Rab. Lev.* 15:2; Burge, *Anointed*, 84. Recall the examples cited in Chapter Three from Philo concerning the temporary possession of the spirit by prophets such as Moses.

[145]Burge, *Anointed*, 84.

[146]Moloney, *Gospel*, 147-48.

established in their midst and recalled by the μένω vocabulary, results in their correct confession and, presumably, indwelling.

In the stories of Nicodemus and the Samaritan woman, the audience continues its journey into the identity of Jesus Christ. The implication of this identity for the believer, however, is increasingly emphasized, since it is portrayed as determinative of new life. The door has been opened for the possibility of debate, however, and of the rejection of this identity, as we see completely followed through in the debates of John 5.

Chapter Five intertwines the themes of the identity between the Christ/Son and Jesus as well as the importance of the witness to this unique identity. Jesus is identified as the man (ὁ ἄνθρωπος) working miracles (5:15). In his explication of the miracle, however, Jesus describes the intimacy of the Son with the Father, that he "sees" the Father and does what the Father does (5:19-24). The Son has the authority of the Father for judgment (5:27-29). John the Baptist is again emphatically described as a witness (5:31-36) as is Jesus himself (5:31), the works he does (5:36), the Father (5:37), and the Scriptures (5:39). Note the confluence of important vocabulary, identical to that in 1 John 5:38: "you do not have his word remaining in you (τὸν λόγον αὐτοῦ οὐκ ἔχετε ἐν ὑμῖν μένοντα) because you do not believe in the one whom he has sent." Confessing this identity, which is clearly supported by reliable witnessing, is crucial to having eternal life (5:39-43).

In describing the course of Jesus' ministry, the Gospel writer also warns that the lack of confession of the permanent incarnation leads to division. While these conflict situations are often described as against or among "the Jews," the characterization of opponents in the Gospel often echoes the characterization of the opponents in the Epistles.[147] Already in the prologue the contrast is made between the light and the dark, between the Logos and the world (1:5; 9-13); the progressives were characterized as walking in darkness, and as being from the world (1 John 3:18-22). To the "Jews," he says, "and you do not have his word abiding in you (ἐν ὑμῖν μένοντα), because you do not believe him whom he has sent" (5:38; 1 John 2:22-24; 4:13-15; 5:10-12, 20-21; 2 John 7-9).

John 5, therefore, provides the other side of the belief coin. While the Nicodemus and Samaritan woman pericopes expand the "how" of the sharing of life and Spirit from the savior to the believing humanity, this chapter shows the possibility of schism if some do not hold to the correct Christology. In the following chapter, the elements in the narrative supporting the salvific implications and logistics of the indwelling Christology come unmistakably to the fore.

---

[147]Talbert, *Reading John*, 141-42. Schnelle sees the acute conflict in the Fourth Gospel as one with docetism rather than Judaism as well, but he interprets "the Jews" as "representatives of an unbelieving world" (*Antidocetic*, 36).

Flesh Expanded: The Bread of Life Discourse

This discourse has received renewed attention recently in response to Peder Borgen's 1965 monograph *Bread from Heaven*.[148] The significant works of Borgen and of Paul N. Anderson[149] have demonstrated satisfactorily, by means of quite different approaches, that John 6 should be read as a unity.[150] While these and other works raise interesting issues in themselves, our focus remains on how the permanence of the divine/human union, as well as its salvific results, is underscored as the text moves forward.

Jesus is yet again identified (and yet again, inadequately) as a prophet on account of a sign that he performed (6:14). The true import of the sign, however, begins to be unpacked with a renewed connection between "seeking" and "remaining" in 6:26-27: "You seek me not because you saw signs, but because you ate the loaves and were filled. Do not work for food that perishes but for food that remains (μένουσαν) to eternal life."[151] The connection to the death of Jesus becomes undeniable with Jesus' statement that he has "come down from heaven" to do the will of the Father, to lose nothing of what the Father has given him, and "to raise it up on the last day" (6:38-39). Spatial and existential intertwine here to introduce the expansion of the "how" of salvation. The identity of this person who comes down, works, and provides for resurrection is consistent.

Immediately an identification is made in the merely human sphere by the Jews who do not understand (6:42): "Is this not Jesus, the son of Joseph, whose father and mother we know? How does he say now, 'I have come down from heaven?'" They cannot believe, to use 1 John's phrase, that the Christ is Jesus. If there is any doubt that the full identification between the human and divine being is intended, that doubt is banished with the dramatic statement, "the bread that I will give for the life of the world is my flesh" (σάρξ, 6:51).

---

[148]Borgen, *Bread from Heaven: An Exegetical Study of the Concept of Manna in the Gospel of John and the Writings of Philo* (NovTSup 11; Leiden: Brill, 1965).

[149]Anderson, *The Christology of the Fourth Gospel.*

[150]That is, without a reordering of the text, so that the "tensions" that led previous interpreters such as Bultmann to redesign the text are unsubstantiated.

[151]Wilckens acknowledges here that "remaining" is a keyword of John's thought, but he reads the theological emphasis on the unity between the Father and Son, and the believers' participation in that divine life, rather than in the unity of the human and divine in Jesus Christ. Though our positions are certainly not incompatible, I suggest that the Gospel's emphasis on the continuity of the human and divine identities in Jesus Christ is fundamental to the enablement of the believers' remaining in the divine life. Ulrich Wilckens, *Das Evangelium nach Johannes* (NTD 4; Göttingen: Vandenhoeck & Ruprecht, 1998), 100; for Wilckens' arguments that the Gospel emphasizes the unity of the Father and Son in light of the charge of blasphemy, see also 170-72, 220-22, 332-36.

This is the first reference to the flesh of Jesus Christ since 1:14, and it is a dramatic expansion. The audience first heard "flesh" in 1:13, that those who received the true light were born not of the "will of the flesh," but of God. Then came the powerful yet enigmatic 1:14, that the Logos became flesh. Again in the Nicodemus pericope, what is born of flesh is inadequate compared to that which is born of Spirit. These meanings come to fruition in the six uses of "flesh" in this chapter (6:51, 52, 53, 54, 55, 56), all of which emphasize the "truth" of the flesh and its salvific effects. The possession at the baptism is central, not as anti-metamorphosis, but as anti-inspiration. It is only because of the indwelling union that the flesh can be given.

The expansion of the "flesh" continues as flesh is associated with blood and life: "unless you eat the flesh of the Son of man and drink his blood, you do not have life in you" (6:53). The opponents described in 1 John come to mind (water *and* blood), especially when we recall that Ignatius' opponents objected to the Eucharist as well.[152] We see here, then, the importance of the permanence of the relationship initiated in the baptism – the continuity during the crucifixion will be the glory, the salvific provision.[153]

This interpretation is strengthened in verse 56, with the appearance of μένω to express the mutual indwelling that will result from the union of Father and Son: "he who eats my flesh and drinks my blood remains (μένει) in me, and I in him." The relation to the baptism/possession is revealed in 6:63: "it is the spirit that gives life, the flesh does not profit. The words I have spoken to you are spirit and life." The flesh alone is merely flesh (echoing 3:6), but when enlivened by the spirit (baptism), enabled salvifically by the death, it is enlivened eternally.

Next, the ascending is stressed and connected with the spirit and life (6:62-63). Flesh only is of no avail, but the Spirit must be added, the same Spirit that entered the picture at Jesus' baptism and that comes through baptism (6:63). This passage does not indicate a contradiction[154] but the difference between the flesh of the unified being, divine with human, and that regular and inadequate flesh of the human that cannot be salvific in itself.

Later, when Jesus says he is the bread of life come down from heaven, the "Jews" complain, asserting that they know that this is Jesus, "the son

---

[152]Cf. Brown, *Gospel*, 292.

[153]While Brown (*Gospel*, 286) sees the Eucharistic meaning in vv. 51-58 as primary, he acknowledges that v. 51 both echoes the incarnation and looks toward the death (v. 51).

[154]Günther Bornkamm sees a contradiction between v. 63 and the other instances of "flesh" and concluded that 51c-58 were later sacramental additions; "Die eucharistische Rede im Johannes-Evangelium," *ZNW* 47 (1956): 161-69. Werner Stenger ties it to the merely "human" messianic expectation that Jesus is attempting to dissuade; "'Der Geist ist es, der lebendig macht, das Fleisch nützt nichts,'" *TTZ* 85 (1976): 116-22.

of Joseph, whose father and mother we know" (6:42). The spatial and existential once again closely intertwine as the importance of correct Christology for the enablement of permanent community is underlined. The discussion about Jesus' flesh and blood, which one must eat and drink to have life, causes murmuring and offense among the disciples and a statement from Jesus about future division (6:66-71). This theme fits well with the concept of the opponents in 1 John as docetists of some sort, since, as mentioned earlier, some docetists rejected any sacramental meaning in the Eucharist (6:50-69).

Just as the baptism of Jesus described the "how" (indwelling) of the "who" and "what" described in the prologue, the Bread of Life discourse describes in detail the "how" of the salvific results of this incarnation. The pericope, moreover, describes the "how" of schism, since those who reject the full identification of human and divine through the crucifixion and resurrection certainly cannot participate in the salvific consequences that impart life. The division seen in John 6 grows in the next chapters; surely the audience would hear echoes of opponents like those described in 1 John.

Community Rejected: Identity in John 7-8

The question of identity is the obsession of the pericopes in John 7, of Jesus' brothers (7:5) and some Jews (7:15) and some people in Jerusalem (7:25-27). The possibility of identifying the Christ with this human remains, at best, clouded. The spatial aspect is not neglected, as "the Jews" puzzle over where "this man" is going that they cannot find him (7:34-35).

Verses 37-38 present a problem. The so-called "western" punctuation of the verse provides a full stop after ὁ πιστεύων εἰς ἐμέ in 7:38, with no punctuation following πινέτω in 7:37, so that the passage would imply that Jesus, rather than the believer, is the source of living water." The "eastern" punctuation, on the other hand, provides the full stop after πινέτω, implying that the rivers of water will flow from the believer.[155] While the issue is difficult,[156] preference should probably be given to majority reading, that the water comes from Jesus, given the close ties with 19:34 (the blood and water issuing from the pierced side of Jesus).[157] Baptism, water, spirit and

---

[155]Talbert (*Reading John*, 148), for example, has recently argued for this interpretation given the "nearly exact parallel of 4:13-14, where Jesus gives the water that then becomes a spring within the believer."

[156]See, for example, the extended discussion in Brown, *Gospel*, 320-23.

[157]See esp. Schnelle, "Geisttheologie," 24. The verse will then tie closely with the baptism of Jesus on the one end of the narrative, and with the crucifixion on the other. It is possible, of course, for the audience to hear both meanings in the grammatically ambiguous statement, which would tie the verse with 4:13-14 as well. For the connection with 4:13-14 and a decision for the minority reading, see Talbert, *Reading John*, 148. For the "ambiguous

belief are, as usual, intertwined with correct christological confession, as the division among the people continues over identity: "Is the Christ to come from Galilee?" (7:41).

The images identifying the Logos/Christ with the human come thickly intertwined with existential and spatial images. John 8:13-14 relates that, once again, Jesus is witness of himself. In 8:12-20, the spatial aspect is highlighted as Pharisees ask "where is your father?" after Jesus has told them they cannot know from where he has come and where he is going. To Jews who refuse to understand his identity, he teaches them almost directly about the connection between his identity and the crucifixion: "When you have lifted up the Son of Man, then you will know that I am he" (8:28); division in the community occurs over the belief, and lack thereof, in the permanent identity of the human and divine through the crucifixion. To "the Jews who had believed in him," he teaches that if they remain (μείνητε) in his word, they are true disciples (8:31).

In the discussion on the parentage of Jesus' Jewish opponents, Boyarin points out that "the word of God appeared to Abraham" (Gen 15:1) and the Targum of Genesis 15:6, "Abraham believed in the Memra of God and he reckoned it from him as righteousness" shows that this entire Johannine passage is a midrash on Genesis 15.[158] In 8:39-41, "these Jews wish to claim precisely that because their father Abraham had received the Logos, and thereby became a child of God, they too have inherited that very status."[159] When Jesus declares that "your father Abraham rejoiced to see my day" and "before Abraham was, I am" (8:56, 58), these passages, to Boyarin, are "full of echoes of our verse in the Prologue."[160] This interpretation shows not only the connection of the prologue to the rest of the Gospel, but a "filling in" of the details of something only given in broadest outline in the prologue.

The three themes, therefore, that support an indwelling Christology are present in John 7-8. The permanence of the union is underlined particularly with the emphasis on witnessing. The requirement of permanent unity through death and resurrection to provide for salvation is emphasized with the full giving of the Spirit only after these events. The enablement of community depends upon the remaining in his word, though the probability of schism is underlined by the debates concerning Jesus' identity. This last point is highlighted in the next chapter.

---

option," see John Paul Heil, *Blood and Water: The Death and Resurrection of Jesus in John 18-21* (CBQMS 27; Washington: CBA, 1995), 109, and G. Bienaimé, "L'annonce des fleuves d'eau vive en Jean 7, 37-39," *RTL* 21 (1990): 281-310.

[158] Boyarin, "*Memra*," 275.

[159] Boyarin, "*Memra*," 275.

[160] Boyarin, "*Memra*," 276.

Union Rejected: The Man Who Sees and the Blind Pharisees

Chapter Nine stresses the identification between savior figure and the human, though it is a recognition that comes slowly in a context that the audience would have related to the sacrament of baptism.[161] First, Jesus is identified with the Father (9:10). When Jesus heals the blind beggar and people ask the beggar how it came to be that he is no longer blind, the man responds: "*The man called Jesus* made mud, spread it on my eyes, and said to me" etc. (9:11; my emphasis). The identification grows from a "man" (9:16), to a "prophet" (9:17), to Christ (9:22). The healed man's confession grows as well, as he ironically calls upon the spatial christological theme: "you do not know from where he comes, yet he opened my eyes" (9:30). The confluence of knowing and seeing is confirmed in 9:39-41. At the end of his monotonous interrogation by the Pharisees when the formerly blind man is put out of the synagogue, he again meets Jesus and confesses (with a little prompting) that this Jesus is the Son of Man as Jesus claims (9:35-38); here, the union of Jesus and Son of Man is fully acknowledged. The consequences of not holding a correct understanding of the identity of Jesus Christ closes the pericope: "your sin remains" (μένει, 9:41).

Union and New Life: The Shepherd Raises His Friend

Like the Wedding at Cana account, the Lazarus pericope and its surrounding material is striking in its ability to hold in tension the revelation of divinity in the context of an abiding human identity, a strategy necessary to demonstrate to the audience the indwelling pattern. Here, however, since identity has been well-established in the narrative, the audience is treated to an account that fully describes the salvific and communal consequences of the union. This expression in events of time and space prepare the audience for the full explanation of these themes that they will receive in the Farewell Discourse.

In John 10, the good shepherd teaching and the reaction to it prepares the audience for the Lazarus pericope. The intimacy between Jesus and the Father continues to be emphasized, and the salvific fulfillment of the incarnation is expressed again in the laying down of the savior's life (10:15-18). That intimacy is most dramatically emphasized in "I and the Father are one" (10:24); recall that Wisdom, Logos, *Memra* interweave in contemporary Jewish texts. The audience has been gradually prepared

---

[161]Brown (*Gospel*, 381) gives the two primary arguments for the connection with baptism: (1) the man is healed only when he washes in the pool of Siloam, the source of the water for Tabernacles that Jesus now supplants (7:37-38), and (2) the man was *born* blind, so that the contrast with spiritual blindness (9:39) insinuates that the sin with which humans are born can only be removed by cleansing waters.

by the cultural expectations it brought to the text and by the narrative itself for this statement and its implications. The assertion reinforces their knowledge gained through the narrative and wraps up a portion of the Gospel that has spelled out exactly what this means, to which the works bear witness (10:25; cf. 5:36). The "Jews" accuse him of the ultimate identity crisis: though he is a man, he makes himself God (10:33). Jesus repeats his statement of mutual indwelling: "The Father is in me and I am in the Father" (10:38).

Echoes of the opponents in the Epistles can be heard in the identification of Jesus as the good shepherd and the false teachers as wolves (10:1-30),[162] a passage which contains teaching about the necessity of Jesus' death and the resurrection, as well as about his own power to accept or to reject that death (10:15-18); again, there is division on account of this teaching (10:19-21). This conflict passage underscores the unity of the divine being with the human Jesus and the salvific results of the crucifixion. The context immediately turns to baptism as Jesus goes back across the Jordan "to the place where John first was baptizing, and there he remained" (ἔμεινεν, 10:40). I suggest that the appearance of the details of baptism and remaining also serve the purpose of reminding the audience of Jesus' baptism and the indwelling that occurred there.

The story of the raising of Lazarus begins with a framework of very human relationships, as Jesus is told that a friend "whom he loves" is ill (11:3). The point that Jesus remained (ἔμεινεν) where he was for two more days has been interpreted to mean that the day the message came to Jesus, plus these two days, plus the day he traveled to Lazarus equals the four days of verse 17, the necessary time to be sure Lazarus was truly dead.[163] The spatial use of μένω here seems at this point trivial, but it will later prove to be less so. This pericope is both the most profound expression of the power of the Son of Man and also contains the most poignant portrayals of Jesus' humanity, in which Jesus is described as loving his friend (11:3, 5), being deeply troubled (11:33, 38), and weeping (11:35). There is no indication of displacement here: the same person who said "I and the Father are one" and is about to resuscitate someone displays quite human reactions and emotions.

The story continues its stress on the relationship between union and salvation. "I am the resurrection and the life" underlines the resurrection as a necessary witness to the salvific life (11:25). Interwoven in the account is Martha's confession that her friend Jesus is the "Christ, the Son of God, the one coming (ἐρχόμενος; see 2 John 7) into the world" (11:27). "Coming"

---

[162]Talbert, *Reading John,* 166. This connection is strengthened by evidence that other early Christian texts used the term "wolves" for those people with different beliefs who could lead believers astray; cf. Brown, *Gospel,* 1.395-96.

[163]Brown, *Gospel,* 431, 434; Schnackenburg, *Gospel,* 2.324.

shows the continuing identity, as it does in 2 John 7. Again, immediately after some of Jesus' Jewish opponents discuss his (salvific) death (11:50-53), the verb μένω recurs as Jesus goes to the town Ephraim and remains (ἔμεινεν) there with the disciples (11:54). The Lazarus pericope, then, is framed with this verb, a cue to the audience not to stray far from their knowledge of the true christological confession in the face of opposition.

The request to see the human miracle-worker Jesus (12:21) sets off a substantial articulation of identity, existential interwoven with spatial, with an emphasis on the necessary death of this person (12:24; 32). This Son of Man retains the human capacity to be troubled and to understand the human tendency to want to avoid the trial required to be glorified, but in the same breath to pray "Father, glorify your name" (12:27-28).[164] The death by crucifixion as part of glorification is underlined (12:32). The crowd, however, though they have witnessed to him in the sense of a miracle-worker (12:17), does not yet understand the full identification of the human and divine. They argue that "the Christ remains (μένει) forever" (12:34) but ask the identity of this Son of Man who must be lifted up (12:34). Jesus reshapes the terminology to the emphasis on light, recalling the audience's expectations of the light associated with Logos/Wisdom/ Memra; the title Son of Man is by this means brought more clearly than before into this sphere.

For the characters in the narrative, however, the effort is to little avail. When Jesus teaches the crowd in Jerusalem about his salvific death and resurrection that will draw all people to himself, they respond that they "have heard from the law that the Messiah remains forever" (ὁ χριστὸς μένει εἰς τὸν αἰῶνα) so that they do not understand because, while they have the concept of the Christ, they do not understand the incarnation (12:27-36). Immediately Jesus tells them to walk in the light and avoid the darkness (12:35-36), to believe in the one who sent him, since "I have come (ἐλήλυθα) as light into the world, so that everyone who believes in me should not remain (μείνῃ) in the darkness" (12:44-46; 1 John 1:5-7; 2:9-11). Lack of the proper confession leads to division.

To summarize, in John 1:35-12:50, the audience has been presented with an explication in space and time of the dramatic but ambiguous "the Logos became flesh" (1:14) and of the indwelling of divine and human in one person (1:33-34). Repeatedly the divine identity of Jesus Christ has been demonstrated in the context of an abiding human identity. There can be no question of displacement of the human mind, and there are no signs of ecstatic behavior. Nor is any evidence presented that would lead

---

[164]Barker (*Angel*, 97-113; 208) argues that the "Name" is another moniker for the "second god" in Judaism; if this suggestion proves correct, it would fit into the constellation of terms (Logos, Son, Spirit, *Memra*) we have identified already as operative in the Fourth Gospel to describe the divine being who fully indwells the human Jesus.

the audience to think that this union will not survive the suffering and
death of Jesus; on the contrary, the crucifixion and resurrection are quickly
and frequently depicted as necessary for the enablement of salvation and
community. The hypothesis that there are opponents in view has been
strengthened by the narrative's recurring insistence on the division and
lack of understanding caused by making christological errors.[165] The
Farewell Discourse will emphasize these aspects and bind them to a
description of what has until now been described only occasionally and
with brevity: the role of the Spirit.

Enabling Union: The Foot Washing and the Farewell Discourse

As Jesus' public ministry ends and he turns to instructing his followers,
we see the theme of incarnation setting in motion the enablement of unity
in the community. "On arrival at 13:1, the reader is asking crucial questions:
how is it possible that crucifixion can be glorification, gathering, the
revelation of God?"[166] John 13-17 provides a direct and extended teaching
on how these elements relate to crucifixion and to the community by
means of the indwelling model. We will see the payoff for the audience of
the accumulated ideas attained through the hearing of the Gospel.[167]

---

[165]The current scholarly orthodoxy, of course, is that John 2-12 focuses on a controversy
with the synagogue (following the Martyn-Brown reconstruction of the Johannine community).
I would make two additional points in opposition to the majority opinion. First, the attempt to
relate the date of the composition of the Gospel to the *birkat ha-minim*, and the *birkat ha-minim*
to a particular Yavneh council, is a failed one. See, for example, Peter Schäfer, "Die sogenannte
Synode von Jabne," *Jud* 31 (1975): 54-64, 116-24; Ronald Kimelman, "'Birkat Ha-Minim' and the
Lack of Evidence for an Anti-Christian Jewish Prayer in Late Antiquity," *Jewish and Christian
Self-Definition* (Vol. 2; ed. E. P. Sanders, et. al.; Philadelphia: Fortress, 1981), 226-44 and Schnelle,
Antidocetic, 25-31. This conclusion opens the door to a different understanding of the conflict
in John 2-12. Second, another way to understand the controversy of the chapters is to see the
reference to Jewish controversy in the manner of "covert allusion" as described by Demetrius
in *On Style* 5.292: rather than addressing opponents directly, Demetrius notes the advisability
of directing blame to those who have acted in a similar way. The suggestion that "the Jews" are
straw men for christological opponents who have fractured the community has the additional
advantage of helping to explain the odd and inconsistent use of the term "the Jews" in the
Gospel. That the struggle with the synagogue is a past one in reference to the composition to
the Gospel has been suggested by, for example, Ulrich Luz and Rudolf Smend, *Gesetz* (Biblische
Konfrontationen; Stuttgart: Kohlhammer, 1981), 125 and Schnelle, *Antidocetic*, 31-36.

[166]Moloney, "The Function of John 13-17 within the Johannine Narrative," in *"What is
John?" Literary and Social Readings of the Fourth Gospel* (vol. 2; ed. Fernando F. Segovia; Atlanta:
Scholars Press, 1998), 48.

[167]The repetition of material in 13:31-14:31 and 15:1-16:33 has often been considered a
sign of multiple redactions of the text; for an overview of the various solutions, see Brown,
Gospel, 581-86. Moloney ("Function," 44) asserts that "however obvious the literary seams

First, let us review how the five themes have shaped the Gospel to the indwelling pattern to this point. John 1:1-34 provided the audience with a statement of the identities of the divine being and of the human, as well as a description of how the union of the two took place, one that made sense to the audience familiar with the possession pattern of how a god appeared on earth to interact with humans. Within the possession pattern, however, there could be substantial variation. As the narrative progressed, the audience saw no signs of ecstatic behavior nor of the displacement of the human mind of Jesus; rather, the narrative emphasized a continuity of the human identity of Jesus as a framework for the revelations of divinity. The narrative also provided indicators that the union between the divine and human will be permanent; that is, that this union maintained through the death and resurrection is in fact necessary to provide the full results desired for the enablement of permanent salvation and community. Rejecting this identity has been condemned as tragically divisive, just as it was denounced in the Johannine Epistles.

The emphasis on the permanence of the unity between the divine being and human possessed by that being (our third theme) is directly depicted in the introduction to the Farewell Discourse (FD), the foot washing episode in John 13.[168] The foot washing action is described in the context of Jesus' love for his own (13:1, 23) and his troubled spirit concerning the one relationship he knows is already broken (13:21-28). The audience is never allowed to forget the humanity of the one before them: he can be troubled in spirit over Judas just as he is about to proclaim the final teaching of the mutual glorification of the Father and the Son of Man (13:31). Just as in the Wedding at Cana and the Lazarus pericopes, the revelation of divine glory is introduced into a framework through which the human continuity is carefully underscored.

The primary contribution of the FD is the transition from an emphasis on this union and its continuation through death and resurrection to a stress on how this permanence in the correct christological confession leads to unity in the community. This accent is introduced in the foot washing episode (John 13). Brown points out that while many commentators are

---

might be to the eye of the literary and historical critic, a reader is challenged to make something of the last discourse as it stands." Talbert (*Reading John*, 202) is surely correct, however, when he asserts that the repetitions should be seen as consistent with rules of Hellenistic rhetoric as described, for example, in *Rhetorican ad Herrennium* 4.42.54: "We shall not repeat the same thing precisely – for that, to be sure, would weary the hearer and not elaborate the idea – but with changes." Fernando Segovia approaches it as a whole as well, but from the perspective of the genre of a farewell type-scene; cf. Segovia, *The Farewell of the Word. The Johannine Call to Abide* (Minneapolis: Fortress, 1991), esp. 2-20.

[168]For the foot washing as an introduction to what follows, see Talbert, *Reading John*, 189. For 13:1-3 as an introduction to the entire Farewell Discourse, see Ridderbos, *Gospel*, 455-57.

satisfied with the foot washing as an example of humility, the emphasis on the cleansing from sin in 13:10, as well as the assertion in v. 7 that full understanding will come only later (apparently after the resurrection) leave many looking for a deeper significance.[169] Haenchen points out the shift in the narrative from νίπτειν in the washing of feet to λούειν in verse 10, "which seems to refer to baptism, the value of which then surpasses foot washing."[170] Though Brown recognizes this as a secondary interpretation, he maintains that the "simplest" explanation of the event "remains that Jesus performed this servile task to prophesy symbolically that he was about to be humiliated in death," a death that would bring his followers into union with him and cleanse them of sin, since Peter's rebellious question compares closely with his rebellion at the first teaching about the suffering of the Son in Mark 8:31-33.[171] Talbert suggests that the forgiveness of one another's daily trespasses that enables true community is paramount, though the connection with baptism would not be an unexpected connection for the audience to make.[172] What the interpretations share is that this person who has been fully demonstrated as human and divine will maintain this identity throughout a complete giving up of self, symbolized in the "humiliation" of foot washing, to enable community.

The emphasis on the union as necessary to make Jesus' death and resurrection salvific plays out in the FD with the clearest statements to date of the somewhat shocking idea that crucifixion is of one piece with resurrection, and that this unified "hour" equals glorification.[173] This concept is not a denial of the suffering of Jesus but rather a recognition that the means of the divine plan for salvation is defined by its result. In John 13:31 the "glory" from the prologue, first explicated in time and space in the Wedding at Cana, is spoken of by Jesus as achieved in its fullness, displaying the certainty of its fulfillment in this one "hour" that incorporates final teaching, passion, and resurrection: "Now is the Son of Man glorified (ἐδοξάσθη), and God is glorified (ἐδοξάσθη) in him."[174]

At its final occurrence in 13:31, the use of the Son of Man title in the Fourth Gospel and its relationship to the permanent identity of this person

---

[169]Brown, Gospel, 559.

[170]Haenchen, John, 2.108.

[171]Brown, Gospel, 568.

[172]Talbert, Reading John, 194-95; cf. W. L. Knox, "John 13.1-30," HTR 43 (1950): 161-63.

[173]For the audience's preparation for this throughout the Gospel, see Moloney, "Function," 47-48.

[174]Most commentators read this aorist passive ("is glorified") as speaking "of an event that is still future as though it had occurred, so certain is the Johannine Jesus of what is to transpire" (Talbert, Reading John, 198), which some call a "prophetic perfect" (Barnabas Lindars, The Gospel of John (NCB; Greenwood, S. C.: Attic, 1972), 426; Burkett, Son of Man, 125.

may now be examined in light of the indwelling pattern. The spatial and existential emphases of the term fit perfectly into the narrative's demonstration of the identity of the savior. Schnackenburg lists the thirteen occurrences (twelve in the previous narrative and the final one in the FD) and demonstrates that they are a unity in this Gospel.[175] The Son of Man descended from and ascends to heaven (3:13; 6:62) and is exalted and glorified (3:4; 8:28; 12:23, 34c; 13:31).[176] The occurrences of the name in the Bread of Life discourse (6:27, 53, 62) "form a unity, since they link the statements about the bread which Jesus is in person and which he gives believers or the partakers of the Eucharist."[177] These uses fit into the overall schema in the context of the salvific nature of Jesus', the Son of Man's, flesh for community: the Son of Man is "the bread from heaven in person."[178] John 1:51 provides the basis for the later assertions of descent and ascent, while the allusion to judgment in 5:27 shapes the eschatological concept of the Son of Man to the Johannine context of "present salvation or condemnation."[179]

Schnackenburg is certainly correct, and I would only add that the Son of Man title has been adopted into the Johannine system by one other means: by being placed into descent/ascent pattern *and* emphasized as the expression of the union with flesh whose eating is salvific, the Son of Man is integrated into the binitarian images of Logos, Son of God, Christ, and *Memra* that we explored in the discussion on the prologue.[180] Brown points out that comparisons of 13:31 with 17:1 and 3:13-17 "suggest that for John the title 'Son of Man' had become interchangeable with 'the Son

---

[175]Schnackenburg, *Gospel*, 1.530-32. The verses are 1:51; 3:13, 14; 5:27; 6:27, 53, 62; 8:28; 9:35; 12:23, 34 (2x); 13:31.

[176]Schnackenburg, *Gospel*, 1.530; cf. Meeks, *Interpretation*, 147-48. Burkett (*Son of Man*, 127) has added the important note that the return to *previous* glory is best understood as a reference to God in Isa 6:1-3, in which "glory" (LXX: δόξα) appears twice in the description of God on the throne (vv. 1, 3), a text referred to by John in 12:37-41. This addition ties the "servant of Yahweh" who is "lifted up and glorified" (Isa 52:13) to the preexistent one.

[177]Schnackenburg, *Gospel*, 1.530.

[178]Schnackenburg, *Gospel*, 1.531.

[179]Schnackenburg, *Gospel*, 1.531-32. Schnackenburg's reading in the Fourth Gospel is superior to the standard division, as seen in Brown (*Gospel*, 88-89), of the Son of Man sayings into three separate categories primarily on the basis of the synoptic evidence.

[180]Cf. Barker, *Angel*, 225-28. This suggestion coheres with Son of Man studies that see the use of the title in the descent/ascent pattern in John connected to the figure of Wisdom; see, for example, F.-M. Braun, "Messie, Logos et Fils de l'Homme," in *La Venue du Messie: Messianisme et Eschatologie* (RB 6; ed. E. Massaux; New York: Desclée de Brouwer, 1962), 140-47; H. R. Moeller, "The Ascent and Descent of the Son of Man in the Gospel of St. John," *ATR* 39 (1957), 116-17; R. Maddox, "The Function of the Son of Man in the Gospel of John," *Reconciliation and Hope: New Testament Essays on Atonement and Eschatology* (ed. R. Banks; Grand Rapids: Eerdmans, 1974): 188-89.

[of God]."[181] The shaping of the Son of the Man title, then, has become one more thread throughout the narrative connecting various expressions of the union of human and divine in Jesus Christ.[182]

Before the role of the Spirit is described in a radically expanded manner, the indwelling motif is recalled both spatially and existentially in 14:1-14 as Jesus teaches on the place he has prepared for the disciples, in which the indwelling will be made tangible when Jesus leaves, then returns to take them to himself (πρὸς ἐμαυτόν, 14:3). It is possible because of the indwelling between Jesus and the Father, so that if the believer truly sees Jesus, that person is indwelling with the both Father and Son (14:5-11).[183]

The necessity of the union that occurred at Jesus' baptism is recalled in this teaching through the use of μένω. Immediately after giving his disciples the love commandment that played such a large part in the author of 1 John's argument against the opponents, Jesus assures the disciples: "In my Father's house there are many dwelling places" (μοναὶ πολλαί; 14:2). As Brown asserts, the best interpretation of μοναί is to relate it to the cognate verb μένω, "frequently used in John in reference to staying, remaining, or abiding with Jesus and with the Father."[184] The question of where he is immediately going intertwines with the existential "I am the way, and the truth and the life" (14:4-7). "From now on you know him and have seen him" (14:7). The difficulty of believing that divinity exists with the human, continues among the disciples even at this point (14:8-9). "I am in the Father and the Father is in me" (14:10).

Between the uses of μοναί as the rooms in the Father's house and the vine metaphor in John 15, two ways of visually portraying indwelling of the believers with the Father and the Son, is introduced in the role of the Spirit. This emphasis on the Spirit in itself reflects the permanence of the incarnation through the resurrection, since already in 7:39 we read that even though Jesus taught about the Spirit, "as yet there was no Spirit, because Jesus was not yet glorified." Now Jesus tells them that "I will pray to the Father, and he will give you another Paraclete to be with you forever, the Spirit of truth, whom the world is not able to receive, because it neither sees him nor knows him. You know him, because he remains (μένει) in you and you in him" (14:16-17). Knowing, seeing and remaining

---

[181]Brown, *Gospel*, 611.

[182]I have sought to highlight this one function of the Son of Man title in the narrative, of course, and left aside the important questions of its history of religions background and the relation of the Johannine use to that of the synoptics. For a review of those issues, see esp. Burkett, *The Son of Man Debate: A History and Evaluation* (previously cited).

[183]As Brown (*Gospel*, 627) correctly points out, there is no indication in the narrative that this indwelling will take place only in heaven; on the contrary, it is Jesus' body that is the Father's house, "and wherever the glorified Jesus is, there is the Father."

[184]Brown, *Gospel*, 619.

are intertwined with the enabling ministry of the Paraclete in the face of a lack of commitment to christological permanence.

John 14:16 has introduced the dramatic expansion of the role of the Spirit, the same Spirit to whom the audience was introduced as the possessor in the baptism of Jesus, the same Spirit with whom they are familiar from their cultural inheritance as one who possesses humans temporarily or permanently, causing ecstatic behavior or not, displacing the human mind or not. The use of μένω combined with the teaching on the role of the Spirit recalls for the audience the baptism of Jesus. Jesus promises that he will send the Spirit of Truth who "abides with you, and he will be in you" (παρ᾽ ὑμῖν μένει καὶ ἐν ὑμῖν ἔσται, 14:17). "Far from attempting to point to a different figure, the author appears to be stressing the identity of function between the earthly Jesus and the abiding Spirit. Hence he can say in the next verse, 'I will not leave you bereft; I am coming back to you.'"[185] To those who are the in community and are able, or rather enabled, to keep Christ's word, "we will come to them and make our home with them" (πρὸς αὐτὸν ἐλευσόμεθα καὶ μονὴν παρ᾽ αὐτῷ ποιησόμεθα; 14:23; cf. 16:5-16). Note again the interplay between the spatial and existential meanings of μένω. The permanence of the incarnation results in the sending of the Spirit, which enables the enduring unity of God with the faithful community (14:25).

The Paraclete's relation to Jesus supports the hypothesis that the Logos/Spirit permanently possessed Jesus. Isaacs' summary is worth quoting at length.

> Even after Jesus's death the spirit-paraclete is closely connected, if not identified, with him. John uses similar language with which to describe the paraclete and the earthly Jesus, and he also shows them performing parallel tasks. Both were sent by (14:16; 5:30; 8:16) or proceeded from (15:16; 8:42; 13:3) the Father; both are visibly only to the believer (14:17; 1:10, 12; 8:14, 19; 17:8) and are rejected by the world. Just as Jesus taught the truth (7:16f.; 8:32, 40-42), so the paraclete's function will be to lead to all truth (14:26; 16:13). Both bear witness (8:14, 18; 15:26), since they do not speak on their own account (16:13; 7:16f.; 12:49f.; 14:24). The ministry of both is to convict the world of sin (3:20; 7:7; 15:26; 16:8). In relation to the disciples both Jesus and the spirit perform the role of παράκλητος, i.e. helper. The spirit's task is to continue this same helping function as Jesus and therefore it is called ἄλλος παράκλητος (14:17). It is possible with Bornkamm[186] to describe Jesus as the forerunner of the paraclete, if by

---

[185]M. E. Isaacs, *The Concept of the Spirit: A Study of Pneuma in Hellenistic Judaism and Its Bearing on the New Testament* (Heythrop Monographs 1; London: Heythrop, 1976), 123.

[186]Gunther Bornkamm, "Der Paraklet im Johannesevangelium," in *Festschrift Rudolf Bultmann zum 65 Geburtstag überreicht* (ed. E. Wolf; Stuttgart: W. Kohlhammer, 1949), 12-35. Isaacs also cites (n. 93) Brown, "The Paraclete in the Fourth Gospel," *NTS* 13 (1967): 123.

'forerunner' one does not imply any subordination, but wishes to stress
the element of continuity between Jesus and the spirit.[187]

Though Isaacs cites Brown's article on the Paraclete, Brown had already
gone a step farther than Isaacs. Brown combines the Jewish prophetic
understanding of possession by the Spirit with the forensic understanding
of Jewish angelology to help explain the concept of the Paraclete in the
Fourth Gospel, emphasizing "how much the holy spirit, angelic spirit,
and Spirit of Truth had come together in pre-Christian Judaism."[188] In this
period of Judaism one finds all the functions that the Fourth Evangelist
combined into one Paraclete figure:

> [A] tandem relationship of two salvific figures corresponding to the
> tandem relationship of Jesus and the Paraclete; the passing on of his spirit
> by the main salvific figure; God's granting a spirit which would enable the
> recipient to understand and interpret divine deed and word authoritatively;
> a personal (angelic) Spirit who would lead the chosen ones against the forces
> of evil, even as the Paraclete brings about the condemnation of the Prince
> of this world; personal (angelic) Spirits who teach men and guide them to
> the truth. And in the passages describing these various relationships and
> spirits there is much of the vocabulary of witnessing, teaching, guiding,
> and accusing that appears in the Johannine Paraclete passages.[189]

Brown also highlights four correspondences between the ministries of Jesus
and the Paraclete: (1) the Paraclete "comes," is "sent" and "given" just as
Jesus has "come," been "sent" and "given;" (2) the Paraclete is "another
Paraclete," which implies that Jesus was the first Paraclete, an interpretation
supported by 1 John 2:1; (3) the indwelling of the Paraclete with the disciples
is described identically to the indwelling of Jesus and the disciples (described
typically with μένω or εἶναι ἐν), and (4) the world does not recognize and
hates the Paraclete just as it does not recognize and hates Jesus.[190]

Brown concludes that the Paraclete is Jesus: "Since the Paraclete can
come only when Jesus departs, the Paraclete is the presence of Jesus when
Jesus is absent."[191] This conclusion is to my mind strengthened by Isaacs'

---

[187]Isaacs, *Spirit*, 122.

[188]Brown, "Paraclete," 113-32; quotation from 123.

[189]Brown, "Paraclete," 123.

[190]Brown, "Paraclete," 126-27.

[191]Brown, "Paraclete, 128. Cf. J. D. G. Dunn, *Jesus and the Spirit* (Philadelphia:
Westminster, 1975), 350; Porsch, *Pneuma*, 139-45. Brown ("Paraclete," 128-232) suggests
that the evangelist wanted to connected Christ and the church because of the delay of the
parousia and the death of eye-witnesses. George Johnston (*The Spirit-Paraclete in the Gospel
of John* [SNTSM 12; Cambridge: Cambridge University Press, 1970], 119-25) agrees with the
identification of Jesus and the Spirit, but thinks that the intention was to connect the Spirit to
the historical ministry in an effort to combat the de-historicizing effects of docetic thought.

argument that the Paraclete is modeled on the figure of Wisdom.[192] Rather than having to decide whether the Paraclete is modeled on the Christ/ Logos sent from God, or Wisdom, or for that matter, the Son or *Memra*, what we see is the confluence of function and identity in the binitarian conceptual world.

These commentators do not take the final step that makes perfect sense of what they describe, the step that the Fourth Gospel employs an indwelling model in which the permanent possession of Jesus by the Spirit is described in 1:33-34 and controls the interpretation of the relationship between them. The equating of Jesus and the Paraclete in the FD provides the strongest evidence yet of the true union that occurred at the baptism, a possession that was not characterized by ecstatic behavior, a temporary nature, or displacement of the human mind, but something much more extensive. The relationship between Jesus and the Paraclete highlights a radical extension of the traditional pattern, one only vaguely envisioned by the eschatological visions of the full and permanent possession of the Spirit by the Messiah and the outpouring of the Spirit on believers. The humanity of Jesus of Nazareth has been brought into the binitarian understandings previously described in the culture by terms such Logos, Son, angel, Spirit and *Memra*! Jesus can give the Spirit, and remain himself, because the Spirit is not diminished by giving, as Philo points out in the case of Moses sharing the Spirit with the seventy elders (*Giants*, 26-27).

Now that the means of indwelling is clear, the pinnacle of indwelling comes with the vine pericope of John 15, where the term μένω comes to full fruition.[193] The prominence of the vocabulary entertains the ear by the figure of the vine and the branches (15:1-11), as Jesus encourages unity and berates schism using the themes of permanence and impermanence.

> Remain (μείνατε) in me as I in you. Just as the branch cannot bear fruit by itself unless it remains (μένῃ) in the vine, neither can you unless you remain (μένητε) in me...Whoever does not remain (μένῃ) in me is thrown away like a branch and withers...If you remain (μείνητε) in me, and my words remain (μείνῃ) in you, ask for whatever you wish, and it will be done for you (15:4-7).

---

[192]Isaacs, *Concept*, esp. 20-25, 50-55. For an example of the contrasting opinion, see Herman Ridderbos, *The Gospel of John: A Theological Commentary* (trans. John Vriend; Grand Rapids: Eerdmans, 1992), 503-04.

[193]This chapter as the culmination point for me,nw is recognized by Gottlob Spörri, *Das Evangelium nach Johannes* (2 vols.; Zürich: Zwingli-Verlag, 1950), 1.29. Spörri points out in his comments on Jesus' baptism that the pattern of this verb in the Gospel allows the Fourth Evangelist to depict the overcoming of all that is transitory by the saving actions of Jesus.

The indwelling of the believer with the Father and Son is enabled by the indwelling that was initiated at the baptism; here, the full implications of the Spirit that "remained on Jesus" are revealed. It is only appropriate that the importance of witnessing continues as well, with both the Paraclete and the disciples who have been along since the beginning cited as witnesses (15:26-27).

The Spirit's enabling of community is emphasized in John 16 with a focus on the parallel spatial aspects of Jesus and the Paraclete. Both 16:5 ("But I am going now to him who sent me, yet none of you asks me 'where are you going?'") and 16:28 ("I came from the Father and have come into the world; again, I am leaving the world and going to the Father") highlight spatial aspects. They serve as a frame for the disciples' identity that will be defined by the presence of the Paraclete: "It is to your advantage that I leave, for if I do not leave, the Paraclete will not come to you, but if I go, I will send him to you" (16:7), and "When the Spirit of truth comes, he will guide you in all the truth" (16:13).

This insistence on true community is accompanied in the Johannine literature by warnings against succumbing to impermanence, that is, not believing that the Christ and Jesus are fully and permanently united. Throughout the foot washing and FD, allusions exist that would surely be heard against those who are leaving or having left the community. The case of Judas, for example, warns that having been a member of the group (sharing in the reciprocal relationships of meal and foot washing, baptizing and being baptized) does not in and of itself entail that the relationship will be permanent, just as with the opponents of the Epistles. The branches that wither on the vine (15:6) perhaps had names to the audience! The expected hatred of the world warns the disciples of exactly the type of event described in 1 John 3:13 and 4:6. The emphasis on the Spirit and on disciples who have been with Jesus from the beginning as witnesses (15:26-27) could be heard as showing the impossibility of denying that Jesus Christ has come in the flesh (1 John 4:1-2).[194]

Nowhere is the warning more obvious than in John 17, Jesus' final prayer for the community, which may be read as a reflection on how to prevent schism. Jesus' prayers for the unity of the community have such intensity that commentators have noted that the schism in the Johannine community is probably in mind (see esp. 17:11, 20-26).[195] Moloney correctly points out that the audience well-knows the fragility of those for whom Jesus prays (cf. 13:21-30, 36-38): "The reader is well aware that they have succumbed to the attractions of the world on more than

---

[194]Talbert, *Reading John*, 217; cf. Brown, *Gospel*, 2.700-01.

[195]Talbert, *Reading John*, 229, who cites G. R. Beasley-Murray, *Word Biblical Commentary: John* (Waco, TX: Word, 1987), 307.

one occasion and that Judas has already gone out into the darkness."[196] Jesus prays, "as you sent me into the world, so I have sent them into the world" (17:18); it is clear, of course, that the world will hate them. Yet their indwelling with Jesus and the Father in love will enable their love of one another and, therefore, their enduring unity: "The glory that you have given me I have given to them, so that they may be one just as we are one" (17:22; cf. 1 John 1:3).

The consequences of the true human and divine union described in the prologue and the baptism have been fully explained in the FD. It only remains for the final part of the "hour" of glorification to play out in the passion and resurrection, the ultimate proof that the Christ is Jesus and that a permanent status as children of God is therefore possible for the believers who remain in the correct understanding of indwelling Christology.

Passion and Resurrection: Identity Fulfilled

If my hypothesis is correct, that the Gospel asserts the indwelling model over the inspiration model, an intense emphasis on the continued identity between the Christ and Jesus should appear in the account of the crucifixion and continue throughout the resurrection. In the passion, the narrative accentuates the abiding union of human and divine particularly at three points: (1) the exchange between Jesus and Pilate; (2) the scene at the cross involving Jesus, his mother, and the Beloved Disciple, and (3) the issuing of blood and water from the pierced side of Jesus. In the resurrection narratives, the continuing identity of the divine/human savior is depicted with a strategy familiar to the audience, in which the revelation of divinity occurs in the context of the resumption of recognizable human relationships.

Salvific Union: The Passion and Crucifixion

Chapter 18 reiterates the identity of Jesus Christ, beginning with the arrest of Jesus. The existential answer is underlined thoroughly in 18:1-3, which provides a context of human relationships and leaves no doubt that this person is the same one the audience knows from the entire narrative. Jesus twice asks those who come to arrest him, "whom do you seek?" (18:4, 7; echoing 1:38). Twice they ask for the man Jesus of Nazareth (18:5, 7), yet when he says "I am," they fall to the ground (18:5), recognizing the sudden revelation of divinity in what has appeared to this point to be a merely human situation.[197]

---

[196]Moloney, "Function," 60.

[197]Falling down at the mention of the divine revelation is found in Dan 2:46, 8:18; Rev 1:17 (Brown, *Gospel*, 818).

During the Roman trial, Pilate initiates a discussion of identity: "are you the king of the Jews?" (18:33). Jesus responds, "For this I was born (γεγέννημαι) and for this I have come (ἐλήλυθα) into the world, to witness to the truth" (18:37). This is the first reference from Jesus to his birth, though we have seen forms of ἔρχομαι as a christological term in the Epistles and Gospel. The two statements reflect, I suggest, not the same moment of origin, but two successive moments of the coming into the world of the beings, human (at birth) and divine (at baptism), now united in one "moment," a similar strategy as the crucifixion and resurrection united into one "hour." The spatial element of existential identity is introduced with the charge that Jesus has "made himself the Son of God" (19:7), which prompts Pilate's question, "where are you from?" (19:9). Pilate's question makes little sense except as the thematic culmination of the active questioning of Jesus' origins. At this point, silence rather than argument is the appropriate response, since the events taking place will culminate in the definitive demonstration of his identity.

Before moving to the telling scene at the foot of the cross, we should note that an anti-docetic assertion has been considered possible in the insistence that Jesus himself bore his own cross (19:17), given the involvement of Simon in the synoptic accounts and the stories of docetic metamorphosis Christology (cited in my Chapter Four) in which Simon was said to have been crucified instead of Jesus. If, however, the baptism of Jesus defines the "how" of the incarnation announced in 1:14, the audience has yet to hear a direct argument in the narrative against metamorphosis Christology. Schnackenburg's analysis, therefore, is closer the mark within the Johannine strategy: this motif accentuates the complete control and self-surrender of Jesus in this situation, just as he met those sent to arrest him (18:4-8) and will die of his own free will (19:30; cf. 10:17-18) after fully drinking the cup his Father has given him (19:28-29; cf. 4:34; 18:11).[198]

The mutual giving over by Jesus of his mother and the Beloved Disciple at the foot of the cross (19:26-27) has been variously interpreted. Schnackenburg, for example, after surveying several options, decides on the interpretation of Mary as the representative "of all who seek true salvation" and a reminder of the Jewish source of the community.[199] Brown notes well the connection with the Wedding at Cana story and describes Mary as the new Eve/Lady Zion, mother of the new community founded at the foot of the cross and symbolized by the Beloved Disciple.[200] I suggest

---

[198]Schnackenburg, *Gospel*, 3.270; cf. Heil, *Blood and Water*, 84; Ignace de la Potterie, *The Hour of Jesus: The Passion and the Resurrection of Jesus according to John* (N.Y.: Alba, 1989), 93; F. F. Bruce, *The Gospel & Epistles of John* (Grand Rapids: Eerdmans, 1983), 366.

[199]Schnackenburg, *Gospel*, 3.276-83.

[200]Her role had been "rejected" at Cana because it was not yet the proper time; Brown, *Gospel*, 923-27; cf. Heil, *Blood and Water*, 96-97.

that at its most basic level, the passage provides the human framework for the revelation of divinity that is about to occur on the cross in 19:30. The connection in this manner with the Cana story, as well as with the stress on the continuing human identity and relationships provided for the Farewell Discourse, is apparent. The founding of new community is also present, but is only enabled by the abiding union of the human and divine through the crucifixion.

When Jesus died, he "handed over the Spirit" (19:30). As Moloney argues, "the Greek must be taken seriously," rendering as "handed over," "delivered," or "entrusted," rather than "gave up" and "the Spirit" rather than "his spirit."[201] Brown recognizes that the phrasing emphasizes Jesus giving over the Spirit to those standing at the foot of the cross, especially to his mother ("the Church or new people of God") and to the Beloved Disciple ("the Christian"). "In 7:39 John affirmed that those who believed in Jesus were to receive the Spirit once Jesus had been glorified, and so it would not be inappropriate that at this climactic moment in the hour of glorification there would be a symbolic reference to the giving of the Spirit."[202] Brown sees it is both "evocative and *proleptic*, reminding the reader of the *ultimate* purpose for which Jesus has been lifted up on the cross."[203]

Just as the author's trump card came at the end of 1 John, so the best hand is held in the Gospel until the end. The final push toward indwelling Christology comes with the blood and water from the pierced side of Jesus:

> But one of the soldiers pierced his side with a spear, and immediately came out blood and water. The one who saw it has witnessed, and his witness is true, and he knows that he tells the truth, so that you may also believe. For these things happened so that scripture might be fulfilled: "Not a bone of him will be broken." And again another scripture says, "they will look on the one whom they have pierced" (19:34-37).

The accent on the eyewitness and the emphasis on his "truth" (a theological term already in 1:9, 14, 17) points the audience to the theological importance of the scene.[204] What the audience should gather from it, however, is a matter of intense controversy among commentators.

Opinions on the interpretation of blood and water may be divided into two broad categories; we should sample each before attempting

---

[201]Moloney, *Gospel*, 508-09.

[202]Brown, *Gospel*, 931.

[203]Brown, *Gospel*, 931.

[204]The placement of the eyewitness statement (v. 35) shows that it is not the fulfillment of scripture that is of primary importance here; if that had been the case, the eyewitness statement would have followed the scripture quotations.

interpretation. The first sees both elements together as a statement about the real human death of Jesus, usually with an antidocetic interest. Ancient Greek thought advised that the proper balance of blood and water in a person was necessary for health, showing that the human body was thought to contain both.[205] The Homeric legend (*Il.* 5.340-41; cf. Plutarch, *Mor.* 180e) that the gods had not blood but ἰχώρ in their veins (a mixture of blood and water), as well as the description in 4 Maccabees 9:20 of both blood and fluids issuing from a dead body, leads Talbert to suggest that the careful mention of blood and water as separate elements emphasize the humanity of the crucified Jesus.[206] Loader concurs with the interpretation of blood and water emphasizing Jesus' humanity "as though [that humanity] were being called into question," which he thinks "quite odd" and asserts that the passage

> has all the signs of a footnote added to the gospel to counter doubts or doctrines which called into question Jesus' real humanity and death. If this had been a major issue for the evangelist we should have more indication of it in the dialogue and discourses, but in these we find none, unless 6:51c-58 be read in this way.[207]

Schnelle concurs that 19:34b-35 are insertions, which he judges to come from the evangelist rather than from a post-Johannine redactor, that emphasize Jesus' real human death and that also have a sacramental meaning (see the second category below).[208]

The second category includes those commentators who see the emphasis on the two elements with a salvific reference to both, though they generally acknowledge that it is the real death of Jesus that makes those elements effective. Witherington, for example, says that 19:34 shows that Jesus was human and not an apparition, but he also adds that "Barrett is right that the theological point is that Jesus' death and our life paradoxically come together. The blood shed symbolizes his life poured out in death; the water, as elsewhere in this Gospel, symbolizes the life that comes from Jesus to his followers. Jesus had to die so others might have life and have it abundantly."[209] He rejects the sacramental reference

---

[205] Brown, *Gospel*, 947.

[206] Talbert, *Reading John*, 245-46. Brown (*Gospel*, 947) notes that the evidence concerning ἰχώρ led P. Haupt (*AJPhilology* 45 [1924], 53-55) and Eduard Schweizer (*EvTh* 12 [1952-53], 350-51) to assert that this blood and water revealed the *divinity* of Jesus.

[207] Loader, *Christology*, 216; cf. Richter, "Blut und Wasser aus der durchbohrten Seite Jesu (Joh 19, 34b)," *Studien*, 134-40, and C. K. Barrett, *The Gospel according to St. John* (2nd edit.; Philadelphia: Fortress, 1975), 556-57.

[208] Schnelle, *Antidocetic*, 208-09. For a list of those commentators who see these verses as an addition by the evangelist or by a later redactor, see his 209 nn. 196-97.

[209] Witherington, *Wisdom*, 311; cf. Barrett, *Gospel*, 556-57.

proper because: (1) he sees no interest in baptism and no interest in the Passover meal in John, and (2) "blood by itself is never a symbol for the Lord's Supper, any more than bread and fish are."[210]

Moloney, on the other hand, cites C. H. Dodd approvingly, that "from the crucified body of Christ flows the life-giving stream: the water which is the Spirit given to believers in Him (7:38-39), the water which if a man drink he will never thirst again (4:14), and the blood which is ἀληθὴς πόσις (6:55)."[211] Moloney goes on, however, to defend the sacramental reading, saying that the life that the new family of Jesus at the foot of the cross receives includes baptism and Eucharist.[212]

Other commentators as well take pains to connect 19:34 with the previous narrative. Burge, for example, sees 19:34 as a fulfillment of that promise given in 7:37-38, especially since 7:39 specifically refers to Jesus' glorification.[213] Since some Jewish tradition (found in *Mid. Rab Exod.* and *PT* on Num 20:11) also views blood as issuing from the rock of Meribah, "the eschatological waters expected from the temple thus flow from the cross."[214] This entire interpretation is certainly strengthened when we note that 7:39 links the cross and the Spirit and makes the connection with Jesus' death:

> Here in 19:34 is a proleptic symbol of the release of the Spirit. The actual bestowal of the Spirit upon the disciples is yet to come (20:22). But for the present symbolism, water flows, as it were, only when it joins the blood/ death of Christ. Paradoxically, the spear thrust was meant to insure the death of the victim; yet instead it made available the living water within. The living Spirit must seemingly await its host's death to be released. That is to say, the living Spirit is none other than the life of its Lord.[215]

---

[210]Witherington, *Wisdom*, 311.

[211]Dodd, *Interpretation*, 428. Cf. Schnackenburg (*Gospel*, 3.294): "the blood is, presumably, a sign of Jesus' saving death (cf. 1 Jn 1:7) and the water is symbolic of Spirit and life (cf. Jn 4:14; 7:38), but both are most intimately connected.

[212]Moloney, *Gospel*, 509; cf. Jean Zumstine, "L'interprétation johannique de la mort du Christ," *The Four Gospels 1992: Festschrift Frans Neirynck* (3 vols; ed. Frans van Segbroeck, et. al.; BETL 100; Leuven: Leuven University Press, 1992): 3:2132-33. Potterie (*Vérité*, 1.316), similarly, sees a "secondary" aspect to the elements primarily due to the eccelesial orientation of the Calvary scene and also in reference to the sacramental reference of blood already seen in 6:53-56.

[213]Burge, *Anointed*, 95.

[214]Burge, *Anointed*, 94; cf. Manns, *Symbole*, 291-92. In the realms of contemporary understandings of Jewish ritual as the primary background for the symbols, see B. Grigsby, "The Cross in John," *The Johannine Writings* (ed. S. E. Porter & C. A. Evans; Sheffield: Sheffield Academic Press), 91, who cites from OT, Rabbinic and Qumran texts examples of the motif of living water as a cleanser of sin and the outpoured blood of the sacrificial victim particularly from the *Akedah* tradition, and, for parallels with the Passover tradition in Rabbinic writings, see J. M. Ford, "Mingled Blood from the Side of Christ (John 19:34)," *NTS* 15 (1969): 337-38.

[215]Burge, *Anointed*, 95. For the connection between 7:38 and 19:34, see also Schnelle, "Geisttheologie," 23-24: "Die deutliche Korrespondenz zwischen Joh. 7:38 und Joh. 19:34…

Brown also finds a connection with 7:38-39, and he also turns to 1 John 5:6-8 for assistance. He observes that it is the issuing of water that is peculiar, that certainly anyone would expect blood to come forth from the human body.[216] He decides on the water as a "proleptic symbol of the giving of the Spirit, carrying on the theme of vs. 30" and as a fulfillment of the prophecy of 7:38-39.[217] To discern the symbolic meaning of the blood, he turns to 1 John 5:6-8, where "in the poetic phrasing of the First Epistle the water had to be mingled with Jesus' blood before the Spirit could give testimony...Thus, it would seem that in the Gospel picture of a flow of blood and water from the side of Jesus, John is saying that now the Spirit can be given because Jesus is obviously dead and through death has regained the glory that was his before the world existed (17:5)."[218]

Heil reads the passage as a climax of narrative symbols that have a salvific nature due to the life and death of Jesus.[219] His summary of the narrative "experience" of the audience to this point is worth citing at some length.

> The God who sent John to baptize with water told him that the one upon whom he saw the Spirit descending and remaining on him is the one who baptizes with the holy Spirit (1:31-33). But there was no giving of the Spirit before Jesus was glorified (7:39). Now that he has been glorified by death, however, Jesus "baptizes," that is, cleanses or washes, with the water that flows from his pierced side (19:34), the living water of the rivers that now flow from within him (7:38), the water that symbolically represents or contains the Spirit he handed over as he died (19:30).
>
> The Jesus whom God revealed to John as the one who baptizes with the holy Spirit, (1:33), John himself had just previously pointed out as the Lamb of God who takes away the sin of the world (1:29)...The cleansing water of the holy Spirit that now follows and flows together with the blood from the pierced side of the crucified Jesus empowers that blood to wash or take away the sin of the world as the sacrificial blood of the true Passover Lamb of God.[220]

---

lässt einen kreuzestheologischen Akzent: Als der Gekreuzigte und Auferstandene wird Jesus zum bleibenden Lebensquell für alle, die an ihn glauben."

[216]Brown, *Gospel*, 948-49.

[217]Brown, *Gospel*, 948-50.

[218]Brown, *Gospel*, 950-51. Brown concedes (951-52) that there may be a secondary sacramental reference, but he is particularly unsure about the blood/Eucharist connection.

[219]Heil, *Blood and Water*, 106; cf. Potterie, *Vérité*, 2.316.

[220]Heil, *Blood and Water*, 106. Cf. Larry Paul Jones, *The Symbol of Water in the Gospel of John* (JSNTSS 145; Sheffield: Sheffield Academic Press, 1997), 211-15, and Edward Malatesta, "Blood and Water from the Pierced Side of Christ (Jn 19,34)," *Segni e sacramenti nel vangelo di Giovanni* (Studia Anselmiana 66; ed. P.-R. Tragan; Rome: Editrice Anselmiana, 1977): 174-75.

The interweaving of various elements from the Gospel in the hearing of the blood and water event, which is given such weight by the assertion of a direct witness, has a strong appeal.

Everything highlighted by these commentators could have been part of the cultural expectations the audience brought to the text. To discern what interpretation they would have placed on this passage, therefore, we should consider how the narrative has guided the audience. Here, the analyses of those commentators who have searched the text and found salvific allusions to blood/death and water/Spirit are especially helpful. I would like to add to their analyses an emphasis, as I have maintained throughout this discussion of the Fourth Gospel, on the baptism of Jesus as a guide for the audience's understanding. In this consideration, the analysis of Heil seems especially telling. The sacrificial Lamb (blood) and the Spirit (water) as developed through the text, especially with 7:37-39, tie 19:34 closely to the baptism. In this reading, 19:34 provides a type of closure for the indwelling argument: he who was united in life remains united in death. The culmination of this union for the life of the community is poured out for them from the death/glorification.

This interpretation connects with the indwelling motif as seen in Jewish eschatological texts cited in my Chapter Three, in which the Spirit will be poured out onto the people of God. The blood, we might say, symbolizes not a generally human death (versus a "phantasm"), but the death of *that same human* the audience knows from the narrative, who was fully united with the divine being by means of possession and who promised to share that divine life with those who believe. This interpretation means that Loader and others who see this verse as an addition would have a good point *if* the blood and water could only be interpreted as a human, "anti-metamorphosis" motif. If the Gospel argues for an indwelling over an inspiration pattern, however, the strategy presented by the blood and water, and the thread of these symbols that weaves through the Gospel, provides the audience with a substantial testimony.

Once we introduce the connection to the indwelling argument, we are back to the realm of 1 John.[221] I suggest that the reversal of elements makes sense in *each* context: the cross context describes the expected blood of the human death now transformed. Both arguments, citing water, blood, Spirit, and witnessing, argue for the permanent possession of human by divine, but using different strategies. The nature of 1 John is such that a summary statement is most effective, while the Gospel, having had the luxury of an extended narrative, can bring to fruition the themes of

---

[221]For commentators who see 1 John 5:6-8 and John 19:34 as at least being part of the same "conceptual school," see, for example, Burge, *Anointed*, 95 (who uses that phrase); Porsch, *Pneuma*, 333-37; Barnabus Lindars, *The Gospel of John* (NCB; Grand Rapids: Eerdmans, 1981), 588; F.-M. Braun, "L'eau et l'Esprit," *RevThom* 49 (1949): 20-30; Klauck, *Erste*, 294.

indwelling presented to the audience throughout the text. That "the Christ
is Jesus," however, is consistent in both passages.

In the passion narrative, the audience has been treated to a confluence
of symbols and strategies that brings to fruition the knowledge about the
indwelling of the Christ and Jesus they have acquired by attention to the
story. The narrative has asserted the abiding union of human and divine
during the exchange between Jesus and Pilate *and* at the cross, both in the
scene at the cross involving Jesus, his mother, and the Beloved Disciple,
and also with the issuing of blood and water from the pierced side of
Jesus. Inspiration is refuted and indwelling established. The resurrection
narratives will provide the icing on the cake.

Abiding Union: The Resurrection

In the form of possession I have called "inspiration," the possession
tended to be temporary. Some early theologians employed this pattern, we
recall, to protect the divine Christ from suffering and death, insisting that
he left the human Jesus before the crucifixion. For the audience to perceive
that the union was permanent, that continuing identity of the Christ with
Jesus would need to be recognized through the crucifixion. If, moreover,
the identity continues in appearances of the resurrected savior, the final
nail is in the coffin of temporary possession. Indeed, the audience will
now hear verification of the continuing identity of the baptized, crucified
and risen savior particularly in three areas: (1) the human relationships
that continue; (2) divinity revealed within those parameters, and (3)
the continuing and intimate connection between Jesus and the Spirit.
Implications for the unity of community are present in the resurrection
accounts as well.

The disciple "whom Jesus loved" is a reminder that this is still a human
being with emotions that continue, mind and identity not displaced (20:2).
Like the Wedding at Cana, the Lazarus story, and the scene at the foot
of the cross, a context of abiding human relationship is provided for the
revelation of divinity. Even the risen Jesus Mary Magdalene can mistake
for a gardener (a human), but when she recognizes him, she can believably
call him by a human title ("Rabbouni," 20:15-16). She could touch him, a
possibility revealed by the explicit warning not to do so, showing that
even the risen Jesus is of some kind of material substance (20:17); recall
Ignatius' statement that Jesus was not a *daimon* without a body (*Smyrn.*
3:1-2). He continues to be addressed by name, underlining the permanent
identity (20:19, 26; 21:4, 13, 15, 23); he shows his hands and side to assure
the disciples that he is the same Jesus (20:20).

Immediately following the evidence of the identity that he is indeed
the crucified one comes the imparting of the Holy Spirit. "As the Father
has sent me, so I send you. And after he said this, he breathed on them and

said, 'Receive the Holy Spirit. If you forgive the sins of any one, they are forgiven, and if you retain the sins of any one, they are retained'" (20:21-23; recall 7:39). How are we to understand the giving of the Spirit at this apparently late point?

Moloney points out that the giving of the Spirit at the cross and resurrection should be seen as all that same "hour" that the narrative has been moving toward.

> At the hour of the cross and resurrection Jesus pours down the Spirit upon the community of his followers (19:30) and breathes the Spirit into its members that they might be in the world as he was in the world (20:22). The oneness of the hour and all that is achieved by and through it is nowhere clearer to the reader than in these two episodes that take place at the hour: the founding gift of the Spirit (19:30; cf. 14:16-17) and the commissioning of the disciples to be his witnesses empowered by the Spirit (20:22; cf. 15:26-27).[222]

The two descriptions of the giving of the Spirit, then, serve to unify the crucifixion and resurrection into one saving moment.

Another key is provided by the verb to breathe (ἐμφυσάω), also used in LXX Genesis 2:7, when God breathed the breath of life into the first man's nostrils, and in Wisdom 15:11, which says that God breathed into him "a living spirit."[223] I suggest, then, that this depiction reveals that the Spirit is not just poured out on the community as a whole, but also "indwelling" each believer. The cross and this event are one "hour;" they highlight different aspects with specific messages in each. Here, the individual's possession by the Spirit equips him to forgive sins, a ministry necessary for true community (John 13).[224]

In the Thomas incident, a division (schism) among the disciples is avoided when Jesus appears with evidence of his ongoing identity: the marks from the nails of crucifixion (20:26-29). While several commentators have suggested an anti-docetic motif in the Thomas pericope,[225] I suggest that it is not the "phantasm" question that is at issue here (docetism, that is, narrowly defined), but rather the enduring identity of the divine and human (indwelling versus inspiration). This interpretation is supported

---

[222]Moloney, *Gospel*, 532.

[223]Brown, *Gospel*, 1037.

[224]The eschatological outpouring of the Spirit was connected to the idea of cleansing from sins (Ezek 36:25-27; 1 QS 4:20f.); Schnackenburg, *Gospel*, 3.325.

[225]See, for example, G. Richter, "Die Fleischwerdung des Logos im Johannesevangelium," *Studien*, 180; Schnelle, *Antidocetic*, 174-75; Hartwig Thyen, "'...denn wir lieben die Brüder' (1 Joh 3,14)," *Rechtfertigung: Festschrift für E. Käsemann* (ed. G. Friedrich, et. al.; Tübingen: Mohr, 1976), 534; Loader, *Christology*, 183.

by the fact that there is no record in the text that Thomas actually touched and discovered the materiality of the risen Jesus: the identification was enough.[226] The ongoing identity of Jesus is underscored to prevent a breach in the community, the same type of breach that I suggested is described in 1 John concerning the ongoing identity of the savior.[227]

The double confession of Thomas "my Lord and my God" (20:28) leads directly into the powerful christological statement of 20:30-31: "Now Jesus performed many other signs before his disciples that are not written in this book; these, however, are written that you may believe that Jesus is the Christ, the Son of God, and that believing you may have life in his name."[228] This statement brings us directly back into the realm of 1 John. Proving that the Christ/Son of God is Jesus, and that confession of this correct Christology (belief) brings life has been the goal of the narrative to this point.

The identity is now being underlined. "None of the disciples undertook to ask him, 'who are you?' because they knew it was the Lord" (21:12). Recognizable relationships from Jesus' earthly ministry continue, especially with the Beloved Disciple and Peter (21:20-23). The validity of the witness to all of these events is the next to last statement in the Gospel, as the witness was the second element (taking 1:1-5 as a unit) at the beginning of the Gospel, and as the witness introduces and closes 1 John (1:1-3 and 5:20). The "remaining" of the Beloved Disciple (21:23) echoes the indwelling of the disciples with Jesus. The Gospel concludes with the abiding relationships and the witness that flows from them.

In this examination of the Gospel of John, we have seen themes appear repeatedly that encourage belief in the permanence of the incarnation, the confession of which leads to unity in the community, and that also warn against impermanence, which leads to division. These repeated themes, along with the use of μένω to underline the permanence of a new spiritual status for those who believe the enduring union of Jesus and the Christ, suggest that the schism was one of the issues the author was addressing. "In John, the foundation document for a community troubled by progressives

---

[226]That there was no need for Thomas to touch Jesus, but that the true lesson is about the faith without it that will become necessary in later generations, is the majority opinion. See, for example, Brown, *Gospel*, 1046; Schnackenburg, *Gospel*, 3.332; Bruce, *Gospel*, 394.

[227]Kohler (*Kreuz*, 183-97) as well points out that the risen Jesus remains the crucified one, and that 20:29c is not a criticism of Thomas but is intended for later generations who must believe based on the testimony of eyewitnesses.

[228]A. Feuillet points out that Thomas' christological language connects closely with that used in the statement of the purpose of the Gospel in v. 31, so that it provides one piece of evidence to suggest that the "les christophanies pascales ont ceci de commun avec les signes du minstere public de Jésus." "Les christophanies pascales du quatrieme evangile sont-elles des signes?" *NRTh* 97 (1975): 579.

who want to avoid an incarnation that continues through Jesus' death, it is important to guarantee the identity of the one known before Golgotha and the one encountered after Easter."[229]

CONCLUSION

The audience of the Gospel of John brings to the text a range of possibilities concerning how a divine being would appear on earth to interact with humans. The prologue to the Gospel, often examined as the final answer concerning how this savior appeared, in actuality, we have seen, must be completed by the baptismal narrative to let the audience know which pattern the evangelist employs. As the story unfolds, importance of this pattern becomes clear: without a permanent indwelling, the sharing of that divine Spirit, the possession of whom enables correct christological belief and true indwelling in the community, would not be possible. The alternative, the solution of "impermanence," can only lead to schism, as the Johannine Epistles warn as well.

We clearly see now why commentators have had such difficulty deciding whether the Gospel is antidocetic or itself borders on docetism. If one defines docetism narrowly, as employing a metamorphosis pattern that emphasizes the nonmateriality of the being who appears on earth, only a few clues as to the direct materiality of this savior could be reasonably argued: 1:14; 6:51c-58; the possible omission of Simon in 19:17, and 19:34. That interpretation of those verses, however, stands in such isolation from the rest of the narrative that commentators have often been led to read them as later, anti-docetic additions. If we recognize, on the other hand, that docetism also involved a possession pattern based on the temporary (hence, incomplete) nature of the union between the divine and human, the narrative makes sense as an extended presentation of the permanence of the union and as a warning against the schism that can result from confessing a "belief in impermanence."

Was John's Christology "orthodox?" If we wish to define the litmus test narrowly to the birth of Jesus Christ as God's Son, we would have to answer in the negative. If, however, the primary fruit of the orthodox path is "fully human, fully divine," this Gospel audience was treated to a foretaste of the formulation of Chalcedon. Seen in this light, an incomplete christological pattern does not equal an erroneous one.

[229.]Talbert, *Reading John*, 255.

CHAPTER 6
CONCLUDING REMARKS

George MacRae once offered a wry analysis of the investigation into the background of the Fourth Gospel: "I have not yet read anyone who argues that John's background was Indian or Far Eastern, but I should not be greatly surprised to do so." I hope that this dissertation has demonstrated that we should not have to go to such lengths to fathom the Gospel background, at least in the realm of Christology. In fact, confined only to the ancient Mediterranean models concerning how a divine being appears on earth to interact with humans, I suggest we have done rather well in pointing to how the authorial audience would have envisioned the Johannine Christ.

This dissertation examined the Christology of the Johannine literature within the ancient Mediterranean audience expectations of divine appearances. Two complex patterns emerged, metamorphosis and possession, and it was argued that the Christology of the author and opponents employed the possession pattern. The evidence suggested that the audience would understand the opponents to subscribe to a temporary mode of possession, which I called "inspiration," while the author would have been heard as urging a permanent form, which I called "indwelling." This chapter will review the findings of each previous chapter and suggest areas for further research.

SUMMARY OF RESULTS

Chapter Two examined the metamorphosis pattern in ancient Mediterranean culture, in which a heavenly being appeared on earth by transforming his/her outer appearance to that of a human. At times, the texts emphasize the non-material aspect of the body that appears, and a polymorphic capability is generally expected. The semantic field that accompanies the description of metamorphosis is varied, but it is generally limited to terms that describe a change of outer appearance rather than one of inward essence.

Chapter Three examined the possession pattern and discovered that this multifaceted phenomenon was best described by three continua. The characteristics of an occasion of possession typically fell into three general patterns: (1) ecstasy, (2) inspiration, and (3) indwelling. In Greco-Roman literature, ecstasy was the most common of the three. In the Jewish literature, the inspiration pattern was somewhat favored, though there was a definite hope expressed for a leader in whom God's spirit would permanently dwell.

Chapter Four inspected the phenomenon of docetism and its relation to the Christologies of the author and opponents in the Johannine Epistles. It was argued that docetism had been generally misrepresented by a "narrow" definition; that is, as consisting only of the metamorphosis pattern with a nonmaterial emphasis. On the contrary, both metamorphosis and possession patterns were used by those early Christians who argued that the human and divine in Jesus only "seemed" to be a full and permanent union. By examining the vocabulary and patterns of the christological statements in the Johannine Epistles, it was suggested that the audience would have most naturally understood the conflict to concern whether or not the possession was full and permanent; that is, the opponents' inspiration Christology versus the authors' indwelling Christology.

Chapter Five argued that the audience would have heard the same christological debate in the Gospel of John. It was further suggested that not only the prologue but also the description of the baptism event of Jesus would have controlled the understanding of the rest of the narrative. That understanding would have colored the entire Gospel as an argument for indwelling, that the union of the divine and human in Jesus that occurred at his baptism would have continued throughout the death and resurrection, enabling a permanence of belief and of community in the followers Jesus left on earth and those they would convert to the faith.

Several overall points can be made about the results of this research, the first three in the areas of early Christianity in general and the Epistles specifically. First, while the appearance of a divine being on earth is generally described in the ancient Mediterranean by the use of two patterns, those patterns are both multifaceted, and the tendencies within them can overlap in various combinations. This recognition should advance the study of these phenomena in this particular cultural context. Second, Christians who held a docetic Christology employed either pattern, and the observations that both patterns are found in both Greco-Roman and Jewish literature will hopefully end the general identification of docetic Christology as an imposition of only Greek thought on Christology. Third, in the Johannine Epistles, if the argument that both authors and opponents subscribe to a possession pattern holds true, not only the differences but also the agreements between author and opponents are clarified. This proposal is an improvement on previous hypotheses in which the choice seemed to be nonmaterial metamorphosis versus incarnation, which led to a fruitless search for a sustained anti-metamorphosis argument in the Johannine literature.

That third point leads into the final three observations concerning the Gospel of John. First, the Brown hypothesis concerning the development of the community seems less probable if the authors of the Gospel and Epistles are fighting on the same christological front. Next, the understanding of the indwelling Christological pattern begins to resolve tensions in the Johannine portrayal of Jesus that have long puzzled commentators. For example, we can see now that what distinguishes Christ from Wisdom, etc., is the human Jesus. What distinguishes Jesus from a possessed leader or prophet is Christ. We see why Jesus in some ways looks so much like an OT prophet yet is described as preexistent. Last, the Christology of the Fourth Gospel is suddenly no longer based on something missing from the narrative (birth stories), or weighted toward the preexistent Logos at the expense of the humanity of Jesus (Logos-Christology rather than Spirit-Christology), but it appears as a far more culturally astute and yet creative expression of a truth that is surprisingly close to the statements of Chalcedon.

OPPORTUNITIES FOR FUTURE RESEARCH

The opportunities for further research in this area are numerous. In early Christianity as a whole, first, the suggested descriptions of the metamorphosis and possession patterns should continue to be investigated and refined. Second, the influence of these patterns on Christology can and should be examined. While the use of the metamorphosis pattern, especially with nonmaterial and polymorphic emphases, has been recognized in early Christianity,[1] the influence of the possession pattern has not been fully appreciated. There is, moreover, fruit to be gathered in comparing the possession Christologies of early Christianity with the with the multitide of cross-cultural work on possession that is now part of the anthropological literature.[2] While considerable progress has

---

[1]See, for example, Cartlidge, *Transfigurations of Metamorphosis Traditions in the Acts of John, Thomas, and Peter* and Riley, "'I Was Thought to Be What I Am Not:' Docetic Jesus and the Johannine Tradition" (both previously cited), as well as Robert M. Price, "Docetic Epiphanies: A Structuralist Analysis of the Apocryphal Acts," *Journal of Higher Criticism* 5 (1998): 163-87.

[2]See, for example, the survey of recent literature in Frederick M. Smith, "The Current State of Possession Studies as a Cross-Disciplinary Project," *RelStRev* 27 (2001): 203-212.

been made in understanding the relationship between "second gods" or angelic figures and ancient Jewish monotheism, there is much more to be done on the overlap between the various titles within this sphere both in Judaism and in early Christianity. Tracing these early Christian trajectories of metamorphosis and possession models through the debates of the ecumenical councils will help understand the sources and nuances of the positions presented there.

In the realm of the Christology of the Fourth Gospel specifically, more detailed work should be done on how indwelling is reflected throughout the Gospel narrative. What effect, for example, does this understanding (possessionist, indwelling Christology) have on the understanding of Jesus' prophetic pronouncements? How does it affect our understanding of the possession of the believer as well? Indwelling Christology, moreover, could positively address other long-recognized Johannine "tensions" such as Jesus' human versus divine origins, and the connection between the descent/ascent pattern and the Son of man terminology.

As Potterie points out, it is necessary after the exegesis of a passage to discern, beyond the semantic field which the text has in common with a previous tradition, if its conception of the truth depends on its sources, or, rather, if it has profoundly reinterpreted the terminology.[3] With this wise counsel in mind, in addition to advances in reconstructing authorial audiences, I conclude that the History of Religions approach, while challenging to implement, still has much to offer the study of the Fourth Gospel. It is well worth the effort to help illuminate the figure of Jesus Christ for all those who seek, in the words of St. Clare of Assisi, to "look at him, think on him, gaze at him and desire to be like him."[4]

---

[3]Potterie, *Vérité*, 2.1004.

[4]St. Clare of Assisi, "Second Letter to Agnes of Prague."

SELECTED BIBLIOGRAPHY

Anderson, G. A. and M. E. Stone. *A Synopsis of the Book of Adam and Eve.* 2d rev. ed. Atlanta: Scholars Press, 1999.

Anderson, J. C. *Matthew's Narrative Web: Over, and Over, and Over Again.* Journal for the Study of the NewTestament Supplement Series 91. Sheffield: JSOT Press, 1994.

Anderson, Paul N. *The Christology of the Fourth Gospel: Its Unity and Disunity in the Light of John 6.* Wissenschaftliche Untersuchungen zum Neuen Testament. Tübingen: Mohr, 1996. Repr., Valley Forge, Pa.: Trinity Press International, 1997.

The Apostolic Fathers. Translated by Kirsopp Lake. 2 vols. The Loeb Classical Library. Cambridge: Harvard University Press, 1970.

Apuleius. *The Golden Ass.* Translated by W. Adlington, rev. by S. Gaselee. The Loeb Classical Library. New York: Putnam, 1935.

Argyle, A. W. "Philo and the Fourth Gospel." *Expository Times* 63 (1952): 385-86.

Ashton, John. "The Transfiguration of Wisdom: A Study of the Prologue of John's Gospel." *New Testament Studies* 32 (1986): 161-86.

———. *Understanding the Fourth Gospel.* London: Clarendon, 1991.

Athanassakis, Apostolos N. *The Orphic Hymns.* Graeco-Roman Religion Series 4. Texts and Translations 12. Missoula: Scholars Press, 1977.

Aune, David E. *Prophecy in Early Christianity and the Ancient Mediterranean World.* Grand Rapids: Eerdmans, 1983.

Barker, Margaret. *The Great Angel: A Study of Israel's Second God.* Louisville, Ky.: Westminster John Knox, 1992.

Barrett, C. K. *The Gospel according to St. John.* 2d ed. Philadelphia: Westminster, 1978.

———. "History." Pages 116-32 in *Essays on John.* Philadelphia: Westminster, 1982.

Bauer, Walter. *Das Johannesevangelium Erklärt.* Handbuch zum Neuen Testament 6. Tübingen: Mohr (Siebeck), 1933.

Bauer, Walter and H. Paulsen. *Die Briefe des Ignatius von Antiochia und der Polykarpbrief.* Handbuch Zum Neuen Testament 18/2. Tübingen: Mohr, 1985.

Baur, F. C. *Kritische Untersuchungen über die kanonischen Evangelien.* Tübingen: Fues, 1947.

———. *Vorlesungen über neutestamentliche Theologie.* Darmstadt: Wiss. Buchgesellschaft, 1973.

Beasley-Murray, G. R. *John.* Word Biblical Commentary 36. Waco, Tex.: Word Books, 1987.

Becker, Jürgen. *Das Evangelium des Johannes.* 2 vols. Ökumenischer Taschenbuchkommentar zum Neuen Testament 4/1-2. Gütersloh: Gerd Mohn and Würzburg: Echter Verlag, 1979-81.

Bernard, John Henry. *A Critical and Exegetical Commentary on the Gospel according to St. John.* 2 vols. International Critical Commentary 29. Edinburgh: T&T Clarke, 1928. Repr., 1998.

Belle, G. van. *Johannine Bibliography 1966-1985: A Cumulative Bibliography on the Fourth Gospel.* Bibliotheca ephemeridum theologicarum lovaniensium 82. Leuven: Leuven University Press/Peeters, 1988.

———. *The Signs Source in the Fourth Gospel: Historical Survey and Critical Evaluation of the Semeia Hypothesis.* Bibliotheca ephemeridum theologicarum lovaniensium 116. Leuven: Peters, 1994.

Betz, Hans Dieter. "Jesus as Divine Man." Pages 114-33 in *Jesus and the Historian.* Edited by F. D. Trotter. Philadelphia: Fortress, 1968.

Betz, Otto. "The Concept of the So-Called 'Divine Man' in Mark's Christology." Pages 220-40 in *Studies in New Testament and Early Christian Literature. Essays Honoring Allen P. Wikgren.* Edited by D. E. Aune. Leiden: Brill, 1972.

Betz, Otto. "Das Problem des Wunders bei Flavius Josephus im Vergleich zum Wunderproblem bei den Rabbinen und im Johannesevangelium." Pages 23-44 in *Josephus-Studien: Festschrift für O. Michel.* Edited by Otto Betz, Klaus Haacker, and Martin Hengel. Göttingen: Vandenhoeck & Ruprecht, 1974.

Beutler, Johannes. *Die Johannesbriefe.* Regensburg: Pustet, 2000.

Bienaimé, G. "L'annonce des fleuves d'eau vive en Jean 7,37-39." *Revue théologique de Louvain* 21 (1990): 281-310.

Bittner, Wolfgang J. *Jesu Zeichen im Johannesevangelium: Die Messias-Erkenntnis im Johannesevangelium vor ihrem jüdischen Hintergrund.* Wissenschaftliche Untersuchungen zum Neuen Testament. Second Series 26. Tübingen: Mohr, 1987.

Boer, Martinus D. de. "The Death of Jesus Christ and His Coming in the Flesh." *Novum Testamentum* 33 (1991): 326-346.

———. "Jesus the Baptizer: 1 John 5:5-8 and the Gospel of John." *Journal of Biblical Literature* 107 (1988): 87-106.

Bogart, John. *Orthodox and Heretical Perfectionism in the Johannine Community as Evident in the First Epistle of John.* Society of Bibilical Literature Dissertation Series 33. Missoula, Montana: Scholars, 1977.

Boismard, M.-E. *Moïse ou Jésus: Essai de christologie johannique.* Bibliotheca ephemeridem theologicarum louvaniensium 84. Leuven: Leuven University Press/Peeters, 1988.

Bonnard, Pierre. *Les épitres johanniques.* Commentaire du Nouveau Testament 13c. Deuxième série. Geneva: Labor et Fides, 1983.

Borgen, Peder. *Bread from Heaven: An Exegetical Study of the Concept of Manna in the Gospel of John and the Writings of Philo.* Novum Testamentum Supplements 11. Leiden: Brill, 1965.

———. "God's Agent in the Fourth Gospel." Pages 136-48 in *Religions in Antiquity: Essays in Memory of E. R. Goodenough.* Edited by Jacob Neusner. Leiden: Brill, 1968.

———. "Some Jewish Exegetical Traditions as Background for Son of Man Sayings in John's Gospel (Jn 3:1-14 and context)." Pages 243-58 in.*L'Evangile de Jean: Sources, rédaction, théologie.* Edited by M. de Jonge. Bibliotheca ephemeridum theologicarum lovaniensium 44. Gembloux: Duculot, 1977.

Bornkamm, Günther. "Die eucharistische Rede im Johannes-Evangelium." *Zeitschrift für die neutestamentliche Wissenschaft* 47 (1956): 161-69.

———. "Der Paraklet im Johannesevangelium." Pages 12-35 in *Festschrift Rudolf Bultmann zum 65 Geburtstag überricht.* Edited by E. Wolf. Stuttgart: W. Kohlhammer, 1949.

Bousset, Wilhelm. *Kyrios Christos: A History of the Belief in Christ from the Beginnings of Christianity to Irenaeus.* Translated by J. E. Steely. Nashville: Abingdon, 1970.

Braun, F.-M. "L'eau et l'Esprit." *Revue thomiste* 49 (1949): 20-30.

———. *Jean le Théologian. Sa Théologie. Le Mystère de Jésus-Christ.* Paris: Gabalda, 1966.

———. "Messie, Logos et Fils de l'Homme." Pages 140-47 in *La Venue du Messie: Messianisme et Eschatologie.* Recherches bibliques 6. Edited by E. Massaux. New York: Desclée de Brouwer, 1962.

Brenk, Frederick E. *In Mist Apparelled: Religious Themes in Plutarch's Moralia and Lives.* Leiden: Brill, 1977.

———. *Relighting the Souls.* Stuttgart: Franz Steiner Verlag, 1998.

Brock, S. P. and J.-C. Picard. *Testamentum Iobi.* Leiden: Brill, 1967.

Brooke, Alan England. *A Critical and Exegetical Commentary on the Johannine Epistles.* International Critical Commentary 43. 1912. Repr., Edinburgh: T&T Clark, 1948.

Brown, E. K. *Rhythm in the Novel.* Lincoln, Neb.: University of Nebraska Press, 1950.

Brown, Raymond E. *The Community of the Beloved Disciple.* New York: Paulist, 1979.

———. *The Epistles of John.* Anchor Bible 30. Garden City, N. Y.: Doubleday, 1982.

———. *The Gospel according to John.* Anchor Bible 29 & 29a. Garden City, N.Y.: Doubleday, 1966, 1970.

———. "The Paraclete in the Fourth Gospel." *New Testament Studies* 13 (1967): 113-32.

———. "The Relationship to the Fourth Gospel Shared by the Author of 1 John and by His Opponents." Pages 57-68 in *Text and Interpretation: Studies in the New Testament Presented to Matthew Black.* Edited by E. Best and R. McL. Wilson. Cambridge: Cambridge University Press, 1979.

Brownson, James. "The Odes of Solomon and the Johannine Tradition." *Journal for the Study of.Pseudepigrapha* 2 (1988): 49-69.

Brox, Norbert. "'Doketismus'—eine Problemanzeige." *Zeitschrift für Kirchengeschichte* 95 (1984): 301-14.

Bruce, F. F. *The Gospel and Epistles of John.* Grand Rapids: Eerdmans, 1983.

Büchsel, Friedrich. *Das Evangelium nach Johannes.* Das Neue Testament Deutsch; Göttiger Bibelwerk 4. Göttingen: Vandenhoeck & Ruprecht, 1934.

Bühner, Jan-Adolf. *Der Gesandte und sein Weg im vierten Evangelium: Die kultur- und religionsgeschichtliche Grundlagen der johanneischen Sendungschristologie sowie ihre traditionsgeschichtliche Entwicklung.* Wissenschaftliche Untersuchungen zum Neuen Testament. Second Series 2. Tübingen: Mohr, 1977.

Bultmann, Rudolf. "Die Bedeutung der neuerscholossenen mandäischen und manichäischen Quellen für das Verständnis des Johannesevangeliums." *Zeitschrift für die Neue Testamentiche Wissenschaft* 24 (1925): 100-46.

———. *The Gospel of John: A Commentary.* Translated by G. Beasley-Murray. Oxford: Blackwell, 1971.

———. *The Johannine Epistles.* Hermeneia. Translated by R. Philip O'Hara, Lane C. McGaughy and Robert W. Funk. Philadelphia: Fortress, 1973.

———. "The History of Religions Background of the Prologue to the Gospel of John." Pages 18-35 in *The Interpretation of John.* Issues in Religion and Theology 9. Edited and translated by John Ashton. Philadelphia: Fortress, 1986.

———. *Theology of the New Testament.* 2 vols. London: SCM, 1955.

Burge, Gary M. *The Anointed Community: The Holy Spirit in the Johannine Tradition.* Grand Rapids: Eerdmans, 1987.

Burkett, Delbert. *The Son of Man Debate: A History and Evaluation.* Society for New Testament Studies Monograph Series 107. Cambridge: Cambridge University Press, 1999.

———. *The Son of Man in the Gospel of John.* Journal for the Study of New Testament Supplement Series 56. Sheffield: Shefflield Academic Press, 1991.

Carson, D. A. *The Gospel According to John.* Grand Rapids: Eerdmans and Leicester: InterVarsity, 1991.

Carter, Warren and John P. Heil. *Matthew's Parables: Audience-Oriented Perspectives.* Catholic Bibilical Quarterly Monograph Series 30. Washington, D. C.: Catholic Biblical Association, 1998.

Cartlidge, David. "Transfigurations of Metamorphosis Traditions in the Acts of John, Thomas, and Peter." *Semeia* 38 (1986): 53-66.

Casey, P. M. *From Jewish Prophet to Gentile God: The Origins and Development of New Testament Christology.* Louisville: Westminster John Knox, 1991.

Catullus. Translated by G. P. Goold. Duckworth Classical, Medieval, and Renaissance Editions. London: Duckworth, 1983.

Charles, R. H. *The Book of Enoch.* Oxford: Clarendon, 1912.

———. *The Greek Versions of the Testaments of the Twelve Patriarchs.* Oxford: Clarendon, 1908.

Charlesworth, James H., ed. *John and Qumran.* London: Geoffrey Chapman, 1972.

———. *The Old Testament Pseudepigrapha.* 2 vols. New York: Doubleday, 1983.

Chester, Andres. *Divine Revelation and Divine Titles in the Pentateuchal Targumim.* Texte und Studien zum Antiken Judentum 14. Tübingen: Mohr, 1986.

Cicero, Marcus Tullius. *Cicero. De senectute, De amicitia, De divitatione.* Vol. 7. Translated by W. A. Falconer. Loeb Classical Library. New York: Putnam, 1923.

Colpe, C. *Die religionsgeschichtliche Schule: Darstellung und Kritik ihres Bildes vom gnostischen Erlöser-mythus.* Forshcungen zur Religion und Literatur des Alten und Neuen Testaments 60. Göttingen: Vandenhoeck & Ruprecht, 1961.

Colwell, E. C. and Eric Titus. *The Gospel of the Spirit*. New York: Harper, 1953.

Coppens, J. "Le Fils de l'homme dans l'évangile johannique." *Ephemerides theologicae lovanienses* 52 (1976): 28-81.

Cullman, Oscar. *The Christology of the New Testament*. Rev. ed. Translated by Shirley C. Guthrie and Charles A. M. Hall. Philadelphia: Fortress, 1963.

Culpepper, R. Alan. *Anatomy of the Fourth Gospel: A Study in Literary Design*. Philadelphia: Fortress, 1983.

———. "The Christology of the Johannine Writings." Pages 66-87 in *Who Do You Say That I Am?: Essays on Christology*. Edited by M. A. Powell and D. R. Bauer. Louisville: Westminster John Knox, 1999.

Davies, J. G. "The Origins of Docetism." *Studia Patristica* 6 (1962): 13-35.

De Boer, Martinus C. "The Death of Jesus Christ and His Coming in the Flesh." *Novum Testamentum* 33 (1991): 326-346.

———. "Jesus the Baptizer: 1 John 5:5-8 and the Gospel of John." *Journal of Biblical Literature* 107 (1988): 87-106.

DeJonge, Marinus. *Jesus, Stranger from Heaven and Son of God: Jesus Christ and the Christians in Johannine Perspective*. Society of Biblical Literature Monograph Series 11. Missoula: Scholars Press, 1977.

Delebecque, Edouard. *Evangile de Jean: Texte Traduit et Annote*. Cahiers de le revue biblique 23. Paris: Gabalda, 1987.

DeMaris, Richard E. "Possession, Good and Bad—Ritual, Effects and Side-Effects: The Baptism of Jesus and Mark 1:9-11 from a Cross-Cultural Perspective." *Journal for the Study of the New Testament* 80 (2000): 3-30.

Dietrich, Bernard. "From Knossos to Homer." Pages 1-14 in *What is a God: Studies in the Nature of Greek Divinity*. Edited by A. B. Lloyd. London: Duckworth, 1997.

Dio Chrysostom. Translated by J. W. Cohoon. 5 vols. Loeb Classical Library. New York: Putnam, 1932.

Diodorus, Siculus. *Bibliotheca historica*. Translated by C. H. Oldfather et al. 12 vols. Loeb Classical Library. Cambridge: Harvard University Press, 1963-80.

Diogenes Laertius. *Lives of Eminent Philosophers*. Translation by R. D. Hicks. 2 vols. Loeb Classical Library. Harvard: Harvard University Press, 1931-42.

Dodd, Charles Harold. *The Johannine Epistles*. Moffat New Testament Commentary. 2d ed. London: Hodder and Stoughton, 1953.

———. *The Interpretation of the Fourth Gospel*. 2d ed. Cambridge: Cambridge University Press, 1978.

Dunn, James D. G. *Christology in the Making: A New Testament Inquiry in the Origins of the Doctrine of the Incarnation*. 2d ed. London: SCM, 1989.

———. "Incarnation." Pages 3.397-404 in *Anchor Bible Dictionary*. Edited by D. N. Freedman. 6 vols. New York: Doubleday, 1992.

———. *Jesus and the Spirit*. Philadelphia: Westminster, 1975.

Ellis, Peter F. *The Genius of John. A Compositional-Critical Commentary on the Fourth Gospel*. Collegeville: The Liturgical Press, 1984.

Epp, Eldon J. "Wisdom, Torah, Word: The Johannine Prologue and the Purpose of the Fourth Gospel." *Current Issues in Biblical and Patristic Interpretation*. Edited by G. F. Hawthorne. Grand Rapids: Eerdmans, 1974.

Euripides. Translated by David Kovacs. 5 vols. Loeb Classical Library. Cambridge: Harvard University Press, 1994-2002.

Evans, Craig A. *Word and Glory: On the Exegetical and Theological Background of John's Prologue.* Journal for the Study of the New Testament Supplement Series 89. Sheffield: JSOT Press, 1993.

Fennema, David A. "Jesus and God According to John: An Analysis of the Fourth Gospel's Father/Son Christology." Ph.D. diss., Duke University, 1979.

Feuillet, Andre. "Les christophanies pascales du quatrieme evangile sont-elles des signes?" *La nouvelle revue théologique* 97 (1975): 577-92.

———. *Le mystère de l'amour divin dans la théologie johannique.* Paris: Gabalda, 1972.

———. *Le prologue du quatrième évangile: Etude de la théologie johannique.* Brussels: Desclée de Brouwer, 1968.

Foley, Helene P. *The Homeric Hymn to Demeter: Translation, Commentary, and Interpretive Essays.* Princeton: Princeton University Press, 1994.

Fontenrose, Joseph. *The Delphic Oracle.* Berkeley: University of California Press, 1978.

Forbes, Christopher. *Prophecy and Inspired Speech in Early Christianity and its Hellenistic Environment.* Peabody, Mass.: Hendrickson, 1997.

Ford, J. M. "Mingled Blood from the Side of Christ (John 19:34)." *New Testament Studies* 15 (1969): 337-38.

Fossum, Jarl. *The Name of God and the Angel of the Lord: Samaritan and Jewish Concepts of Intermediation and the Origin of Gnosticism.* Wissenshaftliche Untersuchungen zum Neuen Testament 36. Tübingen: Mohr (Siebeck), 1985.

Fox, Robin Lane. *Pagans and Christians.* San Francisco: Harper & Row, 1986.

Frey, Jörg. *Die Johanneische Eschatologie.* 2 vols. Tübingen: Mohr (Siebeck), 1997.

Fuller, R. H. "Christmas, Epiphany, and the Johannine Prologue." Pages 63-73 in *Spirit and Light: Essays in Historical Theology.* Edited by M. L'Engle and W. B. Green. New York: Crossroad, 1976.

———. *The Foundations of New Testament Christology.* New York: Scribner, 1965.

Giblin, Charles H. "Suggestion, Negative Response, and Positive Action in St. John's Gospel (John 2:1-11; 4:46-54; 7:2-14; 11:1-44)." *New Testament Studies* 26 (1980): 197-211.

Glare, P. G. W., ed. *Oxford Latin Dictionary.* Oxford: Clarendon, 1982.

Gnilka, Joachim. *Das Johannesevangelium.* Die Neue Echter Bibel 4. 2d ed. Würzburg: Echter Verlag, 1985.

Gnilka, Joachim. "Zur Christologie des Johannesevangeliums." Pages 92-107 in *Christologische Schwerpunkte.* Edited by Walter Kasper and J. Gnilka. Düsseldorf: Patmos, 1980.

Goetchius, E. V. N. Review of.L. C. McGaught, *Toward a Decriptive Analysis of EINAI as a Linking Verb in New Testament Greek. Journal of Biblical Literature* 95 (1976): 147-49.

Goulder, Michael. "Ignatius' 'Docetists.'" *Vigiliae christianae* 53 (1999): 16-30.

———. "A Poor Man's Christology." *New Testament Studies* 45 (1999): 332-348.

Grayston, Kenneth. *The Johannine Epistles.* New Century Bible. Grand Rapids: Eerdmans, 1984.

Grigsby, B. H. "The Cross in John." Pages 69-94 in *The Johannine Writings.* Edited by S. E. Porter & C. A. Evans. Sheffield: Sheffield Academic Press, 1995.

Grube, G. M. A. *A Greek Critic: Demetrius on Style.* Phoenix Supplementary Volume 4. Toronto: University of Toronto Press, 1961.

Grundmann, W. *Der Zeuge der Wahrheit: Grundzüge der Christologie des Johannesevangelims*. Edited by W. Wiefel. Berlin: Evangelische Verlagsanstalt, 1985.

Haenchen, Ernst. *John: A Commentary on the Gospel of John*. 2 vols. Hermeneia. Translated by Robert W. Funk. Philadelphia: Fortress, 1984.

———. "'Der Vater, der mich gesandt hat.'" Pages 68-77 in *Gott und Mensch*. Tübingen: Mohr, 1965.

Hagner, Donald A. "The Vision of God in Philo and John: A Comparative Study." *Journal of the Evangelical Theological Society* 14 (1971): 81-93.

Hahn, Ferdinand. *The Titles of Jesus in Christology: Their History in Early Christianity*. Translated by Harold Knight and George Ogg. London: Lutterworth, 1969.

Harris, Elizabeth. *Prologue and Gospel: The Theology of the Fourth Evangelist*. Journal for the Study of the New Testament Supplement Series 107. Sheffield: Sheffield Academic Press, 1994.

Harris, J. Rendell. *The Origin of the Prologue to St. John's Gospel*. Cambridge: Cambridge University Press, 1917.

Harstine, Stanley D. "The Functions of Moses as a Character in the Fourth Gospel and the Responses of Three Ancient Mediterranean Audiences." Ph.D. diss., Baylor University, 1999.

Harvey, A. E. "Christ as Agent." Pages 239-50 in *The Glory of Christ in the New Testament: Studies in Christology in Memory of George Bradford Caird*. Edited by L. D. Hurst and N. T. Wright. Oxford: Clarendon, 1987.

Hatch, Edwin and H. A. Redpath. *A Concordance to the Septuagint*. 2 vols. Graz: Akademische Druck-U. Verlagsanstalt, 1954.

Hayman, Peter. "Monotheism—A Misused Word in Jewish Studies?" *Journal of Jewish Studies* 42 (1991): 1-15.

Hayward, Robert. *Divine Name and Presence: The Memra*. Totowa, N. J.: Allanheld, Osmun, 1981.

Head, Peter. "The Foreign God and the Sudden Christ: Theology and Christology in Marcion's Gospel Redaction." *Tyndale Bulletin* 44 (1993): 307-21.

Heil, John Paul. *Blood and Water: The Death and Resurrection of Jesus in John 18-21*. Catholic Biblical Quarterly Monograph Series 27. Washington: Catholic Biblical Association, 1995.

Heise, Jürgen. *Bleiben: Menein in den johanneische Schriften*. Tübingen: Mohr, 1967.

Hengel, Martin. *The Son of God: The Origin of Christology and the History of Jewish-Hellenistic Religion*. Philadelphia: Fortress, 1976.

———. *Studies in Early Christology*. Edinburgh: T&T Clarke, 1995.

Herodotus. Translated by A. D. Godley. 4 vols. Loeb Classical Library. New York: Putnam, 1921-24.

Hesiod. *The Homeric Hymns and Homerica*. Translated by H. G. Evelyn-White. Loeb Classical Library. Cambridge: Harvard University Press, 1959.

Hill, Charles E. "Cerinthus, Gnostic or Chiliast?.A New Solution to an Old Problem." *Journal of Early Christian Studies* 8 (2000): 135-72.

Hinrichs, Boy. *"Ich bin": Die Konsistenz des Johannes-Evangeliums in der Konzentration auf das Wort Jesu*. Stuttgarter Bibelstudien 133. Stuttgart: Katholisches Bibelwerk, 1988.

Hoffman, Daniel L. "Ignatius and Early Anti-Docetic Realism in the Eucharist." *Fides et Historia* 30 (1998): 74-88.

Holladay, Carl. *Theios Aner in Hellenistic Judaism: A Critique of the Use of This Category in New Testament Christology.* Society of Biblical Literature Dissertation Series 40. Missoula: Scholars Press, 1977.

Holtzmann, H. J. *Lehrbuch der neutestamentlichen Theologie II.* 2d ed. Tübingen: Mohr, 1911.

Homer. *The Iliad.* Translated by A. T. Murray. 2 vols. Loeb Classical Library. Cambridge: Harvard University Press, 1946.

———. *The Odyssey.* Translated by A. T. Murray. 2 vols. Loeb Classical Library. New York: Heinemann, 1919.

Horace. *The Odes and Epodes.* Translated by C. E. Bennett. Loeb Classical Library. Cambridge: Harvard University Press, 1952.

Hoskyns, Edwyn C. *The Fourth Gospel.* Edited by F. N. Davey. London: Faber & Faber, 1947.

Hunt, Allen R. *The Inspired Body: Paul, the Corinthians, and Divine Inspiration.* Macon, Ga.: Mercer University Press, 1996.

Iser, Wolfgang. *The Act of Reading.* Baltimore: The John Hopkins University Press, 1974.

———. *The Implied Reader.* Baltimore: The John Hopkins University Press, 1978.

Isaacs, M. E. *The Concept of Spirit: A Study of Pneuma in Hellenistic Judaism and Its Bearing on the New Testament.* Heythrop Monographs 1. London: Heythrop, 1976.

Jauss, Hans Robert. *Toward an Aesthetic of Reception.* Translated by Timothy Bahti. Minneapolis: University of Minneapolis Press, 1982.

Johnson, S. E. "Parallels Between the Letters of Ignatius and the Johannine Epistles." Pages 327-38 in *Perspectives on Language and Text: Essays and Poems in Honor of Francis I. Andersen's Sixtieth Birthday.* Edited by Edgar W. Conrad and Edward G. Newing. Winona Lake, Minn.: Eisenbrauns, 1987.

Johnston, George. *The Spirit-Paraclete in the Gospel of John.* Society for New Testament Studies Monograph Series 12. Cambridge: Cambridge University Press, 1970.

Jones, Larry Paul. *The Symbol of Water in the Gospel of John.* Journal for the Study of the New Testament Supplement Series 145. Sheffield: Sheffield Academic Press, 1997.

Josephus. Translated by H. St. J. Thackeray et al. 10 vols. Loeb Classical Library. Cambridge: Harvard University Press, 1926-1965.

Kanagaraj, Jey J. "Did the Word Not 'Become' Flesh?.A Response to J. C. O'Neill." *Expository Times* 110 (1999): 80-81.

Käsemann, Ernst. "The Structure and Purpose of the Prologue to John's Gospel." Pages 138-67 in *New Testament Questions of Today.* London: SCM, 1969.

———. *The Testament of Jesus.* London: SCM, 1968.

Keck, Leander. "Derivation as Destiny: 'Of-ness' in Johannine Christology, Anthropology, and Soteriology." Pages 274-88 in *Exploring the Gospel of John: In Honor of D. Moody Smith.* Edited by R. Alan Culpepper and C. Clifton Black. Louisville: Westminster John Knox, 1996.

———. "Toward the Renewal of New Testament Christology." *New Testament Studies* 32 (1986): 362-77.

Kimelman, Ronald. "'Birkat Ha-Minim' and the Lack of Evidence for an Anti-Christian Jewish Prayer in Late Antiquity." Pages 226-44 in *Jewish and Christian Self-Definition*. Volume 2. Edited by E. P. Sanders, et. al. Philadelphia: Fortress, 1981.

Kisch, Guido. *Pseudo-Philo's* "Liber Antiquitatum Biblicarum." Notre Dame, Ind.: University of Notre Dame Press, 1949.

Kittel, G. and G. Friedrich, eds. *Theological Dictionary of the New Testament*. Translated by G. W. Bromiley. 10 vols. Grand Rapids: Eerdmans, 1964-76.

Klauck, Hans-Josef. *Die Erste Johannesbrief*. Evangelisch-katholischer Kommentar zum Neuen Testament 23.1. Zürich: Benziger, 1991.

———. *Der Zeite und Dritte Johannesbrief*. Evangelisch-katholischer Kommentar zum Neuen Testament 23/2. Zürich: Benziger, 1992.

Knox, John. *The Humanity and Divinity of Christ: A Study of Pattern in Christology*. Cambridge: Cambridge University Press, 1967.

Knox, W. L. "John 13:1-30." *Harvard Theological Review* 43 (1950): 161-63.

Koester, Craig R. *The Dwelling of God: The Tabernacle in the Old Testament, Inter-testamental Jewish Literature, and the New Testament*. Catholic Biblical Quarterly Monograph Series 22. Washington, D. C.: Catholic Biblical Association, 1989.

———. "Hearing, Seeing, and Believing in the Gospel of John." *Biblica* 70 (1989): 327-48.

Kohler, Herbert. *Kruez und Menschwerdung im Johannesevangelium: Ein exegetisch-hermeneutisher Versuch zur johanneischen Kreuzestheologie*. Abhandlungen zur Theologie des Alten und Neuen Testaments 72. Zürich: Theologischer Verlag Zürich, 1987.

Koschorke, Klaus. *Die Polemik der Gnostiker gegen das kirchliche Christentum*. Leiden: Brill, 1978.

Kruse, Colin. *The Letters of John*. Grand Rapids: Eerdmans, 2000.

Kügler, Joachim. *Der Andere König: Religionsgeschichtliche Perspektiven auf die Christologie des Johannesevangeliums*. Stuttgarter Bibelstudien 178. Stuttgart: Katholisches Bibelwerk, 1999.

Kuhl, Josef. *Die Sendung Jesu und der Kirche nach dem Johannes-Evangelium*. St. Augustin: Steyler, 1967.

Kysar, Robert. *The Fourth Evangelist and His Gospel: An Examination of Contemporary Scholarship*. Minneapolis: Augsburg, 1975.

———. "The Fourth Gospel: A Report on Recent Research." *ANRW* 25.3:2389-2480. Part 2. *Principat*, 25.3. Edited by H. Temporini and W. Haase. New York: de Gruyter, 1985.

Lagrange, Marie-Joseph. *Evangile selon saint Jean*. Etudes bibliques. Paris: Gabalda, 1936.

Lalleman, Pieter J. "The Adversaries Envisaged in the Johannine Epistles." *Nederlands Theologisch Tijdschrift* 53 (1999): 17-24.

Lampe, G. W. H. "The Holy Spirit and the Pre-existence of Christ." Pages 111-30 in *Christ, Faith, and History: Cambridge Studies in Christology*. Edited by S. W. Sykes and J. P. Clayton. Cambridge: Cambridge University Press, 1972.

Lataire, B. "The Son on the Father's Lap. The Meaning of εἰς τὸν κόλπον in John 1:18." *Studien zum Neuen Testament und seiner Umwelt* 22 (1997): 125-38.

Lau, Andrew. *Manifest in the Flesh: The Epiphany Christology of the Pastoral Epistles.* Wissenshaftlich Untersuchungen zum Neuen Testament 86. Tübingen: Mohr, 1996.

Levison, John R. "The Angelic Spirit in Early Judaism." Pages 464-93 in *SBL Seminar Papers, 1995.* Society of Biblical Literature Seminar Papers 34. Atlanta: Scholars Press, 1995.

———. *Of Two Minds: Ecstasy and Inspired Interpretation in the New Testament World.* Dead Sea Scrolls & Christian Origins Library 1. N. Richland Hills, Tex.: BIBAL, 1999.

———. "Prophetic Inspiration in Pseudo-Philo's *Liber Antiquitatum Biblicarum.*" *Jewish Quarterly Review* 85 (1995): 297-329.

———. *The Spirit in First Century Judaism.* Leiden: Brill, 1997.

———. "Two Types of Estatic Prophecy According to Philo." *Studia Philonica Annual* 6 (1994): 83-89.

Liddell, H. G. and Robert Scott. *A Greek-English Lexicon.* 9th ed. Oxford: Clarendon, 1990.

Lieu, Judith. *The Theology of the Johannine Epistles.* Cambridge: Cambridge University Press, 1991.

Lindars, Barnabas. *The Gospel of John.* New Century Bible. London: Oliphants, 1972.

Lindblom, J. *Prophecy in Ancient Israel.* Philadelphia: Fortress, 1963.

Livy. Translated by B. O. Foster. 14 vols. Loeb Classical Library. Cambridge: Harvard University Press, 1919-59.

Loader, William R. G. *The Christology of the Fourth Gospel: Structure and Issues.* Beiträge zur biblischen Exegese und Theologie. Rev. ed. Frankfurt am Main: Peter Lang, 1992.

Longenecker, Richard N. *The Christology of Early Jewish Christianity.* Grand Rapids, Mich.: Baker, 1981.

Lucan. Translated by J. D. Duff. Loeb Classical Library. Cambridge: Harvard University Press, 1943.

Lütgert, W. *Die Johanneische Christologie.* 2d ed. Gütersloh: Bertelsmann, 1916.

Luz, Ulrich and Rudolf Smend. *Gesetz.* Biblische Konfrontationen. Stuttgart: Kohlhammer, 1981.

MacMullen, Ramsey. *Paganism in the Roman Empire.* New Haven: Yale University, 1981.

MacRae, George. "The Fourth Gospel and *Religionsgeschichte.*" *Catholic Biblical Quarterly* 32 (1970): 12-24.

———. "The Jewish Background of the Gnostic Sophia Myth." *Novum Testamentum* 12 (1970): 86-101.

Maddox, F. "The Function of the Son of Man in the Gospel of John." Pages 186-204 in Reconciliation and Hope: New Testament Essays on Atonement and Eschatology. Edited.by R. Banks. Grand Rapids: Eerdmans, 1974.

Maillet, H. "'Au-dessus de', ou 'sur'? (John 1, 51)." *Etudes théologiques et religieuses* 59 (1974): 207-13.

Malatesta, Edward. "Blood and Water from the Pierced Side of Christ (Jn 19,34)." Pages 165-81 in *Segni e sacramenti nel vangelo di Giovanni.* Edited by P.-R. Tragan. Rome: Editrice Anselmiana, 1977.

Malatesta, Edward. "Blood and Water from the Pierced Side of Christ (Jn 19,34)." Pages 164-81 in *Segni e sacramenti nel vangelo di Giovanni*. Studia Anselmiana 66. Edited by P.-R. Tragan. Rome: Editrice Anselmiana, 1977.

———. *Interiority and Covenant. A Study of einai en and menein en in the First Letter of St. John*. Analectica Biblica 69. Rome: Biblical Institute, 1978.

Marshall, I. Howard. *The Epistles of John*. Grand Rapids: Eerdmans, 1978.

Martyn, J. Louis. "Glimpses into the History of the Johannine Community." Pages 149-75 in *L'Évangile de Jean: sources, redaction, thélogie*. Edited by M. de Jonge. Gembloux: Duculot, 1977.

———. *History and Theology in the Fourth Gospel*. 2d ed. Nashville, Tenn.: Abingdon, 1979.

McCown, C. C. *The Testament of Solomon*. Leipzig: Hinrichs, 1922.

McGrath, James F. "Going Up and Coming Down in Johannine Legitimation." *Neotestamentica* 31 (1997): 107-18.

McNamara, Martin. "Logos of the Fourth Gospel and Memra of the Palestinian Targum." *Expository Times* 79 (1967-68): 115-16.

Meeks, Wayne A. "The Divine Agent and His Counterfeit in Philo and the Fourth Gospel." Pages 43-67 in *Aspects of Religious Propaganda in Judaism and Early Christianity*. Edited by Elisabeth Schüssler Fiorenza. Notre Dame: University of Notre Dame Press, 1976.

———. "The Man from Heaven in Johannine Sectarianism." Pages 141-73 in *The Interpretation of John*. Issues in Religion and Interpretation 9. Edited by J. Ashton. London: SPCK, 1986. Repr. from *Journal of Biblical Literature* 91 (1972): 44-72.

———. *The Prophet-King: Moses Traditions and the Johannine Christology*. Leiden: Brill, 1967. Repr. from Journal of Biblical Literature 91 (1972): 44-72.

Menken, Maarten J. J. "The Christology of the Fourth Gospel: A Survey of Recent Research." Pages 292-320 in *From Jesus to John: Essays on Jesus and New Testament Christology in Honour of Marinus de Jonge*. Edited by Martinus C. De Boer. Journal for the Study of the New Testament Supplement Series 84. Sheffield: JSOT Press, 1993.

Merwe, D. B. van der. "The Historical and Theological Significance of John the Baptist As He Is Protrayed in John 1." *Neotestamentica* 33 (1999): 267-92.

Michaelsen, Peter. "Ecstasy and Possession in Ancient Israel: A Review of Some Recent Contributions." *Scandinavian Journal of the Old Testament* 2 (1989): 28-54.

Michaud, J.-P. "Le signe de Cana dans son contexte johannique." *Laval Théologie et Philosophique* 18 (1962): 247-52.

Minear, Paul S. "The Idea of Incarnation in First John." *Interpretation* 24 (1970): 291-302.

Miranda, Juan P. *Die Sendung Jesu im vierten Evangelium*. Stuttgarter Bibelstudien 87. Stuttgart: Verlag Katholisches Bibelwerk, 1977.

———. *Der Vater, der mich gesandt hat*. Frankfurt: Lang Bern, 1972.

Moeller, H. R. "The Ascent and Descent of Son of Man in the Gospel of St. John." *Australasian Theological Review* 39 (1957): 116-17.

Moloney, Francis J. "The Function of John 13-17 within the Johannine Narrative." Pages 43-66 in Vol. 2 of *"What is John?" Literary and Social Readings of the Fourth Gospel*. 2 vols. Edited by Fernando F. Segovia. Atlanta: Scholars Press, 1998.

————. *The Gospel of John.* Sacra Pagina 4. Collegeville, Minn.: Liturgical Press/ Michael Glazier, 1998.

————. *The Johannine Son of Man.* 2d ed. Bibloteca di Scienze Religiose 14. Rome: Las, 1976.

Morand, Anne-France. "Orphic Gods and Other Gods." Pages 169-82 in *What is a God? Studies in the Nature of Greek Divinity.* Edited by A. B. Lloyd. London: Duckworth, 1997.

Morris, Leon. *The Gospel according to John.* New International Commentary on the New Testament. Rev. ed. Grand Rapids: Eerdmans, 1995.

————. *Jesus is the Christ: Studies in the Theology of John.* Grand Rapids: Eerdmans, 1989.

Müller, Ulrich B. *Die Geschichte der Christologie in der johanneischen Gemeinde.* Stuttgarter Bibelstudien 77. Stuttgart: Verlag Katholisches Bibelwerk, 1975.

————. *Die Menschwerdung des Gottessohnes: frühchristliche Inkarnationsvorstellung en und die Anfänge des Doketismus.* Stuttgart: Verlag Katholisches Bibelwerk, 1990.

Neyrey, Jerome. *An Ideology of Revolt: John's Christology in Social-Science Perspective.* Philadelphia: Fortress, 1988.

————. "'My Lord and My God;' The Divinity of Jesus in John's Gospel." Pages 152-71 in Society of Biblical Literature Seminar Papers 25. Atlanta: Scholars Press, 1986.

Nicholson, Godfrey C. *Death as Departure: The Johannine Descent-Ascent Schema.* Society of Biblical Literature Dissertation Series 63. Chico: Scholars Press, 1983.

Nock, A. D. *Conversion: The Old and the New in Religon from Alexander the Great to Augustine of Hippo.* Oxford: Oxford University, 1961.

North, Wendy Sproston. *The Lazarus Story within the Johannine Tradition.* Journal for the Study of the New Testament Supplement Series 212. Sheffield: Sheffield Academic Press, 2001.

O'Grady, John F. "The Human Jesus in the Fourth Gospel." *Biblical Theology Bulletin* 14 (1984): 63-66.

O'Neill, J. C. "The Word Did Not 'Become' Flesh." *Zeitschrift für die neutestamentliche Wissenschaft* 82 (1991): 125-127.

Overholt, Thomas W. *Channels of Prophecy: The Social Dynamics of Prophetic Activity.* Minneapolis: Fortress, 1989.

Ovid. *Metamorphoses.* Translated by F. J. Miller. 2 vols. Loeb Classical Library. Cambridge: Harvard University Press, 1950.

Painter, John. "Christology and the History of the Johannine Community in the Prologue of the Fourth Gospel." *New Testament Studies* 30 (1984): 460-74.

————. "The 'Opponents' in 1 John." *New Testament Studies* 32 (1986): 48-71.

————. *1, 2, and 3 John.* Sacra Pagina 18. Collegeville, Minn.: Liturgical Press, 2002.

Patrologia latina. Edited by J.-P. Migne. 217 vols. Paris, 1844-1864.

Patrologia graeca. Edited by J.-P. Migne. 162 vols. Paris, 1857-1886.

Percy, C. E. *Untersuchungen über den Ursprung der johanneischen Theologie zugleich ein Beitrag zur Frage nach der Entstehung des Gnostizismus.* Lund: Gleerup, 1939.

Peterson, E. "Urchristentum und Mandäismus." *Zeitschrift für die neutestamentliche Wissenchaft* 27 (1928): 55-98.

Perkins, Pheme. "Gnostic Christologies and the New Testament." *Catholic Biblical Quarterly* 43 (1981): 590-606.

Pervo, R. I. "Johannine Trajectories in the *Acts of John.*" *Apocrypha* 3 (1992): 47-68.

Pétrement, S. *Le Dieu séparé: les origines du gnosticisme.* Paris: Cerf, 1984.

Philo. Translated by F. H. Colson and G. H. Whitaker. 10 vols. Loeb Classical Library. New York: Putnam, 1929-62.

Philo. *Supplement I: Questions and Answers on Genesis.* Translated by Ralph Marcus. Loeb Classical Library. Cambridge: Harvard University Press, 1953.

Philonenko, Marc. *Joseph et Aséneth.* Leiden: Brill, 1968.

Plato. Translated by H. N. Fowler, W. R. M. Lamb, and R. G. Bury. 10 vols. Loeb Classical Library. New York: Putnam, 1917-1929.

Plutarch. *Moralia.* Translation by F. C. Babbitt. 15 vols. Loeb Classical Library. Cambridge: Harvard University Press, 1927-28.

Porsch, F. *Pneuma und Wort: Ein exegetischer Beitrag zur Pneumatologie des Johannesevangeliums.* Frankfurter theologische Studien 16. Frankfurt: Knecht, 1974.

Potterie, Ignace de la. *The Hour of Jesus: The Passion and the Resurrection of Jesus according to John.* New York: Alba, 1989.

———. *La vérité dans Saint Jean.* 2 vols. Analectica Biblica 73. Rome: Pontifical, 1999.

Rabinowitz, Peter J. "Truth in Fiction: A Reexamination of Audiences." *Critical Inquiry* 4 (1977): 121-41.

———. *Before Reading: Narrative Conventions and the Politics of Interpretation.* Ithaca: Cornell University Press, 1987.

———. "Whirl Without End: Audience-Oriented Criticism." Pages 81-100 in *Contemporary Literary Theory.* Edited by G. Douglas Atkins and Laura Morrow. Amherst, Mass.: University of Massachusetts Press, 1989.

Rahlfs, Alfred. *Septuaginta.* Stuttgart: Württembergische Bibleanstalt, 1979.

Reiling, Jannes. *Hermas and Christian Prophecy: A Study of the 11th Mandate.* Novum Testamentum Supplement 37. Leiden: Brill, 1973.

Rhea, Robert. *The Johannine Son of Man.* Abhandlungen zur Theologie des Alten und Neuen Testaments 76. Zürich: Theologischer Verlag, 1990.

Richards, Lawrence O. *Expository Dictionary of Bible Words.* Grand Rapids: Zondervan, 1985.

Richardson, Cyril Charles. *The Christianity of Ignatius of Antioch.* New York: AMS Press, 1967.

Richter, Georg. "Blut und Wasser aus der durchbohrten Seite Jesu (Joh 19, 34b)." Pages 134-40 in *Studien zum Johannesevangelium.* Biblische Untersuchungen 13. Regensburg: Pustet, 1977. Repr. from *Münchener theologische Zeitschrift* 21 (1970): 1-21.

———. "Die Fleischwerdung des Logos im Johannesevangelium." Pages 149-198 in *Studien zum Johannesevangelium.* Biblische Untersuchungen 13. Regensburg: Pustet, 1977. Repr. from.*Novum Testamentum* 13 (1971): 81-126; 14 (1972): 257-76.

Ridderbos, Herman N. *The Gospel according to John: A Theological Commentary.* Translated by John Vriend. Grand Rapids/Cambridge: Eerdmans, 1997.

Riedel, H. *Zeichen und Herrlichkeit: Die christologische Relevanz der Semeiaquelle in den Kanawundern Joh 2, 1-11 und Joh 4, 46-54.* Regensburger Studien zur Theologie 51. Main: Peter Lang, 1977.

Riley, Gregory J. "'I Was Thought to Be What I Am Not:' Docetic Jesus and the Johannine Tradition." Occasional Papers for the Institute for Antiquity and Christianity Occasional Series 31. Claremont, Ca.: Institute for Antiquity and Christianity, 1994.

Ringe, Sharon H. *Wisdom's Friends: Community and Christology in the Fourth Gospel.* Louisville, Ky.: Westminster/John Knox, 1999.

Rinke, J. *Kerygma und Autopsie: Der christologische Disput als Spiegel johanneischer Gemeindegeschichte.* Freiberg: Herder, 1997.

Robinson, John A. T. "Destination and Purpose of St. John's Gospel." Pages 191-201 in *New Testament Issues.* Edited by R. Batey. New York: Harper & Row, 1970.

———. "The Relation of the Prologue to the Gospel of St. John." *New Testament Studies* 9 (1962-63): 120-28.

Sanders, J. N. *The Fourth Gospel in the Early Church.* Cambridge: Cambridge University Press, 1943.

Schäfer, Peter. "Die sogenannte Synode von Jabne." *Judaica* 31 (1975): 54-64, 116-24.

Schlesier, R. "Daimon und Daimones bei Euripides." *Saeculum* 34 (1983): 267-79.

Schnackenburg, Rudolf. *The Gospel according to St. John.* 3 vols. Herders theologischer Kommentar zum Neuen Testament IV/1-3. Translated by Kevin Smyth. New York: Crossroad, 1968-82.

———. "Die johanneische Gemeinde und Ihre Geisterfahrung." Pages 277-306 in *Die Kirche des Anfangs. Festschrift für Heinz Schürmann zum 65. Geburtstag.* Erfurter theologische Studien 38. Edited by R. Schnackenburg, J. Ernst, and J. Wanke. Leipzig: St. Benno, 1977.

———. *The Johannine Epistles: Introduction and Commentary.* Translated by Reginald and Ilse Fuller. New York: Crossroad, 1992.

———. "Logos-Hymnus und johanneischer Prolog." *Biblische Zeitschrift* 1 (1957): 69-109.

Schnelle, Udo. *Antidocetic Christology in the Gospel of John: An Investigation of the Place of the Fourth Gospel in the Johannine School.* Translated by Linda M. Maloney. Minneapolis: Fortress, 1992.

———. "Johannes als Geisttheologie." *Novum Testamentum* 40 (1998): 17-31.

———. "Recent Views of John's Gospel." *Word and World* 21 (2001): 352-59.

———. "Die Templereinigung und die christologie der Johannesevangeliums." *New Testament Studies* 42 (1996): 359-73.

Schoedel, William R. *Ignatius of Antioch.* Hermeneia. Philadelphia: Fortress, 1985.

Scholtissek, Klaus. "Johannine Studies: A Survey of Recent Research with Special Regard to German Contributions." *Currents in Research: Biblical Studies* 6 (1998): 227-59.

———. "Johannine Studies: A Survey of Recent Research with Special Regard to German Contributions." *Currents in Research: Biblical Studies* 9 (2001): 277-305.

Schlüssler Fiorenza, Elisabeth. *Jesus: Miriam's Child, Sophia's Prophet: Critical Issues in Feminist Christology.* New York: Continuum, 1994.

Scott, Martin. *Sophia and the Johannine Jesus.* Journal for the Study of the New Testament Supplement Series 71. Sheffield: Sheffield Academic Press, 1992.

Seaford, Richard. "Thunder, Lightening and Earthquake in the *Bacchae* and the *Acts of the Apostles*." Pages 139-51 in *What is a God? Studies in the Nature of Greek Divinity*. Edited by A. B. Lloyd. London: Duckworth, 1997.

Segal, Alan F. *Two Powers in Heaven: Early Rabbinic Reports about Christianity and Gnosticism*. Studies in Judaism and Late Antiquity. Leiden: Brill, 1977.

Segovia, Fernando S. *The Farewell of the Word. The Johannine Call to Abide*. Minneapolis: Fortress, 1991.

Seneca. *Ad Lucilium epistulae morales*. Translated by Richard M. Gummere. 3 vols. Loeb Classical Library. Cambridge: Harvard University Press, 1917-25.

Skulsky, Harold. *Metamorphosis: The Mind in Exile*. Cambridge: Harvard University Press, 1981.

Slusser, Michael. "Docetism: A Historical Definition." *The Second Century* 1 (1981): 163-72.

Smalley, Stephen S. *1, 2, 3 John*. Word Biblical Commentary. Waco, Tex.: Word Books, 1984.

———. *John: Evangelist & Interpreter*. New Testament Profiles. Downer's Grove, Ill.: InterVarsity Press, 1978.

———. "What about 1 John?" *Studia Biblica* 3 (1978): 337-343.

Smith, Frederick M. "The Current State of Possession Studies as a Cross-Disciplinary Project." *Religious Studies Review* 27 (2001): 203-212.

Smith, Jonathan Z. "The Prayer of Joseph." Pages 253-94 in *Religions in Antiquity: Essays in Memory of E. R. Goodenough*. Studies in the History of Religions 4. Edited by Jacob Neusner. Leiden: Brill, 1968.

Solodow, Joseph B. *The World of Ovid's Metamorphoses*. Chapel Hill and London: University of North Carolina Press, 1988.

Sophocles. Translated by Hugh Lloyd-Jones. Loeb Classical Library. Cambridge: Harvard University Press, 1994-96.

Sparks, H. F. D. *The Apocryphal Old Testament*. Oxford: Oxford University Press, 1989.

Spörri, L. G. *Das Evangelium nach Johannes*. 2 vols. Zürich: Zwingli, 1950.

Stagg, Frank. "Orthodoxy and Orthopraxy in the Johannine Epistles." *Review and Expositor* 67 (1970): 423-32.

Stanton, Graham. "Incarnational Christology in the New Testament." Pages 151-169 in *The Myth of God Incarnate*. Edited by John Hick. Philadelphia: Westminster, 1977.

Stenger, Werner. "'Der Geist ist es, der lebendig macht, das Fleisch nützt nichts.'" *Trierer theologische Zeitschrift* 85 (1976): 116-22.

Strecker, Georg. *The Johannine Letters: A Commentary on 1, 2, and 3 John*. Edited by Harold Attridge. Translated by Linda Maloney. Minneapolis: Fortress, 1996.

Stibbe,.M. W. G. *John*. Readings: A New Biblical Commentary. Sheffield: JSOT Press, 1993.

Stone, Michael. *Fourth Ezra: A Commentary on the Book of Fourth Ezra*. Hermeneia. Minneapolis: Fortress, 1990.

———. *The Testament of Abraham: The Greek Recensions*. Texts and Translations 2. Pseudipigrapha Series 2. New York: Society of Biblical Literature, 1972.

Stuckenbruck, Loren T. *Angel Veneration and Christology: A Study in Early Judaism and in the Christology of the Apocalypse of John*. Wissenschaftliche Untersuchungen zum Neuen Testament Second Series 20. Tübingen: Mohr (Siebeck), 1995.

Tacitus. *The Histories and the Annals.* Translated by C. H. Moore and J. Jackson. 4 vols. Loeb Classical Library. Cambridge: Harvard University Press, 1937.

Talbert, Charles H. "'And the Word Became Flesh': When?" Pages 43-52 in *The Future of Christology: Essays in Honor of Leander E. Keck.* Edited by Abraham J. Malherbe and Wayne A. Meeks. Minneapolis: Fortress, 1984.

———. "The Christology of the Apocalypse." Pages 166-84 in *Who Do You Say That I Am?: Essays on Christology.* Edited by M. A. Powell & D. R. Bauer. Louisville, Ky.: Westminster John Knox, 1999.

———. "The Myth of a Descending-Ascending Redeemer in Mediterranean Antiquity." *New Testament Studies* 22 (1976): 418-440.

———. *Reading John: A Literary and Theological Commentary on the Fourth Gospel and the Johannine Epistles.* New York: Crossroad, 1992.

Thomas, John Christopher. "The Order of the Composition of the Johannine Epistles." *Novum Testamentum* 37 (1995): 68-75.

Thompson, Marianne Meye. *The Humanity of Jesus in the Fourth Gospel.* Philadelphia: Fortress, 1988.

Thyen, H. "'...denn wir lieben die Brüder' (1 Joh 3,14)." Pages 527-42 in *Rechtfertigung: Festschrift für E. Käsemann.* Edited by G. Friedrich, et. al. Tübingen: Mohr, 1976.

Tobin, Thomas H. "The Prologue of John and Hellenistic Jewish Speculation." *Catholic Biblical Quarterly* 52 (1990): 252-69.

Tödt, H. E. *The Son of Man in the Synoptic Tradition.* Translated by D. M. Barton. Philadelphia: Westminster, 1965.

Trevett, Christine. "Prophecy and Anti-Episcopal Activity: A Third Error Combated by Ignatius?" *Journal of Ecclesiastical History* 34 (1983): 1-18.

———. *A Study of Ignatius of Antioch in Syria and Asia.* Lewiston: Mellen, 1992.

Unnik, W. C. van. "A Greek Characteristic of Prophecy in the Fourth Gospel." Pages 211-29 in *Text and Interpretation: Studies in the New Testament Presented to Matthew Black.* Edited by Ernest Best and R. McL. Wilson. Cambridge: Cambridge University Press, 1979.

———. "The Purpose of St. John's Gospel." *Studia evangelica I* (1959): 382-411.

Vermes, Geza. *The Dead Sea Scrolls in English.* 3d ed. New York: Penguin: 1987.

Versnel, H. S. *Ter Unus. Isis, Dionysus, Hermes: Three Studies in Henotheism.* Studies in Greek and Roman Religion 6. Leiden: Brill, 1990.

———. "What Did Ancient Man See When He Saw a God?.Some Reflections on Greco-Roman Epiphany." Pages 42-55 in *Effigies Dei.* Edited by D. van der Plas; Leiden: Brill, 1987.

Virgil. Translated by R. Rushton Fairclough. 2 vols. Loeb Classical Library. Cambridge: Harvard University Press, 1950.

Vorster, W. S. "Heterodoxy in 1 John." *Neotestamentica* 9 (1975): 87-97.

Vries, Simon J. de. "The Forms of Prophetic Address in Chronicles." *Hebrew Annual Review* 10 (1986): 15-36.

Waetjen, Herman. "Logos πρὸς τὸν θεόν and the Objectification of Truth in the Prologue of the Fourth Gospel." *Catholic Biblical Quarterly* 63 (2001): 265-86.

Wahlde, Urban C von. "'The Jews' in the Gospel of John: Fifteen Years of Research (1983-1998)." *Ephemerides theologicae lovanienses* 76 (2000): 30-55.

———. *The Johannine Commandments: 1 John and the Struggle for the Johannine Tradition.* New York: Paulist, 1990.

Wallace, Daniel B. *Greek Grammar Beyond the Basics*. Grand Rapids: Zondervan, 1996.

Watson, Francis. "Is John's Christology Adoptionist?" Pages 113-24 in *The Glory of Christ in the New Testament: Studies in Christology*. Edited by L. D. Hurst & N. T. Wright. Oxford: Clarendon, 1987.

Watt, J. G. van der. "Ethics in First John: A Literary and Socioscientific Perspective." *Catholic Biblical Quarterly* 61 (1999): 491-511.

Weigandt, Peter. "Der Doketismus im Urchirstentum und in der theologischen Entwicklung des zweiten johanneischen Schüle." *New Testament Studies* 32 (1986): 31-47.

Weiss, K. "Die 'Gnosis' im Hintergrund und im Spiegel der Johannesbriefe." *Gnosis und Neues Testament*. Edited by K.-W. Tröger. Gütersloh: Gütersloher, 1973.

———. "Orthodoxie und Heterodoxie im 1. Johannesbrief." *Zeitschrift für die neutestamentliche Wissenschaft* 58 (1967): 247-55.

Wengst, Klaus. *Häresie und Orthodoxie im Spiegel des ersten Johannesbriefes*. Gütersloh: Mohn, 1976.

Wicker, Kathleen O'Brien. "De Defectu Oraculorum (Moralia 409E-438E)." Pages 131-80 in *Plutarch's Theological Writings and Other Christian Literature*. Edited by H. D. Betz. Studia ad Corpus Hellenisticum Novi Testamenti 3. Leiden: Brill, 1975.

Wilckens, Ulrich. *Das Evangelium nach Johannes*. Das Neue Testament deutsch 4. Göttingen: Vandenhoeck & Ruprecht, 2000.

Willett, Michael E. *Wisdom Christology in the Fourth Gospel*. San Francisco: Mellen, 1992.

Wilson, R. McL. "Philo and the Fourth Gospel." *Expository Times* 65 (1954): 47-49.

Winston, David. "Two Types of Mosaic Prophecy according to Philo." Pages 442-55 in Society of Bibilical Literature Seminar Papers 27. Atlanta: Scholars Press, 1988.

Witherington, Ben. *John's Wisdom: A Commentary on the Fourth Gospel*. Louisville: Westminster/John Knox, 1995.

Yamauchi, E. M. "Jewish Gnosticism?.The Prologue of John, Mandean Parallels and the Trimorphic Protenoia." Pages 467-97 in *Festschrift for Giles Quispel*. Leiden: Brill, 1981.

———. *Pre-Christian Gnosticism*. Grand Rapids: Eerdmans, 1973.

Zumstine, Jean. "L'interprétation johannique de la mort du Christ." Pages 2132-33 in *The Four Gospels 1992: Festschrift Frans Neirynck*. Vol. 3. Edited by Frans van Segbroeck, et. al. Bibliotheca ephemeridum theologicarum lovaniensium 100. Leuven: Leuven University Press, 1992.

Index of Scripture and Ancient Texts

Old Testament

17:4	39
24:3-7	65
24:8-12	65
24:23-34	65

Sirach

24:3	132
24:3-24:12	123
24:6-7	115
24:8	115

Isaiah

2:1	57
11:2	64, 65
14:24	96
21:3-4	48
28:7	39
40:3	126
40:8	96
42:1	66
48:16	58
59:21	66
61:1-2	58
66:22	96

Jeremiah

| 20:9 | 49 |
| 23:9 | 49 |

Baruch

| 3:37 | 115 |

Ezekiel

3:14	48
cf. 3:24	58
8:3	53
11:5	58
33:22	49
37:14	66

Daniel

4:33	32
5:6	32
6:26	96
cf. 7:28	32
8:18	48
10:16-17	48

Hosea

| 9:7 | 49 |

Joel

| 2:28-29 | 66 |

Zechariah

| 2:14 | 123 |
| 4:1 | 48 |

New Testament

John (continued)

19:17	162, 171
19:25-27	140
19:26-27	162
19:28-29	162
19:30	162, 163, 166, 169
19:34	103,147, 164, 165, 166, 167, 171
19:34-35	104
19:34-37	163
20:2	168
20:17	168
20:19, 26	168
20:20	168
20:21	169
20:22	105, 165, 169
20:26-29	169
20:28	170
20:30-31	170
21:4	168
21:12	170
21:13	168
21:15	168
21:20-23	170
21:23	168, 170

2 Corinthians

| 3:11 | 96 |

Hebrews

| 7:24 | 96 |
| 10:34 | 96 |

1 John

1:1	99
1:1-3	170
1:1-5	70
1:3	161
1:5-7	151
2:1	158
2:18-27	70
2:19	70, 136
2:22-24	144
3:13	160
3:18-22	144
4:1-6	70
4:1-2	160
4:2	78, 94, 95, 101, 102, 104, 120
4:6	160
4:9	78
4:9-11	103
4:14	143
5:4b-12	130
5:5-6	127
5:6	101, 127
5:6-8	166
5:7-8	105
5:10-12	144
5:20	170
14:14-15	14

Index of Modern Authors

Printed in the United States
30827LVS00005B/256-426